BOY

WITH

LOADED

GUN

ALSO BY

LEWIS NORDAN

A MEMOIR

BOY
WITH
LOADED
GUN

BY

LEWIS

NORDAN

ALGONQUIN
BOOKS OF
CHAPEL HILL
2000

The author wishes to thank the Virginia
Center for the Creative Arts, where this
book was written.

Published by
ALGONQUIN BOOKS OF CHAPEL HILL
Post Office Box 2225
Chapel Hill, North Carolina 27515-2225

a division of
Workman Publishing
708 Broadway
New York, New York 10003

Some chapters first appeared in slightly different forms in the following publi-
cations: chapter six in *Southern Living*, chapter seven in *The Oxford American*,
chapter fifteen and the Epilogue in *Harper's*, and chapter nineteen in *Playgirl*.

Library of Congress Cataloging-in-Publication Data
Nordan, Lewis.
    Boy with loaded gun : a memoir / by Lewis Nordan.
        p. cm.
    ISBN 1-56512-199-6
    1. Nordan, Lewis. 2. Novelists. American—20th century—
Biography. 3. Nordan, Lewis—Homes and haunts—Mississippi.
4. Mississippi—Social life and customs. 5. Nordan, Lewis—
Childhood and youth. I. Title.
PS3564.O55Z464 2000
813'.54—dc21   99-33339
[B]   CIP

10 9 8 7 6 5 4 3 2 1

First Edition

FOR

Lewis Eric Nordan

IN MEMORY

Lemuel Alonzo Nordan

Gilbert Russell Bayles

Russell Ammon Nordan

John Robert Nordan

My life has been incredible.

I don't believe a word of it.

—KATHERINE ANNE PORTER

I couldn't decide whether to call this book a Memoir or not, so I put the problem to my wife: I said, "If you were working at the Library of Congress, how would you list this one?"

She said, "Nordan, Lewis."

I said, "No, I mean—"

She said, "ISBN whatever."

"Fiction or Nonfiction," I said. "It seems to fall somewhere between the two."

She said, "You made up your memoir?"

"Names mostly, you know."

She said, "You didn't mention my name, did you?"

"I changed your name, I changed all the names, that's what I'm saying."

"If all you changed was names—"

"And conversations. I made up some conversations."

"Still—I'd say Memoir."

"And maybe I exaggerated some stuff too. Some of the painful stuff, death, and like that."

"Grief Therapy. Excellent! Self-Help, Popular Psychology—"

"No, no—"

"You didn't include any recipes, did you?"

"The book's about me, basically. Who I am, and—"

"I see where you're going with this. A 'How To' Guide for Jackasses."

"Really I'm just trying to decide between Fiction and Nonfiction."

"Okay, okay, give me some chapter titles. That might help."

I said, "There's a chapter called 'The Man I Killed.' "

"Murder mystery!"

" 'Up, Up, and Away'!"

"Comics!"

" 'Zen and the Art of Mail Order.' "

"Eastern Religions!"

"One on Emmett Till."

"Historical!"

" 'Tell Me, Ramon Fernandez, If You Know.' "

"Poetry!"

" 'The Amazing Technicolor Effing Machine.' "

This stopped her.

"Say what?"

"There's a chapter called 'The Amazing Technicolor Effing Machine.' "

"Musical comedy?"

"Probably not."

"What's an effing machine?"

"Effing. It's a euphemism, you know. I'm embarrassed. The f-word. Jeez."

"That's the title of one of your chapters? You wrote a book about you being an effing machine?"

"Not—"

"Nonfiction is pretty much off the table at this point."

"Honey, listen—"

"We might be looking at Fantasy here."

"It's not me. I'm not the effing machine. It's a machine. An actual machine."

"You wrote about a machine that—"

"Right."

"You're telling me you've written a Science Fiction memoir? A Science Fiction memoir is impossible to catalog, I hate to tell you."

"No, this part is not fiction, it's real, the effing machine is true."

For a long time she only looked at me.

"All right, all right," she said at last. "Let's move on. More chapter titles, let's go."

" 'The Land of Dreamy Dreams.' "

"Travel."

" 'Violence in America.' "

"Sociology."

It was pretty clear we were getting nowhere.

She said, "So anyway—"

I said, "Yeah."

She said, "So about this machine."

"The effing machine?"

"Right, right."

I said, "Yeah?"

She said, "Where do you keep it?"

ONE

1

Voodoo

DURING THE DAY, WHILE my mother worked, I moved with ease across the small property where we lived. A brindle cow bellowed from a neighbor's yard. Mr. Alexander, next door, stopped by with a honeycomb from his hive, which he shared with me; the crunching in my ears as I chewed the comb were only bee carcasses, he told me, some of the best eating. An old lady down the street yelled at me not to throw persimmons onto her sidewalk. In a corner of the yard stood what we called the arbor, really a large wooden frame draped with fragrant grapevines, muscadines, which attracted an enormity of tuneful bumblebees into the foliage; beneath the shade of these vines I stood with my eyes closed and breathed deep and drank in the purple fragrance of the swollen grapes and of the sweet leaves that, after summer rain, smelled like green peas. The bees were as loud as a stringed orchestra, and when I grew up and read a poem by Yeats about a "bee-loud glade," I was certain I had heard what the poet heard, and heard it again simply by remembering. On the other side of the house stood great, dark pecan trees, their shade so deep and constant that, no matter the weather, the side yard never fully warmed up during the day, and though I played there from morning to suppertime beneath those trees, as the sun passed across the blue sky above me, the light that reached me there was forever dim as twilight. Now half a century later the images beneath those magical trees glimmer and ripple and change as if viewed through water, as it seems to me they did even then. All such images, though they occur to me only in beauty, are really images of loneliness. My father was dead, my mother was away somewhere, somewhere behind me toiled a nursemaid hired to look after me, and I sat all alone in the crook of a willow tree that grew in a ditch alongside a dirt road, looking outward, outward from my perch for the end of longing, for rescue from grief, for which I had no word or even memory.

When I was just eighteen months old, my father died suddenly and left my young mother and me alone, just at the beginning of World War II. He had never been sick before, the story goes—"Never sick a day in his life." So when he came home early from work that day, my mother didn't even take the illness seriously and left to go to a meeting of some kind. The two of them had thought he had indigestion. He died while she was out. When my mother got word at her meeting that her husband, who she had only just seen and spoken to, was dead, she says she didn't cry at all, not until much later, so unreal was the news. She says she only came home and sat and stared out a window at a stand of pine trees out from the house. That was the only response she says she could muster.

I wish I could remember the day of my father's death. If not my father, at least the day that he died. Whether it was cloudy or sunny, who was looking after me, whether I missed him when he was not in the room that night, or the next. I have looked at

4

photographs of myself and of my mother and father during that time, a blond boy-child with a serious, furrowed brow. In some pictures, I am wearing a gown sometimes, a dark sailor suit in other pictures. My mother is a pretty 1940s woman with short hair and spit curls, wearing a sassy dark dress with big white polka dots. Her smile is as bright as sunshine. There is one picture of my father, in which he holds me. He is wearing a hat. He has taken off his suit jacket and wears a white shirt and tie and vest. The sleeves of the shirt are bright against the dark vest. He is wearing glasses, which along with the hat brim, prevent me from seeing his eyes.

I try to see something of myself in his face, but there is nothing. The shape is different, the set of the eyes, the chin, the cheekbones. Our body shapes are different as well. As a grown man I am slender and of average height, he was short and barrel-chested. I look like my mother, I have her blue eyes, her chronic cough, her sense of humor, her straight back and high arches, and though these things I am pleased to share with her, they too are a loss to me, as they provide no purchase on that invisibility in my past. My son looks like my father, I am told, and this gives me some comfort. I look and look at him, and on the rare occasions when current feeling does not merely magnify the beauty of his presence, I do, once in a while, break through into the old abyss and catch a glimpse of what may have been the man I never knew. This is rare and not very trustworthy evidence.

The old car that my father drove on his rural mail route sits in the background of one or two photos, a dark coupe with running boards, looking like an escapee from a period movie. The family dog, a serene and silky old girl, appears in the far-back of another photograph. None of it do I remember. None of it, therefore, convinces me of its reality. Maybe it's obvious that I should not remember, from such an early age, but it seems even so that I should. Some small thing, at least. To want a thing so much—just one memory—ought to confer some entitlement. It has been hard for me to tolerate the mechanical recording of my father's existence without the full proof of my own memory.

I remember that war well enough, the one that was just beginning when he died, and so if I can remember that, then the birth of memory would seem not be far behind. Clearly I remember the news reports on the old Philco radio, the room it sat in, the blackouts and scrap metal drives (I threw a tea kettle onto a pile in front of the train depot) and ration books, the absence of young men from our town, the absence of my own uncle, a physician away from home and at risk, serving as he did in Patton's army in North Africa. So close! I want to exclaim. I am so close to remembering.

I remember angry talk of "Krauts" and "Japs." Men came home from the war with souvenirs, swastikas, German helmets, bayonets, shell casings. I remember the end of the war. My mother and I happened to be visiting an aunt in Louisville on VE day. The soldiers on the train flirted with my grieving mother, and I was surprised to observe the pleasure of her smile as she rejected them. I remember the day the Baptist preacher's daughter appeared all in tears at our back door to report the death of Roosevelt.

But my father is an invisibility. The space that he occupied has always been a significant blank spot in my imagination. I know a few things about him, not many, but I hold to them, with varying degrees of positive effect. He was nearly twenty years older than my mother, which means he was born in 1892, another century. Victoria would reign as queen of England for almost another decade. He first drew breath only twenty-seven years after the surrender at Appomatox Courthouse. He was born, in other words, about the same distance in time from that war as we are now from Vietnam. I frame the chronology in these terms in order to emphasize to myself the distance between my world and his. No wonder I can't remember him. He might as well have lived on another planet. Mark Twain was writing books when my father was born. My father served on a navy ship in the war—but not the war I remember. He was in the First World War. It's unfathomable to me.

AT MY FATHER'S DEATH my mother and I were forced to move out of the little house my parents had built and out of the gentle hills of Forest, Mississippi. We moved a hundred-some miles north to the Mississippi Delta, a vast alluvial plain in a crook of the Yazoo River. In these lonely backwaters and days of grief my memory begins.

One of my nurses during this time was a woman named Lily. Of all the child-care help my mother employed in those early years, Lily is the only one whose name has stayed with me. She was old and large-bottomed and walked with a limp, which I learned much later was the result of a beating she took as a child. Lily practiced voodoo and kept many powders and potions and herbs that were used almost always for purposes of healing and good health, but sometimes in anger, it was rumored. It was said of Lily that she removed a frog from a man's stomach.

One day Lily played a sort of joke on me. She turned on the water at the kitchen sink just enough that only air and very little water could get through the old plumbing. The pipes set up a howl, the sad, strange old groaning that I had heard and been frightened by before. Lily had her back to me. She was a large woman, always wearing an apron. Her hair was long gray and greased and wild. She told me was working a spell, a hex. She turned around suddenly, and out of her big broad nose was protruding a thick foliage of green leaves and twigs. It scared the living daylights out of me. It was a joke, but not one that I could appreciate. I thought a tree was growing out of her nose.

Whyever Lily may have thought to scare me like that, I know that I loved her. She is the first person on earth that I am sure I felt love for. I can't for the life of me remember my father, but I can identify the moment that I knew what love was, and the person I loved was Lily. When Lily moved away, I did not imagine that I would live through the loss. The loss of Lily was the loss of love. I still long for her this half century later. I still feel the soft warmth of her body as she held me. I still smell the corn bread–clean fragrance of her skin, the fruity sweetness of the pomade in her hair. I can hear the low melody of her voice calling me Sugar. I have lost other loves since this time, including two sons, so I don't mean to say that my heart still grieves for Lily. Other grief has eclipsed this, and time does heal, after all. I'm saying that when I want to get back as close to my father as memory and metaphor can take me, I call up that vivid memory of loss when Lily moved away, and I know that this is what I felt on that day before memory when my mother sat at the window and stared at a stand of loblolly pines and I was sitting or standing somewhere in a world in which, forever after, I would be a fatherless child.

2

Home in the Woods

A SIGN ON THE outskirts of town welcomes travelers down old Highway 49 to ITTA BENA, HOME IN THE WOODS. In the autumn the little town still holds its annual reunion called Home in the Woods Day, and usually a band is hired to play in the city park, hot dogs and Cokes are sold from carts, old friends gather. High school class reunions are held on this day. *Itta Bena* is a Chickasaw word meaning "home in the woods." This was the story we learned in fifth grade anyway, and it is still widely believed by those who care. Recently I looked up Itta Bena in a Chickasaw/English dictionary and found that the word is actually a verb meaning "to build a house of crossed logs." Basically it means to build a log cabin. The romanticizing and poeticizing of its more accurate meaning was probably a publicity gimmick to make the place seem attractive to potential businesses and residents. It is a meaning now that is unchangeable, after long tradition.

The person whose mission it was to carry the legend was our fifth grade teacher, Miss Alberta, a heavy-set old woman who wore a mask of heavy face powder, a gold watch pinned to her blouse. Miss Alberta was rumored to have no vagina. People paid little attention to the rumor. There seemed no end of the silliness and inaccuracy of local legends. The children in Miss Alberta's classroom anticipated the Mississippi history lesson that told of our origins. I sat in a desk just behind a honey-haired girl named Milly. I was absurdly in love with her. On the playground, I became her virtual stalker. She made not a move without my shadow covering hers. She was short and blond and sturdily built and freckled with sunburn, she had white teeth and laughing eyes and near-breasts and a huge older brother whose nickname was Joy Boy, for some unknown reason. Later, Joy Boy shot off some fingers in a hunting accident. Milly was the first girl I ever kissed. We were at a birthday party on the moonlight-softened banks of Roebuck Lake. I bought a dollar's worth of penny stamps in a game of post office and we stood at the lakeside beneath tupelo gums, serenaded by mosquitoes as loud and as large and tuneful as violins, and sent out our extravagant mailing to the stars. Tight-lipped and sweaty we kissed until all our stamps were gone and we were covered with chiggers and mosquito bites. There was another kid at the party as in love with Milly as I was, but Milly assured me that he held no interest for her. She had heard that he sometimes crawled up on the refund-gas tank—which stored the tax-free gasoline allotted to farmers for farm machinery—and inhaled the fumes until he passed out and fell off the tank and injured himself. Once he broke his arm. I told her I would never do such a thing.

Miss Alberta was always neatly dressed—she is, in fact, the only schoolteacher I ever had whose clothing I can actually remember with certainty—crisp cotton dresses, often with a broad collar; in winter a sweater draped over her shoulders like a cape; a pair of glasses depending from her neck by a gold chain;

sometimes a strand of pearls; and always, always that fascinating gold watch pinned to her bosom. To check the time she tipped the watch up and snapped open the case and squinted down through her bifocals. There was also a fat alarm clock on her desk. I often wondered why she was so fascinated with the time of day, as all daytime seemed the same to me.

MISS ALBERTA STOOD BEFORE us at her desk, and the lesson in Itta Bena history began. She made the scene palpable: ancient Roebuck Lake, its cypress-darkened waters, the overhanging branches of wild pecan and tupelo gum, turtles on every half-sunken log, cottonmouth moccasins draped on every green twig of willow, alligators mooing like cows from their fecund nests. And then, the white man's house, the first the native Chickasaw had ever seen. The house was real, not romantic legend. A log cabin that probably did inspire the name of the town. The first governor of the state, B. G. Humphries built the little home beside Roebuck Lake. This house I never actually saw, though my mother remembers it. In my mind I can see it, though. In my mind Miss Alberta's vivid tale becomes true. It was a house built of notched logs, lying one across another and cemented with the hardened buckshot and gumbo of the swampbed. The class sat in the silence of awe. We were impressed—I was, certainly. B. G. Humphries, she said. My head reeled, I almost swooned, I clung to every word. She told of the canoe that floated upon those silent waters. I felt it sway beneath me. A dugout, she said. Two barebacked braves knelt in the canoe, dipped their slow paddles. Their braided hair hung down their backs and glistened with animal fat. Each wore a single feather. The sunlight that fell upon their dark shoulders was the same light that flowed through the bank of tall windows into our schoolroom on that yolk-rich-yellow afternoon. They let the boat drift, they squinted their eyes, shaded their brows, each with his hand. One brave pointed in the direction of the clear lane through the forest. An armband with a single feather encircled the upper portion of his arm. Blue herons fished along the shore. An old gar rolled upon the surface of the flood. Through the gap in the trees, they saw the log house. "Itta Bena," the Chickasaw brave said. "Home in the woods."

This was the story Miss Alberta told. She told it well. Mound-building tribes floated upon familiar waters, as if before my eyes. The lake, the governor's house of notched logs, the wilderness, the clearing—I saw them all. I heard wild birds in the trees, saw them wading in the shallows. Then the strangest words came into my ears. They came as if from inside my own head, they were so clear, so distinct. Miss Alberta said, "I was born with no vagina—" Those are the words that I am certain she spoke. With no other education than the bad magic of this moment, I knew the meaning of the word that signified for Miss Alberta an absence. Vagina made sense. I looked up. I looked about me, at the faces of my classmates. Had others heard the same words? I could not tell. No one broke into hysterical laughter. No one wept. No one seemed to react at all, except with the awe one expected from the telling of a tale of our sweet origins. I saw small spots before my eyes. *Born with no vagina.* The words formed in the air. She had said what she said. I missed hearing what came after this, the phrase that completed her thought. Maybe she recalled all her losses—the handsome boy (there must have been one!) she had wanted to marry but could not because of her unholy handicap. In the silence a song found music in my head. *I was born with no vagina and a banjo on my knee.* I tapped my foot. *Nothing could be finer than having no vagina in the morning.* When I asked others they had no idea what I was talking about.

Somebody said, "Maybe she said she was born in Virginia."

I said, "Well, did she say Virginia or didn't she?"

He said, "I didn't hear her say anything, Buddy. I'm just trying to help you out."

3

Up, Up, and Away

THE FIRST TV SET I ever saw sat in a large bare room in a business establishment in Itta Bena called Spock Butane Gas Company. Spock Butane was a prosperous little corporation in this farming community, and it furnished propane fuel to farmers for tractors and home-heating and other purposes. The building was long and low and held several spaces for rent, including a small apartment and a couple of shops, so it was the closest thing Itta Bena was likely to have to an office building, save only city hall. One Saturday afternoon during the matinee the town was rocked by an explosion. When we ran out of the theater to see what had happened, one end of Spock Butane had been blown to smithereens, bricks were everywhere, and a man had been killed. That would happen later, though, and has nothing to do with the television set, except that once Itta Benans had laid eyes on the magic tube, no strangeness or suddenness, even of violence, seemed surprising to us again. An explosion and death seemed, to me anyway, a part of the logic of the expanding universe, once television had been introduced into it.

The Spock Butane building housed the first businesses on one of two main streets in the town center. Near it stood Mr. Hooten's shoe shop, which still had cowboy-style wooden sidewalks. The Dixie Theater, for blacks only, was next. Then the Strand Theater for whites only, except in the balcony. There was a ten-cent store; three Chinese-owned groceries; a Jewish-owned dry goods store; a Sicilian-owned dry goods place; two drug stores; the bank; city hall; the jail; the dry cleaners; the frozen food locker; the VFW hut, which had slot machines and poker tables; Dr. Moore's hardware; Belk's; Dr. Hightower's medical office; and the Kingfisher Cafe, for blacks only. Roebuck Lake, a beautiful snaky body of water, ran through the middle of town. For a while, there was a soap factory near the jail and every day the alley between would be filled with billows of soap suds. Itta Bena was a prosperous little community, and the Spocks were among the most prosperous citizens. They drove a Cadillac and seemed to me a family with many blessings, the television set among the richest of those blessings. They raised Great Danes, which they allowed to run free (this was common and safe in the small-town South), ponylike creatures with slobbering mouths and India-rubber tongues and gleaming coats. The Spocks had two handsome sons a year or two older than me, who in high school drove a new red Mercury coupe.

The TV set had a seventeen-inch screen, the biggest available at the time, and was housed in a large wood cabinet. The room where it sat, with its long expanse of concrete floor and overhead fluorescent lights, was deep and long, and so the set sat at a good distance from where you stood to watch. Someone explained that the farther away from the screen you stood, the better the reception was. This theory I have never fully parsed. The TV was kept playing day and night. In a sense it was impossible to miss anything, in any case. People didn't watch programs. Expectation of programming had not yet entered our intellectual purview. Content was unimportant. We watched the set. What the set was doing by being turned on was really all that mattered. The idea of a picture appearing there before us was far more interesting than anything we might actually see on the screen, and so no one cared what the program at any given time might happen to be.

The nearest television stations to Itta Bena were WLBT in Jackson, a hundred miles to the south, and WMCT in Memphis, slightly farther to the north, so although the television played day and night on one of those two channels, it was a rare day that a recognizable picture ever actually appeared before a viewer's eyes. A few times on Saturday afternoons I actually saw an inning or two of baseball being played somewhere—the reception and sound were never good enough to discern which teams were playing or whether there was a ball or strike or hit or foul, but it was baseball, you could tell this clearly, and that knowledge was enough.

To correct the problem of poor reception Mr. Spock constructed an outside antennae for the set—no, not merely an antenna, but a tower, the most impressive solution to poor television reception or any other problem that Delta eyes had ever imagined. He had built, on top of Spock Butane, upon a massive base of concrete, a two-hundred-foot steel tower, standing upon four wide-stretched steel legs and reaching to heaven. It was the tallest structure within a hundred miles. I was awestruck by the sight of it. I could not take my eyes away. The Spock antenna was, I should have thought, a virtual close encounter. If little green men had been espied scampering up and down its imposing legs, I for one would not have been surprised. Its girth and height made clear, once and for all, that invisible forces existed everywhere around us. For the first time we began to see real pictures. Pictures floated invisible upon the air we breathed, and were given shape by Spock's antenna. Men and women in conversation, men reading the news, sports games that you could actually follow. Programming made sense. Pictures were everywhere around us. I was breathing pictures into my very lungs. I wanted to gasp for breath. Pictures down inside the air sacs, pictures up my nose, pictures gliding in and out between my legs like ocean fish in Gulf waters. Pictures were all over me, even when the TV set was not on, in my ears, in my eyes, on the food. At meals I was eating pictures, I swallowed them in the sweet tea. I pissed and shat pictures. I washed electrical pictures from my flesh with my Saturday night bath. Herb Philbrick, Milton Berle swirled away down my drain. The guy wires, those taut thick cables of twisted steel, fairly sang in a strong breeze. The tower swayed and rocked and creaked like a goose's bones. My head swam. The world changed. Itta Benans were no longer content to stop along the sidewalk to watch a television at the end of a long room. Now we had to have them in our own homes. That summer television sets began to spring up everywhere, as the crocuses had done in the spring. We were resigned to poor reception. Ownership was the key to happiness, not reception.

Looking back on this time it seems odd that my new father shared such ambitions as I am describing. My mother had remarried only two years before the day I am describing. My new father seemed to have no imagination. He was not one to tell stories. He didn't care much for movies. When he was not too drunk, he read Western novels, but with no comment. He had no gift of narrative. He was one of the few men in town who did not stop by Spock Butane and gawk at the television screen. His life was simple and narrow. He was a quiet, small man, a house painter who retired early each night and drank beers in his room until he passed out. He rose each morning at four-thirty and began a ritual of his bathroom ablutions, which he called "clearing out his pipes." This included hideous coughing and hawking up phlegm and gagging and spitting and vomiting into the toilet. This was a daily occurrence, which I listened to with a pillow clamped tightly over my head. Later, when I was in the navy and slept in tight quarters on a ship with men whose habits were similar, I understood that I would forever be more comfortable in a woman's world than in one inhabited primarily by my own gender. The noise he made in the bathroom was only a part of my new father, though. What I loved about him was his insubstantiality. Most of the time he hardly seemed to exist. He moved like a shade through my life. He rarely spoke, and when he did his voice was soft. He dressed quietly in clean white painter overalls, and wore on his head a soft paper cap with the words MURRAY LUMBER YARD printed on it. This white outfit rendered him tiny-seeming—he was about five feet six, 120 pounds —and when I woke during those early morning hours and secretly watched him from my bed as he moved from room to room off a central hall, he seemed scarcely real, a specter almost, and on the paint-speckled crepe-soled shoes that he wore he seemed rather to be floating than walking, so silent and soft were his steps. This near-invisibility in him I admired above all else. His wispy corporeality seemed to me a form of gentleness, a trait or habit or magic trick I often wish I might have learned from him, the value of silence in any life.

For all these reasons my father seemed the last person on earth to want to buy a television set. They were expensive and noisy and there were only hints of pictures to watch in any case. My mother did not encourage him, of this I am almost certain. Her life was very full. Her outlook, despite the early death of her first husband, was optimistic and comic. Her intellectual interests were many, she had many friends. She was not herself ambitious in any material way. As a woman, she had had no occasion to stop by the Spock Butane showroom and so could not have become enchanted, as local males had done. My mother taught bookkeeping and typing at the local high school. She was a popular, well-liked teacher, who was often asked to sponsor the senior class, and so she directed the school play, attended various student-centered banquets and other dress-up events.

Something in her may have cried out for TV before she had ever laid eyes on a set, something at the core of the play director, the performer on the stage of a classroom, the adult who is still enough of a child to attract the devotion of children. Maybe my quiet, strange father knew this, intuitively. So, anyway, a TV set was ordered. I was half crazy with anticipation. When is it coming, I wanted to know. Can I watch it as soon as it comes, can we call and ask what time it will be here, can I invite friends over to watch it, to wait with me, can I go out to the highway and watch for the truck, what will the truck look like, can I walk to Greenwood and ride in the truck with the TV?

My mother said, "Go play."

I said, "No."

She said, "Go swimming."

I loved to go swimming at the town pool. In the summer I went twice a day, seven days a week. I said, "No."

She said, "Maybe you need a polio nap."

I said, "I'll read comic books."

"Anything," she said.

I went out on the front porch, which had a concrete projection out into the front yard that resembled, in my mind anyway, a diving platform. I thought about whether I should go on to the pool. I walked out onto the platform. I stood barefoot on the edge of the porch extension and curled my toes against the edge and crouched as if I were about to dive. I held my arms out then and said, "Sploosh," pretending to dive. I stood up and walked away. Just then my father's father, who we called Pop, walked past on the sidewalk, beneath the pecan trees. Pop was blind from some kind of face cancer. Later on he lived in a spare bedroom in our house, though at this time he still lived in his own house several blocks away. He dressed up in fancy clothes with suspenders and a straw hat and expensive kangaroo-hide shoes and walked with a gold-handled cane and smoked ten cigars a day, which is probably why he had face cancer in the first place.

I said, "Hey Pop."

He was caught off guard and didn't know who had spoken to him. He stopped and cocked his head to one side.

I said, "It's Buddy."

He straightened up then and steadied himself with his cane. He said, "Why aren't you swimming?"

I said, "I'm pretending to dive off the porch."

He said, "You be careful now, you hear?"

I said, "We're getting a television set."

He said, "What do you want to do that for?"

I said, "Watch it, you know. Watch *Superman*. Stuff like that."

He said, "You don't know how to listen to the radio. You ought to try to pick up radio first, then ease on into television. One step at a time. That's the way I'd do it if I was you."

I said, "I know how to listen to radio."

He said, "No you don't."

I said, "It's easy. You just listen."

He said, "Well, that's where you're wrong."

I said, "How do you do it, then?"

He said, "Oh no you don't. You're not going to lure me into one of your traps."

I said, "Big John and Sparky. Boston Blackie. Buster Brown. Charlie McCarthy. I know how to listen to radio."

He said, "If you call that listening."

I said, "Do you want to watch it with us sometime, after we get it going?"

He said, "Well, I'm blind."

I said, "Oh yeah."

Pop walked on down the sidewalk, in the direction of town, stepping smartly behind his walking cane. He was walking up to the Southern Cafe to drink coffee and play the punchboard. He would have to pass Spock Butane on the way, it was only a block or two from the house, so I practiced one more dive pose on the porch and then followed him down the street, far enough behind that he didn't know I was there. He came to Spock Butane and stopped at the big window. A few other men were standing there, staring in the direction of the TV, which had a good picture on the screen. It was Dave Garroway and that monkey, it was still as early as that. I eased up behind the men and watched my grandfather watch the news. I was invisible, as children were then, no one looked at me. We watched, Pop and the men and I, for several minutes.

After a while Pop said, "That J. Fred Muggs is a smart little motherfucker, ain't he?"

A little time passed. One of the men said, "How smart do you have to be to be a monkey?"

That was all, they just kept on watching.

I went back to the house and found Mama in the kitchen. I said, "Pop ain't blind, he's faking."

She said, "Really, don't start. I'm a little nervous myself, all this talking and thinking about the new TV."

I said, "He knows how to watch TV. Blind people ain't supposed to know how to watch TV, are they?"

I went and lay down on my bed and pulled out my comic book collection. *Donald Duck, Little LuLu, The Spirit, Frontline Combat, Tales from the Crypt* yikes *Scribbly, Jingle Jangle Tales*. I picked through a big stack and didn't find anything I wanted to read. I went through another stack and pulled out a few *Supermans*. *Captain Marvel, The Green Hornet, Batman, Plastic Man, Hydroman, Wonder Woman, Sandman*—I liked them all, but *Superman* was my favorite. Captain Marvel looked just like Fred MacMurray. I liked Superman for all the usual reasons, looks, strength, ability to fly, magic tricks. I liked Superman to the point of obsession. My mother had made me a Superman outfit—long johns dyed royal blue with Rit Dye, red bikini briefs and a broad gold belt, and of course a red-dyed cape with Superman's initial at the center. I took the cape from a chair beside my bed and tied it by its braided rope about my neck. I liked Superman because of his parents. His father had died when he was a baby, just like mine. We were both raised by step-fathers. Who were okay, but they weren't quite the right person. He tried many times to imagine Jor-El, his real father, and I tried to remember mine. Superman's real mother died in the explosion as well. In a way I believed that my real mother might have died, even though I knew she hadn't. Sometimes I pretended that she had. I believed my step-mother had sewed special clothes for me, like the cape I was wearing. My real parents were named Jor-El and Ka-El, just as Superman's were. My real birthplace was their exploding planet Krypton. My real parents loved me in the same way as his parents loved him. I went to sleep there on my bed in the sunny morning, wearing my red cape and surrounded by comic books, dreaming about Superman's loving parents on Krypton, and in this way dreamed the death of the father I had never known, the explosion in his heart that had killed him.

The TV was on the way. I knew this in my dream. I woke suddenly from my nap and sat up on the edge of the bed. My head spun from the sudden movement, I was confused. I said, "Mama, is the TV here yet?"

She answered me from a farther room. She said, "I thought you had fallen asleep."

I got out of bed and hurried up the hallway to the living room. I looked at the empty space at the end of the room that had been cleared for the television to be placed. The space was still empty. I was still wearing the cape with the large *S* at its center. I went out the front door and onto the porch. I stood out on the concrete extension of the porch where earlier I had pretended to dive. Now in my cape, still barefoot, I stood at the edge again and pretended to fly. I was Superman. The Goodyear truck rounded the corner by the Methodist church just then, just down the block from where I stood. It was a blue-and-white pickup with a big new television set anchored firmly in the truck bed by ropes. The segments of metal poles and the antenna tubing were visible there as well. My father was Jor-El. He was the handsome doomed stranger from a faraway planet, yet able from death to work his magic. Except that it was not Jor-El who had sent the TV. It was my daddy, my step-father. His imagination, such as it was, had produced this apparition that now, as if in a dream, was turning into our gravel driveway and pulling to a halt before my very eyes. I was screaming, literally screaming. I could not contain myself. My mother rushed to the front of the house, out the door, onto the porch, to discover what on earth could be happening. She thought I had fallen under the wheels of a car, had somehow set myself on fire, she was frantic, she couldn't imagine. The TV the TV the TV, I kept on screaming in a shrill voice, completely unhinged with delirious emotion. She said, "Buddy, for heaven's sake!" In her face was both fear and anger. She must have believed I was losing my mind, as indeed I was. Why I did what I did next, I'll never know. I took flight. I leaped a tall building in a single bound. The tallest thing in the area was the Spock Butane television tower, maybe that is what I imagined I was leaping. I went up up and away. I leaped as if there really were magic in my cape, in the world's unfathomable structure. I bent my knees and pushed off from the porch, leaped outward into space as if to fly to some necessary rescue. I leaped fully extended, my cape fluttered out behind me, my arms were crooked and slightly apart like my hero's in flight. My forehead hit the concrete unchecked. I was knocked unconscious by the force of the fall.

I remember a few things, not many. The pain was quite intense, despite the fact that I was mostly unconscious. My head hurt so bad I imagined I would die. My eyes were wet and then I was aware of a flow of blood from my head. I remember my mother's aggrieved wails when she saw me lying there. Her hands were on me. The Goodyear guys had let down the tailgate of the pickup and were lifting the TV cabinet down from the truck bed to the ground. I think I remember that part, maybe I only supplied it later. I remember thinking I had just waked up from the nap I had recently taken. I looked around me—maybe

I only dreamed this in unconsciousness—and saw my comic books helter-skelter across the sidewalk. I remember the Goodyear guys helping my mother press a towel to my head and lead me through the house to the bed. They swept away the comic books with their hands to make a clear space for me. My mother said, "Sit up. Don't go to sleep." Her voice was stern, efficient, angry, though she was terrified, of course. She called her father, the old doctor in town, my other grandfather, and soon he too stood beside my bed. He was a short warty man, with weak pink eyes and white eyelashes, porcine in appearance, and had stiff white bristles of hair protruding from his ears. He was adenoidal and snuffled when he breathed. He lifted my eyelids, he shined a light in each eye. He helped me sit up on the edge of the bed. I saw his thick, short-fingered hands work deftly with the wound, with gauze and tape. He cleaned the wound, which was more an abrasion and bruise than cut or puncture, and he medicated and bandaged it expertly. While I was ministered unto by my mother and grandfather, the Goodyear guys were installing the new television in the living room. They hauled it in the door and stuck it in the cleared-out corner and plugged it in. Outside they anchored the new antenna in the ground and extended it to its full height above the house. They anchored the guy wires, twisted the pole so that the rack of tubing at the top was positioned at just the proper angle to catch the signals that could theoretically be translated into pictures on a screen. Someone turned on the TV for its maiden voyage, the test run. The TV worked. Not only worked, a picture flickered there where no picture had been expected. Not snow, not a snowy picture even. A vivid sharp picture in amazing shades of black and white. Some disturbance or anomaly or other configuration of the atmosphere found television signals in the photo-polluted clouds and carried them lovingly into our home and translated them into programs for me to watch. My mother moved my sickbed into the living room. She brought out white-fresh pillows and fluffed them up to their full size. She hooked up the oscillating fan and set it on a table and turned it on me. The strong signal stayed not one day, not two, but a week. She turned on the TV and left it on for me. She brought my meals to the sofa. I watched and watched and watched. For short periods my father and my mother, sometimes separately sometimes together, watched with me. We spoke few words. The fewer the better, for me. Loretta Young, *Cameo Theater, I Led Three Lives, Boston Blackie, Dragnet,* Garry Moore, Steve Allen, *Name That Tune, Dialing for Dollars.* I watched them all. It was the happiest week of my life. My new father had nothing to do with this event. He was not there when it happened, he made little comment on it afterward. And yet, this is a memory of my new father. Inexplicably the arrival of the new television set, and its perfect reception, are linked inexorably with my sudden acceptance of his weird love in my life. He was not my new father after this, not my step-father, he was my father. He was himself, of course, and also my old father as well, the invisibility in my past. TV had made me whole, as Superman would never be. Jor-El and Mr. Kent were not the same.

4

"Welcome to Itta Bena, little lady"

ONE DAY MY FATHER made the surprising announcement that he was having company over to the house. This had never been done before. I knew of no friends my father had beyond the men he drank with, some of them steady fellows no doubt and others profane and vulgar men. Mother could not stand any of them. Doctors, mail carriers, plantation owners, grave diggers, men who had not drawn a meaningful breath since catching the winning touchdown pass in the 1940s, as well as the likes of my father, drank together at Shiloh's Store, standing on the rough unpainted boards of the store among the meager groceries that Mr. Shiloh also had for sale, cans of Vienna sausages, Dinty Moore stew, crackers and sardines. Mr. Shiloh had a meat case that housed only a long string of fierce-colored hot dogs that never changed position in the case.

Some of these men were violent drunks who once in a while threw fists, or ax handles, or even pulled a pistol, and no doubt there was plenty of racist and sexist and homophobic talk that went on among them. My father was by far the most gentle and

tolerant of the lot, but I don't blame my mother for her conten-
tion that Shiloh's Store was not an excellent place for Daddy to
spend his leisure hours. Her objection, I suspect, had more to do
with the bad light such company cast on her standing as a citizen
and schoolteacher and the local doctor's daughter than on any
moral objection to anything they did or said in the store. To be
more fair, Daddy's alcoholism had robbed my mother of the
movie star kisses and romance with which their life together had
begun, and it was natural for her to focus on the men and the
setting that represented the robbery that had been perpetrated
on her heart. It would not have mattered to my father that others found his scrofulous friends objectionable, for he loved these
men, loved their funny stories and tall tales and big talk and
even their occasional violence, but most especially their gossip
and impossibly ignorant political views. I know that some days
he wished he could have had his family there with him to hear
those excellent discussions so that we could have shared their
value. Some of the interpretations of national politics that he
brought home from Shiloh's Store were so impossibly stupid that
even I had to laugh. Someone had told my father, for example,
that General Bright, a military celebrity in Korea at the time,
and a local farmer named Bright Chisholm, were the same person. My father was impressed, indeed he was awestruck. "A military hero living in our midst!" my father marveled with open
eyes and open heart. It made no difference to my father that he
had known Bright Chisholm all his life, knew him never to have
left Itta Bena for more than a day or two, and indeed that Bright
Chisholm sometimes drank whiskey in Shiloh's Store alongside my
father. For him Shiloh's Store was imbued with a special magic
that, at least for the time he stood inside its walls and lifted its

amber elixir to his lips, anything was possible. This was the kind of nonsense my father brought home as a conversational gift to his family. In such absurdities he was utterly uncritical and believed every impossibility earnestly. My mother laughed but without much mirth. How wise those idiotic notions must have seemed when they were expressed over the tenth or twelfth whiskey, and how appalling they seemed just outside the store's fly-infested screened door. Even my father must have sensed the inadequacy of his social life, so often was it pointed out to him, but Shiloh's bootlegging establishment was where everybody knew his name, and indeed it was the only place where anybody knew his name. It was the only social life he had. But even though he loved those men, I knew he would never bring them into our house. There were good reasons for this. My mother would have fallen over dead if any one of them had tried to set their drunken white-trash foot inside the front door, first of all, and second these were his friends, not hers or mine, and clearly he had no intention of sharing them. We couldn't appreciate them, why would he subject his friends to hostility and misunderstanding? And there was another reason, a better reason really. Outside Shiloh's Store they scarcely spoke to one another, not even at the Southern Cafe or a high school football game. They knew each other over whiskey, that was it, nowhere else. They didn't play softball on weekends, they didn't go fishing together, they did nothing else. They drank. These were not friendships likely to survive transplantation of even the smallest kind, let alone into private homes with women. With children, for God's sake.

So it wasn't one of his drinking buddies who was coming for a visit. Who then? It was a mystery to me. A date had been set for the visit, a Friday late in August, and that date was not far away. He began making preparations, alerting my mother to his intentions. He would straighten up the house, he told my mother, he would come up with some kind of refreshments too he supposed, some Coca-Cola maybe, some crackers and cheese or something, maybe some of that premade onion dip. He didn't expect my mother to take responsibility for his entertaining, he assured her —sweetly, I thought. He did say that he would appreciate it though if, once he got the place spic and span, we would be thoughtful about picking up after ourselves a little. You know, don't take off your shoes in the living room and just leave them there, stuff like that. My mother pooh-poohed his insistence that he should do all the work himself. She would be happy to help out, she told him, and be assured he would not be allowed to serve some greasy combination of cheese and crackers to a guest in this home, next you'll be wanting to open a can of Shiloh's sardines or Vienna sausages. Of course she would help, don't give it another thought. She would take care of all refreshments as well.

"Your guest is traveling a long way for this visit," she said, "and if you won't insist that she spend the night, or at least have dinner with us, well that is your affair I'm sure, but you are not —I repeat, not—serving her cheese and crackers, of that I can assure you."

She? Is that the word I heard come from my mother's lips? She? My father's guest, for which he was suddenly sober and talking about Cokes and crackers and cheese, was a woman? My father didn't know a woman. I mean, did he? What kind of woman? Just a regular one? How could this be? At first I thought they meant some kind of woman he knew at Shiloh's Store. What kind of woman would that be, actually? I tried to picture such a woman and could not. What was going on here? My father was making big plans to entertain some woman in my mother's home, and my mother seemed just as pleased as punch about it.

I said, "Can I watch *A Tribute to the American Negro* on TV tonight if the reception is good enough?" This was a test, of course. My father was loath to allow me to watch Sammy Davis, Jr., on TV, let alone such a documentary.

He didn't flinch. He said, "Okay, sure." Then he said to my mother, "What else would be good? What kind of refreshments did you have in mind?"

This was a woman my father had dated when he was in the army. My mother was fascinated. Because he was so quiet, so rarely revealed anything of himself, the only previous evidence of my father's past was his army uniforms and a few boring drinking stories about Florida. Mother's fascination overwhelmed all fears of threat, and she threw herself into the project of preparing for this person's visit. The woman had been in show business when he knew her, he eventually told us. This fact further interested my mother and more completely enlisted her on my father's side. This woman would be traveling from Sarasota to Chicago to see relatives and when she realized her train would pass through the Mississippi Delta, she contacted my father to see whether a visit would be appropriate. Our visitor's stage name was Mitzi Hayworth, which she had adapted from the actresses Mitzi Gaynor and Rita Hayworth, though her real name was Jane Martynuski, a Polish girl, and my father's pet name for her had been Marty. He said, "I think we should all just call her Mitzi now, though, unless she tells us otherwise. It's been so long. I wouldn't want to presume."

My mother said, "She's welcome in our home, no matter what, but I do have to ask one question: She's not a stripper, is she? It's okay if she is, I just have to know."

"Absolutely not!" my father replied, relieved and grateful for my mother's help and permission, but a little indignant nevertheless.

Even I, at ten or eleven, had sense enough to know that Mitzi Hayworth had once been my father's lover. When the thought of the two of them "doing it" entered my head, I all but dove under the couch, so terrifying was the image. I had little enough real information about sex but I had plenty of fantasies. I was fascinated by my father as a sexual creature. I watched him carefully about the house. He had never appeared naked in front of me. He went dressed into the bathroom for his bath, and dressed he returned. Occasionally I saw him in his boxer underwear, and I looked at the front fly and willed it to open, but it never did. I saw nothing. I wished we could stand side by side at the toilet and that I might steal a look, but I was never invited, we never stood and peed together. Once we camped out together, on a fishing trip, but even then he stepped modestly behind a tree to relieve himself. What did a grown man's penis look like? What size, color, what shape and configuration, what additions or corrections had been made? Once when he was hospitalized for an appendicitis, I came into his hospital room to find him asleep with the covers kicked to the side, and I badly wanted to push the sheet back another few inches and check him out under there. It seemed easy, who would know, and yet I did not move. I sat instead in an uncomfortable chair with my hands in my lap and stared at the sheet and watched him sleep. I thought guilty thoughts. He woke up as I was sitting there. It startled me when I saw his eyes pop open. I said, "Uh."

He said in a groggy voice, "What's your problem?"

I said, "I didn't pull your covers back. Why are you accusing me of pulling your covers back. Why don't you believe me, you never believe me!" I leaped from the chair and left the room almost in tears.

At home my mother said, "Daddy said to see if you were all right. He said you were acting strange at the hospital."

I said, "He lies! What a liar! Why is he always telling lies about me? I didn't look under his covers. Jeez, what a liar."

She said, "You are the oddest child."

There was no reason for this fascination except that I had so little experience with men at all, I knew no men really, and the one I did know was so shy and careful of his modesty that I had never in all my life seen him without his clothes on. I hungered for information, for imagery. I needed control groups, comparison studies. I wanted some confirmation of myself as a male creature. I suppose that's what I wanted. I would have gladly studied the nakedness of any person on earth who would allow it, so starved was for whatever it was the world was hiding from me.

When my parents were dating, and after they were first married, I was interested in their fond touching, their caresses, their kissing. Often my father would pat my mother's butt; they held hands openly. At the VFW hut they had danced beautifully and romantically together to the heartbreaking voices of the Ink Spots. Much later, when all my father was interested in was drinking whiskey with his buddies at Shiloh's Store, I'm sure my mother longed for those bygone days of sawdust dance floors and movie star embraces. What a dearth of touching there must have been, by comparison. At the time, though, it seemed they would go on forever, that the famine would never come. Sometimes my mother would tease me by saying, "Do you want to see how movie stars kiss?" And then in the hallway or kitchen or sunporch, wherever we happened to be standing, the two of them would fall into a passionate clinch with much open-mouth kissing and movement of hands, the sight of which would both thrill and embarrass me speechless. Then I would screech in a kind of hysterical gaiety for them to stop. I would dive between them, desperately seeking to separate them before I disintegrated in fear and jealousy. Sometimes when I should have been sleeping, I heard the movement of their bed in the night, in the next room, and I could not submerge myself beneath my pillows fast enough, deeply enough, to shut out those vague and frightening sounds of love. And yet I knew so little and longed so deeply, I could tolerate almost anything, so happy was I to have some form of sexual enlightenment, anything at all, about my parents and therefore about myself. My father mainly, not the two of them, was my persistent focus. In him the strength of my obsession centered. I was interested in my mother, of course. I had seen her naked a time or two, dashing from bathtub to bedroom, when she forgot her robe. I had looked down her dress when she bent over, as boys do. My heart leaped, my insides jolted to see her breasts, to behold the amazing patch of hair between her legs. I noted carefully her use of toilet paper after urination, when she left the bathroom door open once or twice, and I managed to steal a glimpse. A couple of times I myself even sat when I peed, and then pulled a few sheets of paper off the roll and wiped myself when I finished, testing something, I'm not sure what. My maleness, somehow. But my mother had been with me since before the advent of memory. I was used to her. I saw her a good deal, day and night. I depended on her constancy. We touched a great deal, she hugged me often, read stories and comic books to me in bed. A certain familiarity was part of the antidote to desire and curiosity. And also, back there in the unknowable darkness of prememory she had shared a life with a man I did not know, and my longing for him, that core invisibility, had overwhelmed the unknowable about her. For complex reasons my interest in my mother's sexuality diminished in the face of what I did not know about my two fathers, and by extension about myself. Despite my unquenchable need of him, I imagined his need of me as well. I felt protective of my now-father. I wanted somehow to be the one who let nothing, especially no sexual slight, harm him. When my mother spoke nostalgically or lovingly about her late husband—my other-father, as I had started to refer to him in my mind—I felt defensive and angry, I wanted to shut her up, I wanted to shield the man who I believed had no defense against my mother's past true love. In a sense this visit by the mystery woman was a kind of leveling of the playing field. For once my father's past seemed to have sufficient substance to compete with my other-father's ghost.

I was determined not to allow my emotions to run rampant when my father's car arrived home from the train station in Grenada carrying Mitzi Hayworth. Too well I remembered the day when the Goodyear truck arrived with the television set in the back. I learned few permanent lessons as a child, but a certain restraint did seem to have settled in me after that nose dive. I could not afford another concussion. My front teeth were still a little loose. I stayed away from my Superman suit and waited nervously on the porch for the appearance of his car on the street. Astoundingly to me, it was not my father who drove to the train station thirty miles away to pick up Mitzi Hayworth, but my mother. My father and I stayed home and waited for her return. This change of plans had been a last-minute decision required by my father. He had started becoming nervous two days before Mitzi Hayworth's arrival. He had stopped going to Shiloh's Store each night after work, in an unexpected purification

ritual of some unnamed kind, and I think the sudden absence of
the alcohol from his system may have done some sort of emotional damage. On the appointed day, he was jittery and miserable and could not sit down. He watched the TV from the French
doors in the dining room and then walked away and paced
through the house and then came back and watched TV again.

My mother said, "Wilbur, for heaven's sake!"

To make matters worse for him, the pecan trees out front
had left everything beneath them sticky as glue with sap. Not
just the windshield but the entire car, and it was potent stuff,
strong enough to take the paint off if you weren't quick. My father stood hopelessly before the sap-varnished car. This was the
beginning of the end for him. The car's appearance suddenly
seemed to overwhelm him. All his strength left him. He looked
very old. He had taken the day off work and dressed himself in
his only suit—his "salt and pepper," as he called it—and put
rakishly upon his head a felt hat, at what he must have imagined
a jaunty angle, with the brim pulled low over one eye, Hum-
phrey Bogart style, a slouch hat that had apparently been stylish
during the war, when he knew Mitzi, and that he had kept for
these many years in the back of his closet, for just such a day as
this perhaps. He had not had a drink in several days now, and
was pale and pasty-faced and terrified-looking. His hands trembled violently. I'm sure he missed his friends, who normally he
saw every day. His identity, I feel certain, was threatened by their
absence from recent days. He was all dressed up, dashing in a
bizarre old-fashioned way, and yet for all that, he might as well
have been stark naked in the presence of his enemies, so vulnerable did he seem. I have never seen a man so frightened.

My mother said to him, "Honey, maybe just one drink
wouldn't be a bad idea."

My father didn't speak just yet. Slow and alien and despairing as a gut-shot bear he turned away from the car and headed around to the side of the house and found the garden hose. He twisted the handle of the spigot and pulled the hose behind him, miserable, to the front of the house and began slowly, hopelessly, humorlessly to wash his car. I was stricken with anguish and grief for him, though I did not know why. I went inside, though no one had asked me to do so, and brought out a bottle of Ivory and a zinc bucket, and together, wordless, my father and I washed the pecan glue from his car. When we were finished, and the car was spotless and rinsed and dried and gleaming, and the hose was put away, and it was time for him to go, he said, "I can't do it."

My mother said, "Of course you can, honey."

He said, "You do it. Will you? Please?"

They spoke in quiet tones in this way for a while, my father pleading softly, my mother offering encouraging words, until finally the hour was so late and his condition seemed to be deteriorating so fast, that my mother took the keys from him and lovingly held him to her breast while he cried, and comforted him with kind words, and then got into his clean car and drove away alone, to the train station in Grenada, where she would pick up Mitzi Hayworth. I never really knew what my father was crying about. It was not a thing I could ask. These years later I think he knew that the past was lost to him forever. The people of his dreams had not waited for him, as he had imagined. They had aged, either well or poorly, they had added to their existence certain new experiences that he would never share. The dreams he had dreamed were stopping by his home on a summer's evening to say that they had moved on, to assert their corporeality and to remind him that he was a drunk, a failure, and that alone, and that what he remembered of the past, whether false or true, served only to deny the futility and despair of Shiloh's Store and the sad pleasures of his hours there. These were not things I believed, either then or now. I have reared two step-sons of my own and I know something of the alienation and heartache of that hard task, so when I imagine my father in heaven—my step-father let me make clear—it is a man who said I love you each night to a boy devoted only to his mama and himself and incapable of returning his love in a way that was recognizable as love. How lonely he must have been in my presence. How difficult to welcome the past into his home in order to hear it say that this loneliness was all he would have forever, for he had chosen it.

My father stopped crying and blew his nose and stood in the driveway as my mother stepped inside the car and closed the door and drove away. He stood there until the car made the turn at the Methodist church, and then out of sight, down little State Road 7 to the main highway, and then he went in the house and sat in his chair and turned on the TV and watched an old black man named W. C. Handy play trumpet for fifteen minutes. I sat with him. I didn't know what to say, so I said nothing. When Mr. Handy's show was finished, we sat through *As the World Turns* and *The Edge of Night,* still in silence, and then he got up and snapped off the TV.

He said, "W. C. Handy is the father of the blues."

I said, "Oh."

He went into his room and did not come out for a long time.

My mother had outdone herself with the refreshments. Everything was all finished before she left the house. I stood at the refrigerator and looked inside as though I were looking into a crystal ball. The food was beautiful, and though some of it was familiar stuff, the celebration that had been planned for this stranger seemed to exist on a separate plane, in a parallel universe. She had boiled and peeled two pounds of fresh shrimp and now they were chilling on a bed of ice in the refrigerator. A tomato-y remoulade sauce, with horseradish, chilled in the center of the shrimp platter. Three different kinds of crackers, olives both green and black, cans of smoked oysters, cheeses, roasted pecans from our own trees with salt crystals gleaming from the meat, some things I had never seen before and that I suspected she had not much noticed either until she picked them up in the Piggly Wiggly in Greenwood, including a couple of little smoked fish with the heads still on. In case Mitzi Hayworth had a sweet tooth, my mother was ready. She had made brownies with home-grown pecans, she made a Karo pecan pie, she had bought an assortment of hard candies and placed them in a big bowl on a table in the living room, and a huge Whitman's Sampler, with the top standing casually open and the chocolates gleaming out of their dark bed like strange diamonds. And just in case Mitzi Hayworth decided to stay for dinner, she had baked a picnic ham, and in case she was staying overnight, she had changed the sheets in the guest room and, on a last-minute impulse, dashed up to Mr. Gold's Low Price Store in Itta Bena and bought a new bedspread, bright yellow, and spread it on the bed. She bought a matching towel set and placed the towels and washcloths on the bed, ready for a guest's use. She looked critically at the old curtains in the room, and I thanked all the gods when she shook her head and dismissed whatever idea she had been entertaining about new curtains.

Mitzi Hayworth had been with the circus. Indeed she was still with the circus. This was the detail that had been left out of my father's story. As soon as I heard it, it made sense, and I wondered why I had not figured this out in the first place. My father's motives were never absolutely clear, and probably never known even to him, so I'm not sure why he didn't mention this fact during all the elaborate preparations, though now I suppose I can guess. It had to do with a certain degree of shame that I wish he had not felt. It explains why he substituted the generic "show business" for the circus. The circus seemed to me then and seems today an honorable profession, though some of its performers are surely held in higher esteem than others. Trapeze artists and lion tamers must be among the most well thought of. But with no advance warning that Mitzi Hayworth was a circus performer, it was no wonder my mother suspected—was possibly titillated by—the possibility that his friend had been a stripper. This guess or interpretation of hers was a revelation to me. I had not understood before this visit just what a vacuum my mother perceived in her life where romance—and maybe I mean sex here as well—had once dwelled in fullness of hope and expression. Maybe my father had held some class prejudice of his own against circus folk, was a little ashamed of Mitzi's profession, despite his affection for the woman personally. Or maybe he had simply surmised that we would have figured it out for ourselves. That was a real possibility. He had often spoken of Sarasota ("Venice, actually," he sometimes corrected himself, "they're practically on top of each other") as the home of the winter circus. I suppose I remembered later all the deadly boring conversations he had engaged me in while drunk in which he told me these things, always in the same drunken words—"winter circus," "Venice, actually." There was a mantralike drone to those sentimental memories, the words themselves seemed to evoke a world for him.

That world now came into our house. It came to us in the form of Mitzi Hayworth, and it left us changed, my mother in particular, though no one was spared. By the time my mother and Mitzi Hayworth arrived in the car from the train station my father was beside himself with anxiety. He was pacing the house like a caged tiger and smacking himself in the forehead with the palm of his hand and letting out piteous and indecipherable groans, which I took to mean "How could I have allowed this to happen!" We heard the car in the driveway. My mother sounded the horn to alert us to come outside to greet them, a few sassy beeps that told me she and Mitzi Hayworth had hit it off well and that she was in an excellent mood. At this point my father was almost prostrate. Without a word I took his hand and led him out the front door to what might as well have been his execution, for all the misery in his face. My mother was still sitting behind the wheel and shutting down the car's engine, but Mitzi Hayworth was nowhere to be seen.

"She didn't come," I said, with both relief and regret.

My miserable father could not even look in the direction of the car, for all his histrionic moaning and head-wagging, and yet he said, "She's there. She's in there all right."

I said, "No, really, look. Mama's in the car alone."

He did look, and just then, mysteriously, the passenger-side door opened up and I saw beneath the door a tiny foot and leg reach out toward the ground. Mitzi Hayworth stepped into view just as my mother made her way out of the other door. Mitzi Hayworth was scarcely more than three feet tall. When she spoke, her voice was not crimped and unusual in the manner of some little people, not a squeak, but it did have that high sweet melody of children's laughter. It was a voice never destined for sultriness but far from comic, rather innocent, sweet, heartbreakingly small and pure. She said, "Hello, Wilbur. Family life seems to agree with you."

I fell in love. I was in love with my father's old girlfriend. Never had I seen so beautiful a person, heard so melodious a voice. She seemed to be around thirty, slightly older maybe. Her hair was long and deep brown, her complexion dusky and dark, her hips were slim, her legs and arms and hands perfectly formed. Her eyes, her lips, she looked like a movie star. She was the perfect size for me. She was the perfect woman. Whenever I had imagined heroic events, in my dreams, my fantasies, it was always really Mitzi Hayworth of whom I was dreaming. I recognized her now, the moment I saw her, the woman of my dreams. My head was spinning. I was in love, I tell you, in love, Lily might as well have put a hex on me, I might as well have had shrubbery growing out of my nose, I made no sense even to myself and I didn't care. Mitzi Hayworth was the woman of my dreams.

The intensity of my feelings prevented me from observing my father's reaction in these crucial seconds of reunion, so it is impossible to say exactly what expression appeared on his face, what language his body began to speak. Upon seeing her he did recover himself considerably, though, I am sure of that much if only because he did not faint dead away in the front yard. Swooning was a possibility in his state and would not have surprised me at all. He said, "Hi, Marty." Mitzi Hayworth walked toward him and he squatted down to greet her as you would a child. She put her arms around his neck and they embraced, awkwardly after so long a time, and then parted.

She said, "I've gone entirely to Mitzi now, hope you don't mind." He was looking hard at her, searching for what I do not know, their past, even his future, and I could tell by his sad eyes that he found one but not the other: The past had left no trace for him, and the future was bearing down on him like a long black train.

He stood up. He said, "Mitzi. Okay. Sure."

My father's recovery of the powers of speech and ambulation were real, but they were only protective coloration and not enough to save him for long. My mother came around from the trunk of the car, out of which she had produced Mitzi Hayworth's little suitcase, and was chattering away about anything and everything, the weather, a man they saw having an epileptic fit in the cinder lot of the train station in Grenada, the car ride home, show business. *Show* business? I had never seen her so happy, so animated, her eyes so brilliant blue. She looked ten years younger, almost like a movie star herself. You would have thought she was the one in love with Mitzi Hayworth.

Once inside the house I began to see that my father had a plan. He was going to bolt. He was getting the hell out of here. He could talk, he could walk, and he was using these powers to set up his escape. I had not seen him with such a positive attitude since he stopped drinking several days earlier. My mother took Mitzi Hayworth into the guest room. It had already been decided she would stay the night, her tickets had already been changed at the train station. Mother showed her the closet and then realized Mitzi would never be able to reach the hangers and so together they cleaned out a low drawer in the chest of drawers. They were like sisters, like girls. My mother showed her the new towels.

Mitzi Hayworth said, "You shouldn't have gone to so much trouble!"

My mother said, "Pshaw, we're just so honored to have you. Now let me show you where you can wash up."

Mitzi Hayworth said, "Have you got a kitchen stool or some-thing, so I can see in the bathroom mirror to put on my face in the morning?"

My mother said, "No stool, but honey, the line of work Wilbur's in, you just know you came to the right house for step-ladders," and again they shared their sweet laughter. My mother's phrasing sounded a little like Pearl Bailey's, I noticed.

The afternoon slid easily past. Mitzi Hayworth loved the shrimp, my mother sliced the picnic ham and put out mustard and cheese for sandwiches. Mitzi Hayworth went straight for the smoked trout, and I could tell this pleased my mother. All of us trailed along as Mother gave Mitzi a tour of the house. Then followed out into the backyard, where she showed her the apple tree, the big toolshed with its neatly arranged hoe and shovel and rake and fork hanging on the wall, my father's fishing poles resting across the rafters. We walked among the fig trees and peach trees and into the vegetable garden. My fa-ther was biding his time. I didn't know this yet, but he was wearing his poker face. The pot was building, and I was the key to his game.

For a while my father feigned an interest in conversation. As long as the girl talk continued, he was all right, was able to nod amiably, ask a question or two, even once to make a witty re-mark. Mitzi Hayworth commented again on the beautiful guest towels and bedspread in her room, and my father said, "Now we don't have to wonder where the yellow went." This was a reference to a popular toothpaste commercial on television: You'll wonder where the yellow went when you brush your teeth with Pep-so-dent. Mitzi and my mother both got the joke and laughed appreciatively. For my part I set upon a campaign to make a complete fool of myself for Mitzi Hayworth's attention. My father had apparently counted on this happening. I laughed too loud at every small suggestion of humor. I would say, "That's funny, man, oh man, that's funny," and then break up laughing again, long after the joke was over. Some of my numerous nervous habits kicked into high gear. I belched and armpit-farted and threw out all my joints, thumbs, fingers, shoulders, cracked my knuckles, and even heard myself telling about the "flatulence artist" I saw in a sideshow carnival.

This faux pas was deemed especially egregious by my mother, since it brought up the otherwise unmentioned topic of "show business" of the particular genre in which Mitzi Hayworth was employed, that is, freak shows. My mother was embarrassed to death and said, "Buddy!"

Mitzi Hayworth was not offended at all. She said, "Oh I've seen that artist, he has an Italian-sounding name, doesn't he? He's excellent. I'm sure it's the same one."

I was ecstatic, I was a success in life, a beautiful woman understood me, I was in love, I said "Hunh, hunh, hunh," like a Mongoloid. I rocked so vigorously in the platform rocker that it bounced on the hardwood floor. I put my feet up on the coffee table. I almost knocked a good dish to the floor. I ate four pieces of candy from the Whitman's Sampler and got chocolate drool on my shirt. When my mother finally admonished me, I slouched down and sat on my spine, rather on my neck, and had to be told to sit up straight. What I didn't know was that I was playing directly into my father's plan. He had not said one word to correct me, no matter how out of control I became, and too late I understood that I was his escape hatch out of this crystal ball in which his meaningless future was the single and constant prediction.

My father said, "I'll tell you what—you girls go on talking, there's plenty of time for me and Mitzi to catch up. I'm going to take Buddy here along with me to run a few errands. Do y'all need anything from town?"

My mother said, "Oh, *would* you? He is driving me straight out of my mind."

Mitzi Hayworth said, "I could use some emery boards if you go anywhere near a drugstore, Wilbur."

"Emery boards it is," he repeated. He was looking better by the second, his voice was strong, his color had returned. "Anything else?" he said, chirped.

I had not even suspected there was a plan, and now here it lay before me, fully executed. I was doomed. Mitzi Hayworth's love was lost to me as quickly as that. My father was an artist himself, I had just not known to watch him. He had let my screw-ups build up so gradually, over the hours of the afternoon, that even I had not seen the progression, certainly not the end-mark, where he could get anything he wanted just by moving me out of the house and from under foot. I wanted to say, Oh, wait, wait, I see now, I can control myself, whoa, let me have one more chance. Too late. He had already laid down his cards and won the game, Royal Flush, suckers, outta here.

There were no errands, of course, and no emery boards would be returning with us. This was an escape, and I was a hostage. I was also by my stupidity an accomplice. I kept saying, "I want to stay, Daddy. Can I stay? Can I? I'll sit still, I'll—." He didn't hear me. We were already in Part Two of his plan. We were already in his car, and I was breathing the last faint traces of perfume that Mitzi Hayworth had left there and hating myself for being young and stupid in so many ways. And maybe if I had understood my father's plan at all I would not have protested it in any case. Another of my dreams was about to come true. I was going exactly where I had always wanted to go, having had no imagination until this point to think of anywhere better.

Shiloh's Store, as I've said, sold illegal whiskey and a few groceries. The store was a rude unpainted building with a broad open porch and a tin roof. It sat in the middle of a large graveled lot on the cusp of the white and black sections of town. The cotton gin, a private home (occupied incidentally by Itta Bena's grave digger), a service station, and a couple of other business concerns—all sat at the same intersection as Shiloh's Store. Nothing was hidden, customers passed in and out without shame. The residents of Balance Due, the black section of town, could walk the short distance from their homes to the store for incidental items. The alcohol sold here was not moonshine but brandname bonded liquor, the same as you could buy openly anywhere else in the country, but sold here "illegally." Such sale was in no way considered a "crime" but only a practical solution to the state's ridiculous laws governing the distribution of alcohol. Most of what was sold at Shiloh's was package goods, but a select clientele of sportsmen or gentlemen or simply hopeless alcoholics like my father was permitted to stand in the store and drink at the counter that Shiloh used for his bar. For the first time in my life, I walked up the steps and entered the cool darkness of Shiloh's Store. I was a man.

Daddy watched Mr. Shiloh pour his first drink in almost a week and his hands trembled like a willow branch as he brought the amber fragrant elixir to his lips. He hesitated, he tipped the glass up, he swallowed, oh yes, he closed his eyes, unhinged his jaw, oh yes my God oh yes. He was well. There was no more need for tears, for fakery, for visions of his hopeless future, he was free at last. At first only my father and Mr. Shiloh and I stood in the store. Mr. Shiloh did not drink at all, that I noticed, and my father drank only because he had to, as a diabetic takes insulin. I knew Mr. Shiloh's two children slightly, they were younger than myself, and I knew their mother to be a pleasant woman who took them to the same Sunday school I attended each week. I was comfortable and happy here. I had lost Mitzi Hayworth, it was true, and it took me a while to accept that I would never have her back, but that was all right, in the long run. I had Shiloh's Store, I was being given all the Coca-Cola I could drink, all the greasy food I could eat, beef jerky and pickled eggs and a can of Vienna sausages, which Mr. Shiloh pronounced Vye-eenas. I was standing in the sanctum sanctorum of my father's days. Except for love, especially the love of a woman in show business, what more could a boy want?

By midnight I was exhausted. I felt ready to cry. A hundred times Mr. Shiloh said he would take me home if I was ready to go, his car was right out front, but I declined. I wanted to keep an eye on my father, for one thing, but mainly I was afraid I would miss something. Mr. Shiloh had discreetly called my mother, early in the afternoon, and told her that I was there with Daddy and would be okay, he would look after me. A half dozen or more hard drinkers had settled into the store to join my father on his path to destruction. Someone told a story about being wounded in France. He pulled up his shirt and showed the scar. Someone else told about his arm going to sleep in a tent and when he woke up and felt the dead arm in the sleeping bag with him he thought it was a snake and beat it to a pulp with a flashlight. Someone else asked whether we had heard that a blue runner snake would chase you down and hide in your asshole. Two men got into an argument about whether a tree was willow or a weed, and one stabbed the other. It was a small knife, and not a deep wound, so neither of the men went home, they just didn't talk to each other for a while. Then they seemed to forget all about it, and before long they were talking about something else. Somebody else took a poll, attempting to decide which was better to have as a friend, "A bad white person or a good nigger." There were arguments on both sides, it went back and forth for a while. I was glad my mother was not present to listen to this one.

For his part my father courageously concluded, "There's something to say for one, and something to say for the other."

I would have died if anyone had singled me out and asked me what I thought. All I wanted to do was to fit in. Which I suppose is all my father wanted as well. The right answer seemed like "good nigger" but I wasn't sure. Eventually my father turned blue and collapsed on the floor and his breathing stopped and Mr. Shiloh, who was a big man, had to pick him up and shake him till he started breathing again, and then he helped him vomit off the store porch and after that he took us both home in his Cadillac. He carried my father in the house in his arms. I went to bed by myself and listened to my mother crying in Mitzi Hayworth's room. Later, when she was finished crying she came into my room to check on me, but I pretended to be asleep. It was a close call for my father, no doubt about that. I was very frightened when he was sick and relieved when he came to life again and very grateful for the gift of being allowed to see all this and to know what I had been missing. I slept till noon the next day, and when I woke my father was still sleeping on the couch on the sunporch and my mother had driven Mitzi Hayworth to the train station, and so neither of us ever saw her again.

There is one more thing I want to tell about this amazing

day, or about its aftermath, I suppose. My mother was changed by it. Immediately this became apparent. Not by my father's close call, for as I was to learn later, this and worse had happened many times. She would go on loving him forever, sometimes in bitterness, sometimes with gentler love, no matter the extravagance of his failure. What was different is hard to define precisely. She stopped sometimes in the yard when I was nearby and when the orange sun was low in the western sky and she would point and say, "In that direction is Texas. If you keep on going you'll come to California." Or we might be sitting together as a family on the screened-in porch my father had built on the back of the house and he might say in his loving, lazy way, "There's a southern breeze tonight," and she would look out in a southerly direction, as if to agree, but from where I sat, shelling peas or shucking corn in my lap, I would see that her eyes were turned inward, not to the south at all, and finally she would say to me, "The Gulf of Mexico, is in that direction, Buddy. Venezuela, Brazil." Nights, at bedtime, I would be lying in my room, and my father would call to me, "I love you," and I would love him as well but I might say this or I might not, and my mother would come into my room with the Sears and Roebuck catalog, or maybe Montgomery Ward's, and we would play a game she had learned that night from Mitzi Hayworth, in which we assigned lives and lovers and destinies to the models photographed there with merchandise. After a while she would put the book aside and her gaze would again turn inward.

One night I said, "I'd like to go into show business when I grow up."

After a silence my mother said, "I wouldn't have minded being in show business myself."

5

Zen and the Art of Mail Order

SOMETIME AFTER SCHOOL STARTED in the fall of that year, I began to order things from mail-order catalogs. Montgomery Ward was my favorite, and my first order was a gift for my parents. Somewhere near the middle of the catalog I found the order sheet, which I ripped jaggedly out, and I began to fill it out in pencil in my pathetically childish hand. I carefully spelled out the letters of my name on the top line of the form, only to discover that I had failed to follow directions and should have noted "last name first" in the first blank. Laboriously I erased and, in the smudged space that resulted, began again. Name, address, telephone, name of item, item number, size, color, price, and so on. For the first time I felt in communication with an exterior geography, almost another world. That was the point of this exercise, far more than the gift that was its immediate object.

After the long night in Shiloh's, after falling in love with my father's midget, the city limits of Itta Bena began to seem a prison to me. I was not ready for my escape, but for the first time I could see beyond the walls. Would Ward's even send me what I ordered? Would my money disappear into the ether? I was not sure. I was not at all confident my message would reach its destination, any more than are those scientists who send out signals to the stars in hopes of contacting extraterrestrial life. They are not surprised or disappointed on a daily basis at the silence of their stars, nor would I be.

My task was made more difficult, though not less thrilling, by the fact that I had hidden myself in the clothes closet of my room, among the must of rubber boots and malodorous shoes and wool clothing on hangers. I don't know why the secrecy of this act was important to me. To have anyone suspect that I was so presumptuous as to believe I could actually make contact with the outside world—well, I had to hide, I couldn't face anyone with such a presumption. There was no light in the closet, so along with my pencil and the catalog I took a flashlight, which with difficulty I managed to balance and to shine upon the page, and with cramped-up joy I copied out the proper item numbers and other information. It was hot in the closet and I sweated like the Missouri.

Later my mother said she had heard me giggling in there, and I am sure this is true, so much happiness did this secret deed, this first communication with the universe, give me. My mother's use of the catalog was to inspire dreams of worlds she did not really believe existed and was resigned to know only in fantasy, but I saw real worlds toward which I might flee, if ever Itta Bena should nod and loosen its firm clutch on me. Montgomery Ward was an escape hatch, its opening as thin as a reed, but somehow I might squeeze through it and pop out the other end into rarer air. In the world beyond, Shiloh's Store and what I had seen there would not exist, or would do so only as a distant memory, itself more dream than true.

Mother's Day was near and Father's Day not far behind, and so when I saw in the catalog two painted oversized coffee cups and saucers, one with an image of a mustachioed, derby-hatted gentleman riding an old-fashioned big-wheeled bicycle, and on the other a lady in a long dress and plumed picture-hat riding a similar vehicle, I had all the excuse I needed to make first contact with whatever planets revolved around Ward's newly discovered sun. "Enclose check or money order," I read aloud, inside the closet, holding steady the flashlight's beam. "Do not send cash through the mail." I would have to figure this one out. Discovering a solution to paying for the gifts would be a valuable lesson, which would come in handy later on, with subsequent purchases.

I remember standing at a window in the old post office that I was scarcely tall enough to see into, and purchasing from the postmaster Mr. Banyon that first money order, or as I would have almost been able to say at the time, my first ticket out. I had money of my own. I had never had any expenses, so whatever money came my way had always been stuffed into a drawer and had been piling up for some time. My mother paid me an allowance for certain small jobs around the house, and occasionally I ran errands for older people in the neighborhood—trips to the market for bread and milk, or to Mr. Beard's Drug Store for a prescription—and sometimes I accepted a dime, a quarter, whatever was offered. We had a push mower that I used to mow our yard, for which task my father paid me more. Later I used the mower for the small yards of our neighbors, and then my father bought a power mower, with a bright yellow frame and a red Briggs & Stratton engine and a pull rope you had to rewrap each time, and my lawn-mowing business increased and made me rich.

By the time the package arrived at the post office—a yellow slip in our home mailbox addressed to me told me to pick it up —I had forgotten that I ordered the cups and saucers and felt a little frightened that somehow I might have done something wrong as I answered the summons of its message.

The gifts were a success, my parents loved them. The painted cups were more gay and fanciful in real life than in the catalog, everyone was impressed and pleased with my self-reliance and good sense and generosity. My mother was practically in tears. "You are the most thoughtful child. I'm sorry I said you were odd." None of that is important. The importance of this event was that it opened a universe to me. There was intelligent life on the stars, and I had made first contact, received the first clear signals. A power of distances built inside me. Now on to the galaxies, wherever mail order dwelled.

Comic books offered a host of send-away possibilities. I joined Junior G-Men, I got the badge, the code, the secret decoder ring, the fingerprinting kit, the collapsible spyglass. I joined the Dick Tracy fan club and got similar items. I joined several fan clubs, in fact, including Little LuLu (which encouraged me to keep a diary), Pogo, and Joe Palooka. I ordered fake money, sea horses, itching powder, invisible ink, a squirt flower, a palm buzzer, a nose flute, jacks and a rubber ball, a book of paper dolls. For a while I stuck with "free" items, which I understood were not really free and that I didn't want in any case —stamp collections, trading cards, Charles Atlas information, art lessons, and Mexican jumping beans. I sent back the stamps and jumping beans and did not follow through on the others. The whole point was to make contact.

At first it was. The world was out there. It knew my name, it knew my address. I went back to Ward's catalog reinvigorated. The items became more expensive. More money was required, so I worked twice as hard. I ordered a magic set. It had a collapsible magic wand, a top hat made of collapsible paper, decks of regular cards, decks of trick cards, in which every card was the same, and a book that described dozens of card tricks, almost all of them too complicated or requiring too much manual dexterity to be of any help to me. It had "magic" water glasses that you could pour water into and then turn upside down and they seemed to be empty. There was a similar trick with newspaper and a milk bottle. The set had steel rings that supposedly you could make come apart and put back together, though I never figured out how. It had colored scarves and devices with long rubber bands that would make those scarves disappear from your hand by jerking them quickly behind your back. I could only do about three of the tricks in this elaborate set. I was not discouraged, not in the least.

I ordered a ventriloquist's dummy. It was an amazing piece of work. I wonder whether such a thing can even be ordered so easily today, let alone priced so that a child in my circumstances might afford to buy it. The head and hands and feet were carved of wood. The dummy already had a name, printed on the box and on a tag around its neck, and coincidentally the name was the same as my own, Buddy. Buddy was painted with freckles and large stationary eyes and resembled Howdy Doody slightly, and eerily it resembled me a little as well. When you put your hand inside him, from the back, and got hold of the controls, the head and mouth moved with almost scary precision and reality. There was an instruction pamphlet describing ways to make the dummy move effectively and to create a comic impression of reality, and another pamphlet describing ventriloquism, which it insisted was an illusion, not a real "voice throwing," though both concepts were somewhat over my head and I got little out of them. The dummy's clothes, I was disappointed to see, were supposed to indicate a "hick" or "greenhorn," which I already knew myself to be, and so this part of the illusion was the opposite of what I had had in mind.

Nevertheless, I loved Buddy and practiced endlessly at throwing my voice and not moving my lips, reading and rereading the puzzling instructions. The reason I finally gave up working with the dummy was that I discovered I had nothing to say. I would hold Buddy and speak in my strained falsetto, but the words that came out were not interesting. "Hello, Buddy," I would say in my regular voice.

"Hello, Buddy," the dummy would say in his falsetto.

"Is there an echo in here?" I would say.

"Is there an echo in here?" Buddy would say.

I wanted more. I wanted the words that would go beyond mere contact with this exterior world. I wanted words that came from so deep inside me that when I heard their sound, perceived their meaning, I would become possessed of a new self, somehow, one that might someday leave Itta Bena and exist, nay thrive, in another world. I poked through the box the dummy came in, looking for a pamphlet telling me what words to speak to produce the interior, spiritual results I so vaguely, and yet so passionately, hoped to effect. I found nothing. There was nothing. I would have to wait for those gifts of the spirit from which words would be formed.

When I understood that the answers were mysterious, far more mysterious than could be decoded by any pamphlet, and more personal than any one being could relate to another, I finally put Buddy aside. I did not put him away, though. He sat in a small chair in my room and looked at me through his perpetually open eyes, and neither of us spoke.

I went about the slow unfolding of my days. I thumbed through catalogs in all my spare time. I ordered a body-building set. It came in a huge flat box. In it were two squeeze devices to build up strength in the hands, and then a similar-looking but much larger squeeze thing that looked a little like hedge clippers, for building up something else, maybe the chest muscles. There was also an adjustable metal bar to fit inside a door frame for chin-ups, and then a series of exercise tools that consisted of steel springs with red plastic handles. These springs you stretched outward to both sides of your body by extending your arms. A longer one you could anchor your foot on one handle and the other handle in your hand and do "curls" for the biceps. After a certain number of repetitions you changed to the other foot and arm. Then you put them behind your back and pulled at them to strengthen other muscles. All these devices I never used, so far as I remember, so bizarre did they seem, except to try them out when they first arrived, and yet this did not matter. I was astoundingly attracted to them. I had them, and that seemed to be the point, ownership. Now they were mine, moon rocks a child of a later generation might have thought, talisman, magic charms, protection somehow against a reality from which as yet there was no final escape.

I see now that I was not merely making contact with the outside universe, as I had initially imagined, but that I was seeking power from those other-worlds, outside the Mississippi state line, as Superman had renewed his powers from by occasional returns to outpost Krypton. I was ordering out for protection, for power. I began with the cups and saucers, gifts to the enemy,

I suppose. I joined clubs in which I became a member with identification as such, exclusive clubs in a way, since you had to cut
out the coupon and send it off with your name to join. I tried devices of trickery, the itching powder, and then went to appara-
tuses promising actual physical strength. It was power I wanted,
far more I suspect than mere confirmation of the larger world.

Power, of course, is what I possessed least of all, and connections with the outer darkness, as geographies beyond Itta
Bena seemed to me, were tenuous indeed. More than anyone I
was a product of my real world, tied to it in ways that were
comfortable and familiar and through which, in fact, I was a
success in life, if one was content with my kind of success. I was
a Mississippian, an Itta Benan, forever thus would I be, there
was no point in my denying it. My mother referred to me as "a
nervous child," "an odd child," and so I was, for all the time that
I was secretly plotting an escape through catalog contacts with
extant societies from the planet Krypton, I was also digging my
own burrow, or ground nest, or grave, in Itta Bena.

I was the poster boy for Itta Bena Elementary School. I was
class clown—the skinny kid with wispy blond hair and a
cowlick and freckles and jug ears and an overbite, small for my
age, the child who brought frogs and crawfish and snakes and
salamanders and bugs into the classroom, the child who pretended to dance the flamenco behind the piano-playing public
school music teacher's back as the rest of the class sang "Ma-
ñana," the child forever in trouble for talking, giggling, poking,
smoking cornsilk or rabbit tobacco or muscadine vines—my
tongue was numb for weeks on end from all my illicit smoking. I
was the one making wanted posters depicting the principal, and
laughing too loud and too long after the joke was over.

Later on, in high school, I was voted Silliest Sophomore. I

was obsessed with sex. It was all I could think about. I made every item of conversation into something sexual. I made up sexual stories about the models in the Sears and Roebuck catalog. These two were "doing it," this guy was a sissy. I nearly busted a gut over the poem "The Owl and the Pussycat." *Oh what a beautiful pussy you are, what a beautiful pussy you are. Oh pussy oh pussy oh pussy my love.* I like to died, as I would have said back then. I thought they were going to have to send me down to Whitfield, I was so tickled. Whitfield was the name of the state mental institution, a sort of snake pit at the time. I had no idea what most sexual words meant. I could not come close to defining the word *pussy,* and yet I used it at every opportunity. I listened carefully to its every utterance in rest rooms and in vacant lots, hoping to catch some clue to its meaning, and yet I could never quite nail down a definition. A boy named Vickers seemed worldly, so I asked him, in an offhand way, "Have you ever gotten any pussy, Vickers?" I was employing a popular usage of the term, so I was able to speak with rare confidence. Vickers had a flattop and large forearms, like Popeye. He was not given to fantasy or exaggeration, so I knew I could trust him.

"No," he answered truthfully, "I have not."

All right, I thought, so far so good. "What would you do if you did?" I said slyly.

He eyed me suspiciously. He said, "What do you think?"

I smiled and winked at him. "Right," I said knowingly. "Right. Same here. Me too." I could not bring myself to say, "But how, Vickers, how? Give me a hint, man, anything."

In the halls of the school, beneath portraits of Lincoln and George Washington, I sang "We are the girls from Norf'lk, Norf'lk, we don't drink and we don't smoke, Norf'lk, Norf'lk," though I had not the slightest idea what the joke was, or for that matter what Norfolk might be. I certainly never dreamed it was a town in Virginia. I did a little hootchy-kootchy dance beneath the great presidents' portraits as I sang. I told sexual lies on almost everybody in school. I was famous for it. Eventually I'd get caught, always, some parent would hear what I had said and come after me, yank me out of the Saturday movie, or off the baseball field, or out of the rubber-gun wars, or off my bicycle as I was cycling behind the town tractor in the DDT spray, or off the piano bench where I sat hammering out "The Volga Boatman" next to my big-bottomed, gentle teacher Mrs. Wilson, and demand that I tell the truth. I expended enormous energy pretending to my accusers that I at least understood what I had been lying about. I encouraged a friend to let me tie him hand and foot with rope before school one morning, and then I left him alone behind the high school gym all day while the whole school worried about what had become of him. I set the alarm of Miss Alberta's desk clock so that it would go off during class and scared the bejabbers out of her. Miss Alberta was the fifth grade teacher who first told us the meaning of *Itta Bena*. I sucked on the skin at the crook of my arm and then stuffed my nose deep into the wet crotchlike place I'd created there and inhaled the near-sexual scent of it deep into my lungs in morbid joy. I bit my nails, stripped my cuticles raw, picked my nose, gouged at my scalp with my fingernails until it bled, crossed my eyes, wiggled my ears, cracked my knuckles and toes and elbows and knees, threw my shoulders out of joint so that I looked deformed, and destroyed school books by unconsciously sucking my thumb and then rubbing my wet thumb on the crease in the opened book until the paper crumbled away to nothing. I did this thing with my Adam's apple that is hard to describe: The Adam's apple would jump wildly in my throat and people would look away. I could whistle an ear-splitting note through my gapped front teeth, I could belch on demand, execute loud armpit farts, and blow dove sounds through my coupled hands. I could fold back my eyelids and bend all my fingers at the first joint and throw both my thumbs out of joint. I lighted farts with a Zippo lighter I had won at a carnival, as boys my age crowded near to see the blue streak fly out of the seat of my pants. At the same carnival I paid a full dollar to enter a tent where a so-called flatulence artist plied his strange trade. I was astonished and impressed, even inspired, by his ability to blow out a series of candles from across the room. I wanted to be like him. Secretly I hoped his vocation might someday also be mine. It was my earliest dream of power, and perhaps metaphorically it has come true. I could hold my breath until I actually fainted and cracked my head against the desktop or tumbled onto the floor. Usually I did this to impress Milly, the girl who sat in front of me and with whom I was absurdly in love. Later, when I had more body hair, I took a meticulously sharpened Barlow knife and shaved my legs in class and then closed my eyes and put my hand on my ankle and pretended it was the stubbly shaven leg of the almost-grown-up and evermore beautiful Milly. I traveled to the stars and beyond. Oh love, oh romance, oh Milly!

So the thing I ordered next, after the body-building kit, makes a sort of sad sense I suppose. I won't try to analyze it or make sense of it, except to say that in some ways the pistol was a mere extension of the body-building kit and of Buddy the ventriloquist's dummy, who sat silent in a chair in my room and found that he, like his master, had nothing to say. The pistol was both an image of the rural world where I lived so successfully, and an attempt to jump clear of the same world, which seemed to hold me against my will.

In the local barbershop, in the back pages of an old magazine of some pulpy ilk that I was thumbing through while waiting for a haircut, *True Stories,* maybe, or maybe something slicker, *Argosy* or *Field and Stream,* I noticed a tiny ad. ARMY SURPLUS. It's a wonder I could read the ad at all, so small was its print. ENFIELD .38 CAL. REVOLVERS. RAF SIDEARMS, BRITISH OFFICERS. DOUBLE AND SINGLE ACTION. SPECIFY EXCELLENT OR GOOD COND. $12.95 AND $14.95. NO C.O.D. MUST BE 21. I read the ad over and over.

There were two barbers, Shorty Grable, the good one, with one leg shorter than the other and a built-up shoe that caused him to rock when he walked, and Mr. Shepherd, the worst barber on earth, who was usually too drunk to finish a haircut properly and so just shaved your head quickly before he passed out. No adult with a brain in his head would allow Mr. Shepherd to touch him, and children feared him, prayed that he would pass out before he got to them in the queue. The ad distracted me from my fear that I would draw Mr. Shepherd. I stopped counting ahead to see how many were in front of me, whether I should leave now and wait until he had drunk more and went into the back room to lie down. Once he was down, Shorty Grable would be mine all mine. I looked at the ad. Fifteen dollars for the excellent. Okay, I would take excellent over good any day. The money was not a problem. I had paid fifteen dollars for Buddy, so fifteen dollars was nothing to me. Well, it was plenty, but not a problem, not when it came to mail order. Just fifteen dollars, for a real pistol? It was like a dream. I had never had a burning interest in firearms, so even I was surprised to see how energized I was by this magazine offer.

Guns were common in Itta Bena, of course, a rural community. People hunted, target practiced, kept them for protection. Mr. Burnside, who lived down on Lake Front Drive near my grandparents, shot and killed a man he thought was trying to break into his house. It was a mistake, a tragedy. It was Hambone Johnson, a Peeping Tom everybody knew and generally liked and tolerated. He was afflicted with narcolepsy and often fell asleep while practicing his peeping in windows and had waked Mr. Burnside with his snoring. In his distress and fear of intruders, Mr. Burnside shot five times straight down through the sash and sill of his window, and one of the bullets hit the sleeping Hambone. That was terrible, of course, but the only serious misuse of a firearm anyone could remember.

There were guns in our own house. My father kept a couple of shotguns in his closet, a .22 caliber pistol in his nightstand beside the bed. He had taught me to shoot them. He and my mother and I would go, some Sunday afternoons, and stand on the Bear Creek bridge near Berclair in the summer sun, and take pot shots at turtles or snakes or maybe just an empty beer can or two he'd throw into the water for targets. Safety was a big concern. He showed us proper loading, proper use of the safety, the safe way to hold a firearm when it was not in use. People who knew nothing about guns were the ones likely to accidentally hurt themselves or someone else, he said. Always assume a gun is loaded, he cautioned. It's the *unloaded* gun that can kill you, he said a hundred times. I suppose I understand his ironic meaning now, but at the time this phrase was a mystery. He showed me proper cleaning, storage, how to take the guns apart to prevent accidents, how to store ammunition in separate places, under lock and key, for the same reason. I enjoyed the outings, but mainly because they were a friendly thing the family did together. I had no other particular interest in guns.

But this ad! How it intrigued me! I read it over and over and over. I considered my financial resources: what I had on hand, how many allowances I would have to wait for, how many yards to mow, how long this industry and husbandry would take. Not long at all! I was almost there! A pistol, a "revolver," of my very own. It would be my secret. Double action, or single action—I didn't know what this meant. This troubled me some. Double was probably better than single. Well, on the other hand, I wasn't sure. Maybe single was better. "RAF," I read. Raf. It was a strange word. I pronounced it many times. Raf raf raf raf raf. If I said it enough times I was sure I would intuitively begin to know what it meant, or so I thought. It meant nothing, no matter how many times I formed it on my lips and tongue. It made me think of a barking dog. It could have been a code of some kind. The *R* could stand for rifle, possibly. That made no sense. It was very frustrating. British, though, that was good. That was like another country, I was pretty sure, close to England. The post office box where I should send my order, along with a check or money order, was in Arizona. Outside myself somewhere, as if in another world, my name seemed to float about me.

Buddy, a voice seemed to say. *It's your turn.* It was the drunken Mr. Shepherd. I had drawn Mr. Shepherd and not Shorty Grable. I was trapped. I could have just bolted, run out the door. I had seen other children do this, without shame. Probably their home lives were different from mine. Probably their violent fathers had promised to beat the shit out of them if they came home with their head shaved. They weren't paying any seventy-five cents for one of Mr. Shepherd's buzz cuts, so don't plan to come home with one. In my home the emphasis was on not hurting anyone's feelings, no matter how much humiliation you yourself were required to endure.

"Poor Mr. Shepherd," my mother would say. "I don't know how he can keep up his home if people won't even let him cut their hair. It's his livelihood, for heaven's sake!"

"Well, sure," my father would add without the slightest trace of irony, "but he's got to realize that if he would exercise a little more willpower over that 'problem' of his, he wouldn't be worrying about scaring kids off." He would use his fingers in the air as quotations marks around the word *problem,* and make a sound like "chick, chick" with his cheek and tongue, to indicate the quotation marks, as if "drinking problem" were too shocking a phrase to say in front of a child.

My mother would agree that my wise father was right, of course, "sad but true," she would say.

I did not run away, as good sense bade me do, but one bold movement was still left in me. Without trying to disguise or hide my actions at all, I sat where I was for another few seconds and ripped the page from the magazine I had been reading and folded it carefully and placed it in the pocket of my shirt. Mr. Shepherd was sweating dangerously, and on his face was plastered an idiotic smile behind eyes as shattered-seeming as busted glass, so much pain did they reveal. I walked slow as a gut-shot bear in the direction of the waiting barber chair.

Mr. Shepherd picked up a grapefruit-sized river stone, smooth as glass, that sat on the ledge behind him beside the combs and bottles of hair tonic and bay rum and talcum-filled brushes. He said, "See this?" He was holding the stone out in my general direction. "Know what this is for? We use this to rub old men's nuts with. Ain't that right, Shorty Grable? We take old men who want their nuts rubbed back in the back room and you know what we do with this here river rock?"

I said, "Rub their nuts?"

He said, "You're goddamn right we rub their nuts. This here river rock is a nut-rubbing motherfucker."

I looked at Shorty Grable to see whether he would save me, but he didn't look away from the head of hair in front of him. A wild horse couldn't have made him look in any direction but straight ahead. There were a lot of people in the barbershop, mostly older kids, high school. None of them looked up either. All were occupied with something of enormous importance. Lazy Bones Wooten was the shoeshine boy, a black man more than sixty years old. He was as drunk as Mr. Shepherd. He was sitting in the enormous shoeshine chair and when Mr. Shepherd's voice reached its final decibels he woke up suddenly from his drunken slumber and sang two lines of "Danny Boy" and fell asleep again.

I sat in the chair and Mr. Shepherd cut my hair. He was careful and slow and did not pass out. When he was finished, he removed the cloth from around my neck and snapped it in the air and dusted my neck and face with a talcum-filled brush.

He said, "You ain't got no nuts. Don't be asking to have your little nuts rubbed. Old men got long nuts. You ain't got no nuts. Not none that needs rubbing."

Later my mother said she thought it was one of the best haircuts I'd ever had. She was surprised to learn that Mr. Shepherd had been my barber. She said, "He must be getting some of that willpower your daddy was talking about, after all."

I said I thought she was probably right about that.

THE GUN ARRIVED BY rail. Even more puzzling than the summons to the post office when my first mail-order items arrived, I had no clue why a notice from the Southern Railroad had come to the house in my name. What on earth could have been waiting for me at the depot? The depot was right in the middle of Itta Bena, in the shadow of the water tower, a long gray building with an unflushed toilet and the most elementary of graffiti on its walls: *Pussy is good. I like thick dick.* And a picture of a single disembodied breast with the word *titty* above it. Nothing on earth that I could attach emotionally to myself could be waiting for me in this depot. Even when I had been assured that a package awaited me, and when I had signed for it and held the heavy-paper envelope in my hand and felt the considerable heft of its contents, I still had no idea. I had not yet celebrated my thirteenth birthday.

I opened the package at home, and fortunately no one was around to see. Inside all the packing and confetti, I finally saw the gun barrel and knew what I had. The revolver was packed in grease. My hands were black with the heavy grease before I realized it, so I went to the bathroom and scraped off what I could and wiped away more with toilet paper and washed away the rest with Lava soap, which my father used after work sometimes. More carefully now I finished unpacking the gun. I found a stash of clean rags among my father's painting supplies and began to clean the grease away. I cleaned the barrel, the trigger guard, everything. I found a small-diameter dowel rod in my father's things and rammed a soft rag through the barrel to clean the inside. I looked down the barrel and saw the well-defined rifling inside.

The pistol was a heavy black revolver, .38 caliber, with a six-inch barrel, and with black plastic hand-grips on the gun butt. On the end of the butt was a black metal ring, for attaching a lanyard of some kind I supposed. When I had finished cleaning the gun, it still felt oily to the touch, but the grease did not now blacken my fingers. I held it, I weighed it in my palm. I spun the cylinder. I sighted along the barrel. I said, "Doosh," the sound kids made back then to indicate shooting. I said, "Ptchoooooee," another such sound, with a sort of whistling at the end, to indicate a ricochet.

I hid all the materials the gun had come packed in. I washed out the sink, to be sure I had left no trace of grease. I hid the pistol in one of the rubber boots in my closet. It was safe there for now. I needed bullets. I didn't have anything in mind to do with them, I just needed them. I wanted to load the gun. Bullets were simple to get. Anybody could buy them, no signature, no waiting period, no age limit, nothing. I went to the Western Auto Store and waited around until Mr. Martin was in the back of the store. There were car batteries and wheelbarrows and high-powered rifles and Kelvinator refrigerators. You could get anything in Western Auto. Mr. Martin would sell me bullets, probably, there was no law against it, but he would also probably mention it to my parents. I was waiting around for the high school kid who worked there in the summer.

The kid finally saw me and said, "Can I help you?" He meant, "Are you about to steal something?" He had real white hair.

I said, "Daddy sent me for some bullets."

He said, "Okay."

"Thirty-eights."

"Okay."

That was it. That's how easy it was. The bullets came in a yellow pasteboard box with the word *Federals* printed on the outside. This was the Western Auto brand. I left and the white-haired boy was no wiser.

I hid the bullets in the other boot, the one the pistol was not in, and couldn't do anything with my prizes for a long time, several days. On the weekend, when I had done my chores and mowed my lawns, I rode my big Goodyear bicycle, with balloon tires and a basket and reflectors and a tinny horn, out to the Bear Creek bridge and blazed away at things in the water, animate and inanimate. The turtles were safe that day. I was not a good shot, so I hit nothing I aimed at, but I loved the heft of the gun in my hand, the shock that jolted through my arm when I pulled the trigger, the ringing in my ears after the report. When I was done, I allowed the cylinder to swing free from the frame and I dumped the empty casings from the cylinder. I held the warm spent shells in my palm and lifted them to my nose and breathed in the beauty of cordite.

EVENTUALLY I TRIED TO kill my father, of course. I loaded the revolver with the blunt copper-jacketed shells, and I lay outside in the dark of night beneath fig trees, the sticky milk of their fruit and leaves brushing against my neck and causing me to itch mightily. I had sneaked from the house and lain in wait beneath this heavy cover specifically for this melodramatic purpose. This was premeditation. They were inside, I was outside. I watched them through the kitchen window, as if on a black-and-white TV screen. They moved, they spoke without sound. I imagined that my father was drinking, though actually I could not see well enough to know for sure. I imagined that my mother was unhappy, though I have no evidence, not a single detail from my hidden vantage point to suggest the truth of such an interpretation. I looked into the window and saw a drama I had already begun to play upon the stage of my mind.

Maybe I shouldn't say I tried to kill him "of course," as if my father somehow deserved such violence, for not once did I ever imagine this to be true. I understood in a rudimentary way at least that the lives my parents lived, the tears they wept, were lives and tears they had chosen. I only mean that my ambush was a natural development in a narrative of power and escape that had long ago begun and now played out to its final scene.

I didn't succeed in my attempt. Maybe I should add "of course" to this sentence as well. This good result will seem to some to have been a result only of luck, or to what some others refer to as the grace of God, which I suppose is pretty much the same thing as the first. I aimed through the window, I pulled the trigger, the gun didn't fire. As simple as that. It had fired every other time I pulled the trigger, when pointed in the direction of the fearless turtles and snakes, but not this time. I don't know why. I have no explanation, I won't try to invent one that takes physics into account.

I never tried again to fire the Enfield revolver, so if a physical explanation were required it could have been anything, the firing pin, the particular bullet in the chamber, the cylinder, which did turn out to be unstable, to rattle this way and that and could have thrown the firing pin off line, really I don't know. The next morning I rode again on my fine Goodyear bicycle to Bear Creek and leaned the bike against the bridge railing and tossed the pistol off the bridge, quickly, before I had a chance to change my mind. I watched it hit the water. I watched the solid splash it made. I watched it sink. I watched the crease that it made on the surface of the brown water close behind and swallow it up forever.

I'll never believe mere anger and Freud led me to that desperate night when I might have killed the man I loved most in the world. I'll not believe that mere luck or mere God saved me from the consequences of my attempt. Something in me had caused that pistol not to fire. This is not mysticism that I mean, it is electrical or chemical or atomic or something as yet unnamed, but I believe in it, know it to be true.

Some instinct deeper than animal and specific to one person on this earth, this Buddy Nordan whose blockhead image was sitting inscrutable in a chair in their shared room, reached from my heart and into the chamber where pin and primer seemed destined to meet and stopped the ignition of the nitrol and saved my young ass from a million billion trillion prisons, not just the one at Parchman but the imprisoned heart, the home-shackled fate, the never-executed great escape.

I wanted out of Itta Bena. This fact was primary, it lay zero at the bone, deeper than anger, deeper than Freud. Though I loved Itta Bena and belonged there in deference to its nurture when my other-father died and left me and no other inn would take me and my mother in, I had by this time turned my back, I had reverted from my roots, I had cast my line through mail-order catalogs and comic books and old barbershop magazines, out into space to Krypton and Arizona, in hopes of snagging a way out, a map with the route marked, a set of clear instructions. A bullet in my father's chest, or even a bullet that missed his body and only cracked a window, punctured the hot-water heater, busted up the plaster on the wall, would have kept me there in Itta Bena, in the cramped spaces of my limited imagination, forever. I could not have survived killing anyone, because my imagination could not have then continued the search for the crease, the hatch, through which to make my escape.

This is what my heart knew, or something more powerful than a human heart, I can't say what, that caused a misfire of the Enfield that night. I don't mean to say I understand more than I do, only this. If Bear Creek still flows with muddy waters through the swamp and into Blue Lake at Berclair, then that black pistol still lies where I dropped it, snakes encircle its barrel, weave themselves through the trigger guard.

6

One Summer Night in Memphis

THE SUMMER I WAS fifteen yeas old, I boarded a Greyhound bus and crossed the Delta on Highway 61, the first time I had ever left home. Though my mother had grown up in Itta Bena and had never ventured far away herself, it was she who decided it was time.

I said, "Memphis?"

She said, "Why not?"

I said, "What will I do when I get there?"

She said, "Look around. I don't know. See what you think."

I said, "Memphis?"

She said, "It couldn't hurt."

I found my way from the bus station to the Gayoso Hotel, where I rented a tiny dark room with an enormous air conditioner in the window. I had a few dollars in my pocket, the money I had earned mowing lawns. In my suitcase I had smuggled, like contraband, a Gillette safety razor and a pack of blue blades, along with a tube of shaving cream, a styptic pencil, and a bottle of shaving lotion. I had never shaved before, but I had been hoarding these items in my room at home for a long time. In the Gayoso I unpacked this equipment before anything else. Though at fifteen I had not one hair on my face, I went into the dark little bathroom and lathered up and shaved.

I shaved the tops off all my acne pimples and actually screamed out loud the first time the styptic pencil touched my raw face, but no child could have been so happy or felt so manly as I did beneath the dim bulb in that bathroom. I doused my face liberally with a weird brand of shaving lotion I had bought in an army surplus store. I turned on the air conditioner and sat on the edge of the bed. I didn't know what else to do. I was afraid to go out on the street, to look around, as my mother had suggested. I read a *Field and Stream* magazine I had brought along in my suitcase, and finally fell asleep with my clothes on and dreamed of ice fishing in a hurricane. When I woke up the room was a cold as Alaska, and the air conditioner sounded like it was about to take off.

The next morning, a Saturday, the city did not seem so intimidating. I got up and shaved again and this time applied scraps of toilet paper to the bloody spots, avoiding the styptic pencil altogether. I took the elevator down and went out into the street and decided on a direction and began to walk. I walked for miles and hours. I grew hungry, but was too shy to go into a restaurant. Maybe it was the effluvium of my army surplus shaving lotion that caused me at last to stop walking and go into a store. An army-navy surplus store, at that. For some unknown reason I spent virtually every penny of my lawn-mowing money on a complete set of navy whites—a whole uniform, thirteen-button, bell-bottom trousers, everything. I spent the rest of my money on a taxi ride to the Memphis zoo and didn't save myself enough for food or for cab fare back to the Gayoso. I walked slowly from cage to cage and stared solemnly at the animals. The panting tiger, the sound-asleep polar bear, the red-butted baboons. A kind family saw me and bought me a hot dog and a root beer and looked at me as if I might have escaped from some place, an asylum.

The woman said, in a kindly voice, "Are you with anyone? Do you have ride home?"

I said, "I'm staying in a hotel. I'm just in town buying sailor uniforms."

She said, "Is your face all right?" and touched her fingers lightly to my freshly shaved acne.

Her husband gave me three dollars and instructions on how to catch the city bus. He said, "You'll look sharp in those navy whites."

I said, "Thank you."

He said, "Or you can mix and match. Wear the jumper with blue jeans."

It was already dark when I stepped off the bus, back in the city.

I walked into a movie theater in sight of the bus stop and watched the last half of *Mister Roberts,* which had already started. I slept for part of the movie, and when I came out I felt rested and a little dazed. I wasn't sure where the hotel was, so I just started walking, hoping to run across it. I walked for a good long time.

And then I walked right smack into the middle of what my mother unknowingly had sent me to see. I was standing at the top of Beale Street. Beale Street on a Saturday night, a radiance, evil maybe, but I didn't care. Everything I had ever failed to notice, I now suddenly saw in one amazing instant. A sea of African faces, my face the only white one among them. Out of every door, it seemed, a vivid music poured, bright and sexual laughter, women and men and even children—hustlers and hookers and preachers and blue-plumed pimps, dice rollers and tap dancers and showmen. It was a party, the biggest party I had ever imagined. This was what it meant to be an adult. No, this was what it meant to be *alive*. Whiskey flowed, dancers danced, dice rolled, money changed hands, the music throbbed. I held on to the package I was carrying with the sailor suit in it. I was swept along the street in the crowd, enveloped in fragrances of musk and perfume that told me my military-issue cologne would go with anything.

I was not on the street long before my fear overcame my amazement and so I walked away and miraculously found the Gayoso. But before I did, a man standing nearby said, quite casually, "Look yonder." I'm not sure he was actually talking to me. He was pointing to a spindly old man in a slick suit. I looked at the old guy. The man said, "That's Mr. Handy."

A great many other things happened that summer to make me think of it as the summer I stopped being a child. My mother went off to summer school at Mississippi State, and my father hired me on a paint crew for the rest of the summer for three dollars a day to paint the old Humphries High School building. I hung out with the painters, their buckets and brushes and radios and talk of booze and women. At the end of the day my father and I smelled like paint and turpentine, and after our baths, we smelled of Lifebuoy soap and Fitch's shampoo, and Wildroot Cream Oil. In Mother's absence we always fixed the same supper, chicken-fried steak and boiled potatoes and milk gravy and a salad with bottled French dressing. We ate in silence at an oilcloth-covered table. The kitchen was fragrant with hot grease and scorched flour. These manly and intimate moments were a kind of fulfillment, a completion of my burgeoning self.

But it was the earlier moment that marked the pivot for me, after which Itta Bena would never quite be enough somehow. It was the moment when I stood on a corner of Beale Street in Memphis and, while the music played and the dice rolled, I laid eyes on W. C. Handy, the Daddy of the Blues.

7

A Body in the River

ONE AFTERNOON IN EARLY September, in our high school football locker room, I heard several boys on the team talking about a dead body that had been found in the Tallahatchie River. The room where the boys were putting on their practice uniforms was long and low-ceilinged. The floor was concrete. It smelled of sweaty socks and sweat-soaked pads and a backed-up toilet. The shower at the far end had a slow drain, and it carried its own unpleasant effluvium. I was the team "manager," a sort of hard-working waterboy and flunky. I busied myself taping ankles or changing cleats or helping this person or that person lace up his shoulder pads. I was not on the team myself only because of a knee injury, I told myself, but in truth I was skinny and slow-footed and uncoordinated, and was lucky to have been given this job of team manager in order to stay close to the more popular boys in school. The boys discussing the death, the body that had been discovered in the water, already seemed to know a good deal about the case—that the dead person's name was Emmett Till, that he was a black teenager who had insulted a white woman, that he had been killed and sunk in the river with a gin fan barbwired to his neck. This was such shocking information that it scarcely seemed real.

I was quiet, a little shy among these football guys—my social standing among the actual athletes was quite low—and so I added nothing to the conversation. Others were quiet too, I suppose; I am mainly remembering a few big talkers. Despite the horror of the content of the conversation, no one seemed horrified. People were laughing. It was a funny story, like a movie plot you remember as having scared you at the time, maybe, but now is a big joke. The tone of the conversation was one of general approval, and even hilarity. I worked hard at not seeming affected by what I was hearing. I added my share of approval by sitting quietly and listening. The theme of the conversation was that a "nigger" had done this thing, wolf-whistled this white woman. They seemed to be saying that this Chicago kid had learned his lesson, he sure got what he deserved! I wish I could report honestly that I was higher-minded and exempt from complicity in the general sense of approval and jocularity, but I cannot. I was jealous that I had no details to add and no social standing that would have allowed my participation in the first place. There was a terrible joke being told as well. The joke was that this "nigger" had tried to steal a gin fan and swim across the river with it and drowned himself. Probably I smiled at the joke, I don't remember. In any case, the thing that happened next remains one of my most vivid memories. The picture of the scene stands frozen in my mind's eye as clearly as a photograph on a table before me.

A boy putting on his shoulder pads turned to the rest of us and said, "I'm for the nigger." He was serious. I could see it in his face. He had not been smiling at the jokes, had not approved of anything that had been done or said. In my memory everyone else stopped talking and looked at him, frozen smiles on our faces. He said, "It ain't right. Kill a boy for that. I don't care what color he is."

When I have had occasion to tell this story in conversation over the years, I have often been asked, "Do you remember the boy's name? Where is he now?" I do remember his name, and I know the town he lives in. But I have always had to say that I am out of contact with him. I have had a fantasy of meeting him again someday and asking him about that moment, this act of unheard of courage when he voiced his disapproval. And courage is what it was. This was not the captain of the team, or the quarterback, who I suppose could have exhibited such outrageous individualism without fear of reprisal or ostracizing; and it was not the team geek, or waterboy, or manager, myself I mean —who had no status to lose anyway and could have been in that way impervious to ridicule. This was simply a boy on the team, a quiet country boy who had everything to lose and nothing except a lifetime of self-respect to gain, and he said, "I'm for the nigger. It ain't right." For forty years I have wished I had been the boy who spoke those courageous words.

The story of Emmett Till is a familiar one to most Americans. In the summer of 1955, traveling by train from his home in Chicago an African American teenager named Emmett (Bobo) Till journeyed to Money, Mississippi, in the Delta, for a visit with his uncle and aunt. Money was a little town just a few miles from my home in Itta Bena. Bobo was warned beforehand by his mother that the rules of etiquette were not the same in Mississippi as in Chicago and that he should be very careful of what he said and how he acted. Any small infraction could be serious.

Living in the same town Bobo visited was a big extroverted man known for violence, J. W. "Big" Milam. He owned a country store operated by his half-brother Roy Bryant and Roy's wife, Carolyn. The store was enough like Mr. Shiloh's in Itta Bena as to have become merged in my mind as one: big unpainted dungeons with bare-board floors and wide porches and a few groceries. Big Milam was admired for being good at "handling niggers." He carried a .45 automatic pistol wherever he went, which he said was "good for shooting or slugging." Shot through the chest in World War II, his body scarred with multiple shrapnel wounds, Milam had pistol-whipped and killed German soldiers and prisoners in the war. He was an expert with the "grease gun" and all other weapons of short-range violence.

On a dare, in late August, Bobo Till went into the country store and asked Carolyn Bryant for a date. He made a couple of insulting remarks and wolf-whistled her, apparently. Later on, in reprisal, Roy and Big kidnapped the child from his Uncle Mose's and Aunt Lizzie's house, drove him around in the dark for several hours to scare him, tortured him, and finally shot him in the head and killed him. Then they barbwired him by the neck to a heavy fan from a cotton-gin motor and rolled his body into twenty feet of water in the Tallahatchie River.

These details and others are available to us because many of them, including the kidnapping, were admitted to, even bragged about, by the defendants before the murder trial, and then the rest were revealed in a paid interview by the defendants to William Bradford Huie in *Look* magazine shortly after the trial. Both defendants were found not guilty of murder, and a grand jury in Greenwood failed to bring an indictment for kidnapping, despite the public admissions.

As a high school boy, in the days after the hilarity in the

locker room, and then later, after I was a grown-up young man, I became obsessed with the case. I thought about it daily, I grieved it, but not with a social conscience, I'm sorry to say, and not with much compassion for Emmett Till or the loving mother who suffered this loss, but with a defensiveness that bordered on neurosis. To my mind, something had been done to me, to us, to the South. And not by Milam and Bryant but by the "Northern" media. I felt personally accused. The fact that what was being reported was essentially what had happened did not mitigate my feelings of betrayal, as if an undeserved attack had been directed at me by the rest of the world. It's impossible for me to understand how I had for so long fantasized escape from the confines of my geography and now, suddenly, with the perfect moral excuse for full emotional detachment and rejection of the place, I clung to it, defended it against "outsiders." For a long time I focused on how "unfairly" Mississippi and the South were treated by other Americans. I hung out in public libraries and read accounts of the murder and of the trial over and over. The whole affair seemed unbelievable to me. Could those men, with familiar names, with a little country store, have really done what the magazines and newspapers were saying? I knew it to be true, but the truth was unacceptable to me. I began to feel torn apart by my loyalties, to what I knew of right and wrong and to the morality of the only home I had ever known.

The obsession was completely private. I talked about my feelings and beliefs with no one, neither friends nor family. My parents spoke not a word. In fact, just last year I asked my mother, who is eighty-seven, how we talked about the trial at the dinner table. Her answer: "Honey, we didn't talk about it at all. We never said a word." Years later, in the navy, and then in college, I still found myself going over the events in my mind. Once in about 1968—for reasons obscure even to me—I copied from microfilm, by hand, onto a legal pad, every word about the trial that *The New York Times* had reported during that summer and fall. The thing I could never admit, and that all my obsessive thinking seems now to have been covering up, was that I did indeed feel culpable. I had sat in the locker room and listened to the jokes. I had smiled. I had wished I had something to add and some status from which to enter the conversation. I had not been horrified at the word *nigger* or sought to correct anything at all, even by removing myself from it. I was as guilty as *The New York Times* had implied I was.

There is, I suppose, one more thing to tell. Forty years later, after publishing a novel based on the Emmett Till murder, I worked up my courage and called information and dialed the number of the boy in the locker room, the child who stood up for what was right when no one else even knew there was an issue of right and wrong. To my surprise, the voice on the other end of the line was not a sixteen-year-old boy, as I had foolishly expected, but rather a man in his middle fifties. I wondered how I sounded to him. He was easy to talk to, we were still friends, after so long. He was glad to hear from me. We talked for a while. He told me he had three children, all grown and gone from home.

"Just me and my wife now," he said.

I asked about another friend, and he had some recent information, so we talked about him for a while.

I said, "Did you make it to the class reunion last year?"

He said no, that was cotton-ginning time, the fall, not the right time of year for him.

I said I was promoting books in the fall, so it was not a good time of year for me either. Though I did not say this to him, as it might have seemed to accuse my hometown of something it was not guilty of, I recalled that the death of Emmett Till had been the final reason, if I had needed one final reason, that I left Itta Bena to try to find a life in the larger world. I was running from myself when I left home, not from the people who loved me.

He said he had heard all about my books and was happy for me.

I said, "Did you know that my new book was about the murder of Emmett Till?"

He said, "Oh yes, I've heard all about it."

I said, "That's why I'm calling, actually. I'm calling to ask you what you remember about those days."

He said, "Well, I remember it, but I don't remember anything very specific."

I said, "Do you remember when you first heard of the murder?"

He said, "No, Buddy, I'm sorry I don't."

I said, "There were some terrible jokes being made, do you remember that?"

He said yes, he did remember, and then he recalled the same awful joke about the stolen gin fan.

I said, "I'm thinking of a day in the football locker room. The team was dressing out, and everybody was talking about the murder. Do you remember that?"

He thought for a few seconds. He said, "No, I don't think I do. I remember people talking about it."

I said, "The day I'm thinking of, we were all talking about the murder, and making jokes, and then you stood up for the dead boy. You said, 'I'm for the colored boy,' or something like that. Do you remember that?"

He thought again. He said, "No, Buddy. I'm sorry. I really don't."

I said, "The way I remember it, you said this and the rest of us just stopped talking. I thought you were so courageous. I wished I had said it. I think about that moment all the time. I've thought of you for all these years. You don't remember?"

His voice was thoughtful and kind. He said, "No, I'm sorry. I don't."

I said, "It took so much courage. I admire you for it."

He said, "Well, thank you. Thank you, Buddy."

We talked awhile longer. Finally he said, "I'm real glad you called. This has been nice."

I said, "I hope we can stay in touch."

He said, "Well, good. That would be fine. That would be real nice."

8

New York City

AFTER THAT NIGHT ON Beale Street the discontent that I had begun to feel settled deep inside me like an old friend. I felt no burning desire to remove myself from my comfortable surroundings, and yet something had changed. This change was a gift from my mother, I now understand. I began to dream of foreign geographies. I dreamed of faraway places and exotic lands. Such dreams became my constant occupation. These fantasies I entertained behind the lawn mower, or behind the soda fountain of the Bena Drug Store in Itta Bena. I imagined myself beneath a tropical sun on the deck of a ship, cutting banana stalks with a machete. Always nearby lay olive-skinned women and tarantulas. My skinny ass and freckles were transformed to bright copper. My muscles grew and rippled beneath beads of gleaming sweat. Or I dreamed of frozen oceans and ice-jammed ships, the icy poles of the earth, white bears and penguins, sealskin parkas and Nor'westers, hardtack and blubber my only rations, scurvy my sometimes friend. A dark-skinned woman generally found her way into this fantasy as well. I mowed the lawns and breathed the fragrance of fresh-cut grass and wild onions. I scooped ice cream from cardboard barrels and served it on cones. I saved my pennies for a time when I might actually leave that patch of Delta soil and make my place in the larger world.

After work there was often time left over to go swimming, to camp out in the Roebuck flatwoods and eat a can of beans by firelight, even to sit behind the schoolhouse in the cab of a Dodge pickup with a friend and share forbidden swigs of whiskey from a bottle. One summer I used some of my saved-up money to go with a pal from high school and his parents to Florida, where I drank some beers and got a sunburn. This was the extent of my traveling, and it did not satisfy.

This was the 1950s. One day, I heard about the beatniks. It was a word as yet undefined, or only vaguely defined for me, but wonderful. Goatees, yes, berets, possibly, dark glasses and dissipation. With so little information it was hard to imagine the beatniks very vividly. I thought they might go around reading the works of Edgar Allan Poe, for some reason. I'm not sure where I got this idea. A rash of beatnik jokes cleared up a few things:

What did the beatnik say when he walked down the railroad track?

"Dig this crazy staircase, man."

What did the first beatnik say when the second beatnik said, "Let's blow this joint"?

He said, "Nah man, pass it on to the waitress."

I didn't know what this meant, but I wanted to be a part of it. I wanted to say "Dig, man." I wanted to say "Cool" and "Coltrane" and "Reefer" and "Go cat, go." Beatniks hung out in coffeehouses, drank espresso, played bongos, read poetry aloud. Poetry seemed better than tarantulas and penguins. Dissipation and E. A. Poe beat machetes and bananas. I believed I could learn to drink coffee. With enough sugar and milk I could do it.

The problem was, the beatniks were in New York and I was in Mississippi. Well, obviously. Why would they be in Mississippi? Everything I had suspected about the inadequacy of my life and geography seemed confirmed. That glimpse of W. C. Handy weighed on me and compelled me outward. More than ever Mississippi became my prison, the details of my own history, my damnation. I longed for New York more than for the banana boats or icy seas. New York seemed farther away and more mysterious than the Amazon. Now when I pushed my lawn mower or dipped ice cream for some redneck's banana split, those dark-skinned women no longer lay about with the tarantula, but sipped bitter coffee and listened to jazz and read the works of Edgar Allan Poe.

I went on with my part-time jobs. Saturday mornings and afternoons I walked behind the rattling little lawn mower with the Briggs & Stratton engine, and Saturday nights I stood behind the Bena Drug soda fountain wearing a paper hat until midnight. I slept hard, hard on Sunday mornings. I took a few other jobs as well. I detasseled corn for Pfeister Hybrids, I worked in Mr. Curry's lumberyard for a while. The money piled up a little at a time. I had no obligations, no rent, no car, no girlfriend, no expenses beyond an occasional movie or a hamburger and a Coke, and so if I had been thinking seriously of leaving town, I had the money. What it took me a while to gain was enough imagination to know that New York need not remain a dream. You didn't need a plane ticket to get to New York, you didn't need a visa. You didn't even need your parents' permission, if you played the right angles. You could get to New York on a bus, for God's sake. You could go down to the Southern Cafe and watch old men play the punchboard, and then you could tell Mr. Pirelli you wanted to buy a ticket, and then you could wait on the curb for the bus driver to show up, a guy in a baggy gray wool suit and a billed cap and whiskey on his breath, wheeling around out of the cinder lot at the depot across the street in a blue and white coach with a picture of a running dog on the side, and take your sorry self to anywhere you wanted to go, become anything you wanted to be. I don't know when all this occurred to me, exactly. I don't know what possessed me, one day, to act upon this startling impulse.

I did the drill. I played a game of pinball, checked the pay phone for nickels, ate a pork barbecue sandwich with slaw, and almost before I knew it, I found that I had bought myself a ticket to become a beatnik. It was true. Without telling anyone, without any clear plan at all, suddenly I was going to New York. Gimme a chocolate milk to go with that barbecue, Miss Sara, hot sauce right. I puked halfway to Memphis and a lady bought me a Coca-Cola in Batesville to calm my stomach down. I slept a long time after that and when I woke up the lady was gone. I discovered that I was frightened, that I had no idea what I was doing, that I didn't know what I would do when I got there. I rode and rode, and a long time and many filthy bus stops later I got off the bus in New York City. Grand Central Station, maybe, who knows, it was so long ago.

I wish this story had a better ending, more conclusive any-way. It's not a bad ending, not tragic. I didn't die, or lose a limb, or even my virginity. Nothing was lost, really, only some hours on a bus. It's not that it's an unhappy ending, just not the ending you might be expecting, where I either find my true self in New

York, or come to realize that my true self was in Mississippi all the time, that my life, despite its limitations was not one to be ashamed of. That's probably what everybody eventually learns in life anyway, if they live long enough and work at it some. So what's the point of leading you this long way just to come to that weary old conclusion. The truth is, nothing really changed. Maybe it did, in some deep-down way, maybe this trip did help set my course, solidify something, but these were not changes that were obvious to me then, and are not obvious even now, I should say. My trip to New York is a mere detail in an unremarkable life story. I was very tired. I smelled faintly of pork barbecue. My parents, back home, were worried half to death and thought they were big failures in life and that if I was ever found safe, I should probably go out to the asylum at Whitfield for a while, for some evaluation at least. My mother must have blamed herself for what may have been only a dangerous extension of the Memphis trip she had promoted. The truth is, there were no great consequences of my adventure and all their concern. I came back home and slept for a long time, and things went on as before.

I don't want to leave out this part, though, the New York part. If anything is remarkable about this time in my life, it is that I actually found the beatniks. They were there in New York, Lord knows what street in Manhattan, but right where rumor and corny jokes had said they would be. Poetry, bongos, a guitar. Beards, bandannas around their necks, cigarettes and espresso. The women were exactly as I had dreamed, dusky skin, leotards, but a few years too old for me. I was a child, almost a foreigner, so I only beheld them, nothing more. The name of the coffeehouse was Your Father's Mustache, which later became famous, probably a chain. It seems a cliché now. At the time, though, the name alone seemed the epitome of everything I had been searching for when I paid the wadded-up handful of dollar bills to Mr. Pirelli for a ticket out of Itta Bena.

There is another strange part that I should tell as well. It's almost unbelievable, in fact. When I first entered Your Father's Mustache, it was so dark and smoky that I could scarcely see. I didn't have allergies yet, so I wasn't miserable, but it was pretty bad. There was a little stage and a few instruments propped around it. A jukebox was playing at the time. Jazz of some sort, though of course I had no idea what or who. Anyway, the place was so dark that when I chose a small table near the door, I didn't notice that someone was already sitting there. A woman—an African American woman, I need to say—maybe ten years older than me. My eyes adjusted sufficiently to the light that I could make out her features. Her eyes were huge and white in the darkness. Her lips were red and moist. She was dark skinned and heavily made-up. She wore an extravagant scarf and large dangling earrings.

It was one of those fictionlike moments that sometimes actually occur, an epiphany, as we say in writing classes. This is the insight that came to me: I realized that I was in New York City sitting at a table in Your Father's Mustache with the dark woman of my dreams. She was not beautiful, but this did not matter. She was beautiful enough for me, beautiful enough to prove herself to be the woman I had been looking for. I had not realized she would be African American, Negro, colored, whatever word I would have used then to identify her—but it didn't matter, of course, it was she. I realized I had never sat in a social setting with a black person before, let alone with the woman I loved. I realized all these things, and yet they are not the reason I am telling this story. What I am saying is that on the table in front of her was a hardbound copy of the *Selected Stories of Edgar Allan Poe*. My heart stopped, or seemed to stop, I swear. All traces and memories of pork barbecue disappeared from the face of the earth. The woman shifted slightly in her chair and placed one long-red-nailed finger on the dust jacket of the book, which carried a famous picture of the author, dark-eyed and fully dissipated.

I said, "Oh, I'm sorry. I didn't see you." I added, "It was so dark."

She tapped her fingernail on the book cover. Her expression did not change.

I said, "I didn't mean that the way it might sound."

She didn't answer.

I said, "I'm sorry."

I didn't know what to do, how to act. I didn't feel welcome. Maybe I should have stayed.

I pushed back my chair. I got up and left Your Father's Mustache and went back to the damp hotel where I had found a room, near the bus station. The next morning I took an early bus back to Mississippi. When we stopped for an hour in Roanoke, I washed my face in the rest room and called my parents from a pay phone and told them where I was. That's when the Whitfield idea surfaced.

And that's where the story ends. I went back home and nothing much changed. Maybe I went through those days and hours for no reason at all. Who can say?

In any case, before I take myself out of Your Father's Mustache and New York and back to more years of obscurity and meaningless longing in Mississippi, I want to tell you about that hotel where I stayed.

Where in the city it lay, I have no idea. The street was noisy with the sounds of people who were not having any fun. How I found it, I don't really remember that either, except that I tried several places before settling uncomfortably there, all of them too expensive for my lawn-mowing budget. The door was solid, unpainted steel, I remember that. The room was tiny and bare. There was a single bulb on a cord, hanging from the ceiling, and it cast harsh light over the tacky, sparse furnishings, a deal dresser, with no lamp or radio, or even Bible. The bedspread was threadbare and dusty. The sheets, when I pulled back the covers, were not clean.

It may surprise you that I had smuggled a half-pint of whiskey with me, all the way from Mississippi, where it was then illegal and could be purchased easily on the black market by minors. I had husbanded it through the many miles of Greyhound travel, hearing its familiar friendly gurgle in my pathetic Boy Scouts of America backpack, over the miles. What exactly I had imagined its uses to be, I don't remember—probably grownup celebrations with dark-skinned women, I'm not sure. I had not imagined that I would retreat to it now, at the end of my first and last day in the city as a refuge against loneliness and despair. I was hungry, I missed my parents, my bed at home. This was the kind of room—indeed, the very room, I am certain—that was rented to carry out suicides. I took off all my clothes. I wrested the whiskey bottle from the backpack and cracked the seal and managed a warm, weird solitary swig and lay back on the dingy pillows and wished I had never left home. There seemed to be a buzz coming from no place outside myself. The room was hot and airless, and I probably should have nipped from the bottle more slowly than I felt compelled to do. I lay on top of the covers of my bed in the harsh glare of the single bulb. I drank more. I got up to go to the bathroom.

There was no bathroom, I remembered now. I had forgotten that there was no private bath. I stood in the middle of the floor. My lips had gone numb. The only bathroom provided was one to be shared by everyone on the hall. I looked out my door. I saw it down there, a door into a tiled cell far, far away. I looked up and down, both directions. No one was in sight. No radios played, no sounds came from the other rooms, no light from a transom. I admit it, I was drunk. I had never been drunk before. Getting dressed seemed an impossible task, fraught with loneliness and despair. My clothes lay in a jumble in the corner. I looked down the hall again. The tiled room at the end seemed, suddenly, as much like freedom and happiness as tall ships and distant seas had seemed only yesterday. The bathroom was ice floes and penguins. It beckoned to me like the geography of a dream. I decided to take a chance. I did it, I ran. I took off, I flew. Bare-assed naked, Mississippi kid, eyes rolling, feet flying, hotfooting it down the carpeted hallway of a midtown dumpy SRO, Yahoo, baby, Dig, man, Go, cat, go! I made it. My feet skidded on the tile as I stopped. The place was empty. Nobody there, nobody in the bathroom, I was naked, I was free, oh Luck be a lady tonight. I walked in, I strolled, I swaggered, I rambled, I bopped—right up to the urinal. No zipper, no hands, nothing. I did my business, swing your partner, oh yes, feeling good, feeling fine, and then, outahere, gone, flying back down the hall, home free.

I was not home free.

The door to my room was locked. It had shut behind me. I rattled the knob. It would not turn. Never had a door been so locked as that steel slab. I stood there. My heart filled with strong feeling. I was young, I was naked, I was drunk, I had found the beatniks, I was locked out my room in New York

City. My heart filled up with joy. I realized my estimable life had begun. I loved New York.

I'VE THOUGHT ABOUT THIS moment in my life a good deal over the years. If this were fiction, the story would be over. The teenage boy would have come into his own, vulnerable and naked to the large world but also for the first time in charge of his life, enjoying the first intoxicating fruits of near adulthood and a freedom bestowed by the greater world of which he had dreamed. The tale would leave its audience at a high point, the boy in the hallway, comic and endearing and suffused with the fullness of possibility. You would understand that all the narrator's protests about nothing much changing were not quite true, that probably he would never see the world in quite the same way again. You would imagine that this moment might, in some way, come to many lives, even one's own.

That's why I like fiction better than autobiography. Fiction has that built-in obligation of irony and its riches. It circumvents the more obvious conclusions that might easily be drawn from the narrative—that this kid is headed for trouble, for example, that he might be in the early stages of a serious drinking problem, that for the rest of his life once the romance has worn off a new situation, he will have a hard time accepting responsibility for its consequences, that those qualities which seem endearing in a naked kid in a midtown hotel won't change much over the years and will come to seem, in a middle-aged man, hideous. We don't think that someday that child in the hallway will grow up and take all these same wrongheaded notions about life and use them to ruin lives, marriages, or worse. I'm not saying I did those things, made those darker turns, participated in those ruinations; and I'm not saying I didn't do them either. I'm saying that in life whatever happens, really and truly, is in fiction always transformed, the possibility of grace for its characters is never lost. And I live my life today, as I did then, in the hope of finding real transcendence, after the manner of fictional characters, though I understand the danger of such hope.

I'VE ALWAYS BEEN QUICK on my feet, a problem solver. I stood in the hallway, holding the doorknob. I thought for a minute. I had an idea. I walked back down to the bathroom. I took my time. A calm had come over me. I had more than an idea, I had a plan. My plan was to wrap myself in toilet paper. That was it. I would use a full roll, if necessary, two rolls. I would spin it off the reel, around and around my body until I was well covered, absolutely modest, and then I would take the elevator down to the lobby, go to the front desk. "I seem to have locked myself out of my room," I would say. I would try to disguise my Southern accent. It was a plan. It wasn't a good plan, but I was happy enough to have it.

The thing is, it didn't work. It should have, but it didn't. The only toilet paper in the bathroom was the kind that comes in a million slick single sheets from a tiny dispenser. I stood and looked at the dispenser. I was discouraged but not defeated. I began to pull out the single sheets, one by one—it takes a very long time to make much progress with one of those dispensers—and to stick them with water to my body. Slap, slap, slap they went on, some more successfully than others. Wet they were not so good a cover as the roll kind would have been, but with enough of them plastered around me, I began to develop a sort of skirt that was more or less opaque. I concentrated entirely on the lower part of my body, though in Plan A I had imagined quite an elaborate modesty, a togalike garment, with an over-the-shoulder feature, to cover large areas of skin. When I had used several thousand sheets of paper, the whole apparatus sagged badly and threatened to slide off in a single soggy mass, around my feet. For this reason, I walked with a peculiar shuffle, as I moved out of the bathroom, and made my slow way down the hall to the elevator.

I was not jailed, screamed at, insulted. I did not have to present myself in the lobby downstairs to ask for a key. I was not arrested. The solution was fairly simple, and I already had it in mind. In those days there was no such thing as a self-service elevator. Every hotel elevator, no matter how lowly the hotel, employed an operator. This person was always male, so my disgrace in nakedness would be minimal, I knew this. In terrible old hotels like the one I was staying in, the late-night elevator operator was usually ancient, could fall asleep easily on the little fold-out stool where he sat to open and close the accordion style gate on the door, and press the buttons. I knew that I could count on being rescued.

I pressed the button and immediately the elevator began to make its clanking noises, groaning up its steel cable in my direction. I stood there in my skirt of toilet-paper sheets. It was holding well. My head was clearing slightly from the alcohol. I straightened my shoulders. I took a couple of deep breaths. I waited. The elevator door opened and revealed the uniformed operator sitting there, fully uniformed as all of them were in those days—a faded and filthy uniform by the way, all wool even in the summer heat, gray in color with what once may have been red trim about the jacket, stripes down the sleeves, around the cuffs, et cetera. Except for the preposterous pillbox hat that he was required to wear, with a chin strap, he looked for all the world like a Confederate soldier after a particularly arduous retreat. He looked this way in his dress, in any case, and he was surely a man in a sort of retreat from the hard battle of his life. He was old, it was true, though not so old as I had imagined. He was sullen and uncommunicative, neither amused nor unamused by what waited for him in the hallway, me I mean, in my absurdity. He knew an easy dollar when he saw one, that was the extent of his expression, the poor light in his dull eyes, as I remember them. He did as I asked, went back down to the lobby for a key to my room while I hid out in the bathroom, and soon enough I was inside the room again and all my money was in this man's hands, and I stayed awake for several more hours, as yet unable to see the humor of my situation.

There is one further detail, though I hesitate to mention it, for I know I risk a violation of political correctness. The elevator operator was what we would call in these more enlightened days one of the little people. I mean he was a midget. He was wearing a midget uniform, a midget pillbox hat. His midgety feet dangled high above the floor from his perch on the elevator seat.

Please do not mistake me: I have no bias against midgets, none at all. I like midgets. I have known several over the years, and each of them I have found to be charming in every way, particularly Mitzi Hayworth, my father's friend. An entire family of midgets lived in a small mobile home on my parents' property for a while, working on a pipeline being laid across the Delta. I mean no harm to midgets, I assure you. They are human beings with the same feelings and hopes as any of us. If you prick a midget will he not bleed, Shakespeare might as well have written.

And yet there he was. His appearance cast me into a terrible and unexpected depression. His materialization before me seemed a judgment upon me. The lesson seemed cosmic, if only I could discover what it was. I was not free of Itta Bena, and never would be, so long as my destiny was in the hands of midgets. It made no sense then, and makes none now, but that was the message that seemed written for me in the stars. I had chosen this hotel, chosen it myself out of a million others, this night, and in this moment I knew, believed anyway, that I was different somehow, doomed, or cursed in a particular way, from which reinvention would never be an effective escape. I had chosen this particular rescuer, I was not sure how. A kid from Pittsburgh, or Ames, Iowa, or Butte, Montana, or anywhere else on earth would not have chosen a hotel in New York where the late-night elevator man was one of the little people, whose name I wish I could say I remember, or ever knew, if only to humanize him for myself now. I was a child of Itta Bena, my father's son. To me, this man was a freak, only that. He was tiny, wrinkled, dirty, alcoholic, he was dressed in a hideous monkey-suit of a uniform, his voice was a bitter squeak. I saw myself in him, or if I did not see it then I see it now. He was my salvation, and in a sense he was me, tragedy and comedy locked in a single human form. He was the hidden part of myself that before I could become an adult I had to accept as my own—solitary, lonely, deformed, drunk, costumed in ways that least spoke of myself, small, out of proportion to what I wanted out of life, but me in any case, the inner self that has nothing to do with the inner child we hear so much about these days. This was the inner midget, my humble self.

TWO

9

Oh Love, Oh Romance

AFTER A BRIEF TOUR of duty in the navy I entered college and almost immediately fell in love with a girl named Elizabeth, who was so cute, so smart, such a good dancer that I never quite believed my good luck. I had never really had a girlfriend before, and now I was dating an absolute prize of a girl. Not only that, I was in love with her, and she was in love with me. We knew immediately that our love was true. We spent every possible hour together, we began almost at once to make plans for a lifetime together. In fact, it wasn't long before getting married had become our only topic of conversation, it was all Elizabeth and I ever talked about. We were crazy to get married, and we liked talking about it more than we liked almost anything else we did together. The Millsaps College campus stood on a hill, and everywhere, at least to our young eyes, romantic walkways wound through the dormitory grounds and golf course. Walks and buildings and the tomb of Major Millsaps himself were shaded by ancient pin oaks and lord knows what other big trees. There were plays and concerts and fraternity boys serenading the girls dorms, and wonderful weather, late-night coffee and eggs and earnest conversation in all-night diners. It was a wonderful place to fall in love.

I was just out of the navy, as I said but still a kid, innocent as I could be. The navy had been my hope of a solution to leaving Itta Bena behind me, but it had not worked. I had been homesick for the whole of my enlistment. I hoped now that, somehow, college would supply what ships and oceans had not been able to do, the escape that geography had not cured. Elizabeth was nineteen. We both had terrible acne and were forever going to dermatologists for the latest treatments, including a painful process that involved freezing the skin with something in an aerosol can.

So we made plans to elope. There is no better logic to it than that. We talked about it so much we found ourselves with nothing more to do than to go through with it. After you've talked about marriage as much as we had, you eventually start repeating yourself. There is only so much you can say about marriage, finally. Elizabeth's parents had the good sense not to encourage our marriage talk, and we took their hesitance and caution as a catalyst to romance. They didn't approve of our marriage? Well then that made marriage all the more exciting, more necessary, even. With parents as disapproving as hers, we figured we were pretty much obligated to get married. Elizabeth was not old enough to marry without her parents' permission in Mississippi, so when we found out that Livingston, Alabama, was our nearest possibility, we were set, nothing could stop us. We shopped for wedding rings, on our small budget, and finally found two that we could afford, simple gold bands for ten dollars each at a jewelry shop called Herman's.

I also found a flower shop on Capitol Street and bought an

orchid to go with the dress that Elizabeth had decided to wear. It was a purple flower, for twelve dollars. The white orchids were twenty dollars, and I could still kick myself for not spending the extra eight. This was the one place where I economized on romance, and it was a mistake. I think Elizabeth was disappointed when she saw that the flower wasn't white.

The main intrigue, though, involved renting a car to drive to Alabama. I had no credit cards, of course, and a fifty-dollar deposit was required to secure the car. It seems a modest deposit nowadays, but it was a fortune to me then. Crafty and resourceful boy that I was—lovesick swain that I was!—I approached a guy in my fraternity who worked at Hertz and convinced him to rent me the car without a deposit. With a bit of sleight of hand on his part, the deed was done. I insisted that the car have air-conditioning. There was no need for air-conditioning, since the weather in April was still cold and rainy, but this was a luxurious detail of our romantic adventure that I did not want overlook, as air-conditioning in cars was more rare then than now and meant, to a boy from Itta Bena, anyway, the difference between romance and just a half-assed or desperate thing to be doing on the weekend. The car was a new Lincoln Town Car, an enormous car, the only one my fraternity pal had on the lot with AC, and it seemed conspicuous sitting in front of the fraternity house the night before the great elopement. The boy who arranged the rental didn't ask why I needed air-conditioning.

Elizabeth and I had been "doing it" in the backseat of borrowed cars for a year before this—usually right in the dormitory parking lot, in sight of other couples doing the same thing—and so even though we agreed that we would restrain ourselves sexually the night before the wedding, it seemed to me a waste of an expensive car to have it sit empty in front of the fraternity house all night, with nobody in the backseat. Once again, romance won out over practicality. We remained abstinent that night, so as not to make the weekend of the big event seem ordinary or typical of every weekend.

Everything was set. On Friday night we "signed out" of the dorm for Saturday with the excuse of going on an all-day picnic. This was the old days, when college girls were required to observe curfews and to account for their every minute. It was an awful system, but in fact it too was one of the details of the adventure that increased the romance. The more lies we had to tell, the more deceit the grown-ups demanded that we practice, the more fine the event. And frankly, I never once thought of our marriage as a beginning, only as an event, an adventure.

The blood tests were complete, the marriage license was purchased and tucked into the pocket of my suit coat, the rings were hidden, the orchid was disguised as a lunch and stored in a small box and refrigerated for the night in Elizabeth's dormitory Frigidaire. Elizabeth's dress was chosen, the car was rented and filled with gas, we were observing our hard celibacy. Everything was set. I marvel now that we got it all accomplished. I was terrible with details, and so I suspect that Elizabeth had taken charge of things up to this point.

The plan was for me to wake up at some specific early morning hour, before daylight, to dress in my suit, and to wheel the big car through the circular drive in front of Franklin Hall, the dormitory where Elizabeth would be waiting for me. She would jump into the car and we would drive away to Alabama to marriage and bliss. That was the plan.

The point of leaving so early was to prevent other students from seeing us all dressed up in our best clothes and an orchid corsage, and of course we didn't want to have to explain the big new car. I had never driven such a fine automobile, or indeed ever ridden in one, and this too seemed a waste, to have no one to show off for. Still, secrecy was the key. What else would we look like but two people driving to Alabama to get married?—the whole point was to prevent anyone's noticing. Or I suppose that was the whole point.

I had a hard time getting to sleep that night. I lay in my narrow bunk and listened to the sounds of my roommate's sleepy breathing above me. I tossed about. I kept my hands above the covers. There was a light rain for a little while, and so I listened to that too and tried not to feel foolish about the air-conditioning that I had insisted upon. I went over the details in my mind, step by step. Sneak out, drive over to the dorm, wait in the parking lot, drive away, get married, got it. I got up out of bed once to check the marriage license in my coat pocket, to be sure it was there. I got up another time to be sure I had the road map that showed me how to get to Livingston, Alabama. I lay in bed. I realized I was very frightened. I thought, What have I done? I didn't want to be married. I had no job. I didn't know whether I loved Elizabeth. I thought, How have I come so far without having thought of these things?

Finally I did sleep, and then I woke early, wondering what time it was. I had only slept a couple of hours. I forced myself to lie in bed until near the time that we had agreed upon. I held my breath for fear of waking my roommate. I crept from my bed and found my clothing and dressed in the dark in my suit and tie. I had no luggage, we would be back before check-in that night. I supposed I was ready. I was going to get married. I went into the bathroom and wet my hair with water and combed it with my fingers.

Outside in the parking lot, when I started the car, the engine seemed so loud that I was certain all the lights in the fraternity house would come on and people would stick their heads out their windows and shout, "What's all the commotion?" This did not happen. I sat with the engine idling. I didn't turn on the headlights, not yet. I took deep breaths and then put the car in Drive and eased away from the curb, headed across campus for Franklin Hall.

Though there was some light coming into the gray sky, it was not much. I checked the car clock. I was right on schedule. It was a short drive to the dorm, and there was no other traffic on campus. I turned on the car's lights and the whole world seemed to grow bright. The car was huge, as I have said. It was a cruiser, an aircraft carrier, at least to someone not accustomed to driving such a car. Actually I was not much used to driving a car at all.

And yet the amazing tonnage of automobile was as light as a feather. I had not driven a car with power steering before. I could spin the wheel with one finger. I was floating on air, I might as well have been. It was a balloon. It was the Goodyear blimp. Alongside it, with me at the wheel, the helm, I might have said, everything else was small and insignificant. No longer was I frightened of marriage. No longer did I consider my joblessness or whether I was in love. Clearly I had made a wise decision. I was the master of my fate, possibly of the universe. I cornered, I signaled, I turned, I checked the gauges, I applied the brakes. In ecstasy I even blew the horn, a great blast that might have been Gabriel, come to wake the dead. What luxury, what ease of handling! Power steering—I hadn't even asked for power steering, and yet here it was, right along with air-conditioning. Like a dream! I believed that I was a shrewd businessman, I believed I would make a good husband.

I wheeled confidently into the circular drive in front of Franklin Hall. I soared in. I sailed in. I glided in for a landing. The car was not only wonderful looking, it was not only wonderful to drive, it smelled wonderful. A brand new air-conditioned, power-steeringed sort of smell. I breathed the good new air into my lungs and felt new and handsome and full of good health.

I parked and turned off the headlights. I looked up toward the front door of the dorm, at the end of a long climb of steps, under Greek columns. The porch light burned in the mist. I waited. Soon I would be driving this fine machine to Alabama. I was getting married. In a car like this, marriage would be easy. I hoped Elizabeth didn't insist on driving. Well, no, she couldn't. They told me that at Hertz. Only me and my wife could drive the car. Oh yeah, she would be my wife on the way back. It was getting a little complicated for me. The problem was, Elizabeth was not there. She was not standing where she said she would be. The front door was not opening. Where was Elizabeth?

I was confused by this. I hadn't turned off the engine. Mist had gathered on the windshield, so I searched around for the wiper button and finally found it and cleared the front window. I sat with the car running and the wipers going. The weather was chilly and wet. The light rain had picked up a little. I thought of turning on the car's heater. It was cold enough for a heater. I did not turn it on. If I had done so, I would have had to admit that the air-conditioning was a mistake. I would have to admit I was a fool.

I sat in the car and looked out the window, up the long flight of steps to the columned verandah of the dorm. I studied the front door and expected it to open. It did not open. I kept looking at the door. I was willing this door open, and still it did not.

There were many cars parked in the lot. I had parked along

the curb, set for a quick getaway. I thought maybe I should just park in a proper space. After I had waited awhile longer, I pulled the Town Car into an empty parking space. I backed in, so that I could keep my eye on the door of the dorm. Still she didn't come. I shut off the engine and started to wait. Any minute, I thought, Elizabeth will come out. She will be beautiful and flustered. She will be wearing the purple orchid, or maybe still carrying it in the Kentucky Fried Chicken box where she had hidden it. We would kiss and laugh. I would say, "Where *were* you? I thought I would have to get married without you!" We would congratulate ourselves in this way on the accomplishment of our intrigue. We would drive into the morning and the rest of our happy lives.

I waited and waited, and still she did not come out.

At first the eastern sky glowed vaguely, then streaks of faintest pink showed in places against the rain clouds, then even that disappeared. Behind the canopy of clouds the sun rose. Now the sky had grown fully light. The rain had stopped but the morning was a lightening shade of gray. I felt foolish and exposed, sitting in this unfamiliar car in front of the girls dorm at this hour on a Saturday morning. It was near time for breakfast to be served in the student union. Shit. Where was she? I wonder now why it did not occur to me that this was a sort of reprieve. I could go back to the fraternity house. I could return the car, save no telling how much on mileage, maybe not have to pay the daily rate, if the right guy was on duty. I didn't think any of these things, though. They never occurred to me. I wonder now what our lives would have been like if I had remembered my fears as I had lain in the bed in the night and realized I might not love this woman, or rather that I had no idea what love was.

At last the front door of the dormitory opened. Well, all

right, I thought, all right, let's go, let's get a move on, let's get on down the damn road. I leaned forward and looked through the windshield. Someone came out the door of the dormitory. Who was it? It was not Elizabeth, it was two other girls, on their way to breakfast. Saturday breakfasts were especially good at our college cafeteria. You could get omelets and waffles. I scrunched down in the front seat of the car and hoped they would not see me. It was no use. They had to walk very close to the car. They saw me and recognized me. They gave me a puzzled look and waved, and so I waved back, but that was all. They went on to breakfast. Oh man, come on Elizabeth, please just come on.

The sun was very high now. The clouds were breaking up a little. I turned off the windshield wipers. I had forgotten they were on. Many girls came out of the dorm on their way to breakfast now. Millsaps is a small school, so I knew most of them. Some of them noticed me, most did not. They were sleepy, the car was gaudy but unfamiliar. One was a girl I had dated for a while before I met Elizabeth. She was what used to be called perky, so she bent down in her sassy way and looked boldly into the car to see just what the heck was going on here. She recognized me. She came over to the car and made small talk. She said, "Whose car?"

I said, "I don't know." I thought she didn't seem as perky as she did when we dated. She just seemed bitter.

She said, "You don't know?"

I said, "A friend. It belongs to a friend."

She said, "Really? Who?" She was getting a little perkier. Maybe I just never noticed the bitter, brittle edge that perkiness carries with it.

I said, "It's sort of a secret."

She looked at me like, Grow up, asshole, and walked away

from the car toward the cafeteria to order a Mexican omelet, or a banana and whipped cream waffle, or some other damn thing that made me dislike her in the first place. Perky bitch. Perk my ass, why don't you.

I could not imagine what had happened to Elizabeth.

For a long time I was worried about her, afraid something really had happened to her. Then I started to get irritated, then pretty mad. I was sick of this shit, actually.

The more girls who crossed campus on their way to breakfast, the less worried and the more hurt and pissed off I began to feel. "Left standing at the altar" was the phrase that kept coming into my mind.

I waited longer. I even talked to several more girls. I found myself flirting with one of them.

She said, "Are you and Elizabeth still going out?"

I said, "Who wants to know?"

She said, "Well, maybe I do."

I said, "Ask me no questions I'll tell you no lies." God.

Still Elizabeth did not show up. I waited and waited.

Then I did a foolish thing. I got out of the car and walked up the sidewalk and out onto the wet lawn and through the grass all the way around to the back of the dormitory. The grass was still wet from the rain, and my feet were cold. I was looking for the window to Elizabeth's room, on the second floor. Never mind that half the student body had already seen me wearing a suit and sitting in a strange car. I could have gone to the front desk and had Elizabeth paged, I suppose.

But something told me that throwing pebbles at her window was the right thing to do, under the circumstances. Without giving words to the thought, the intuition, I believed I was trying to resurrect by a romantic act the romance with which our elopement had been born. Only in that way could I possibly live with what I still supposed I intended to do, once she got her butt down the stairs and into the car, to get married I mean. Otherwise, it made no sense at all. Without romance it was merely a bad idea, her parents were merely right. I found a few small stones and tossed them up at a window on the second floor of the dorm. I thought it might be the right window. It doesn't matter, in any case. The rocks came nowhere close to the spot that I was trying to hit. They bounced irrelevantly off the brick wall. The only result of the attempt is that now my feet were wet and I was angry and felt like a greater fool.

I went back to the car and sat in it. I turned the heater on high and took off my shoes and put my feet under the blower. I folded my arms across my chest. All right, I would wait.

Now the girls I had seen earlier started to come back from breakfast. Some of them spoke to me again and walked on by, back to the dorm. Others snubbed me, this second time around. This was too much. This was insulting.

I checked for safety and waited while a group of eight or more girls crossed the driveway in front of me, and then I pulled out of my parking spot and drove across campus, back to the fraternity house. There was no telephone in Elizabeth's room— there were none allowed in any of the girls' rooms—but I knew that there was a pay phone in the hall on the floor where she lived. Each night after our lovemaking in borrowed cars she called me from this phone and we talked. I had the number, and so now I called it from the fraternity house. A few boys were awake, moving around the house in their underwear, but no one seemed to notice that I was dressed in a suit. I stood in the hallway with the black telephone to my ear and listened as the dormitory phone rang many times. Literally, thirty or forty times. There was no answer.

I went back out to the Town Car and drove over to Franklin Hall again. I was sure she would be there waiting, I was sure of it. But when I looked up at the steps, toward the front door, she was not. I parked again and sat and looked at the dormitory doors again. She did not come out. Other college boys drove in and picked up their Saturday morning dates and drove away. I didn't need the heater any longer, at least. It would be a mild day. My feet were dried out, pretty much.

I drove back to the fraternity house and called again. I let the telephone ring many times. I let it ring so many times that it would have been impossible that somebody should not have picked it up. Finally, somebody did answer the phone, some girl, I forget who. I asked to speak to Elizabeth.

There was silence for a very long time while she was going to get Elizabeth. She was gone so long I was afraid she had lied to me and had simply gone back to bed.

Then a sleepy voice came on the line. "Hello?" the voice asked, a quiet question. This was Elizabeth. She sounded like a person who had not expected to be waked up so early on a Saturday morning.

I said, "Elizabeth, where are you? What's the matter? I've been waiting for hours."

THERE IS NO NEED to draw this out. We drove to Alabama that day, and we were married by a Baptist minister, with the minister's wife as our witness. Afterward we stopped at an out-of-the-way place called the Lakeview Motel, where the door to our unit kept springing open at odd times. We made love as many times as we could—this was our first crack at sex in a bed or in a prone position—and then we watched a television show called *The Defenders*. It starred E. G. Marshall and Robert Reed, and the plot that night had something to do with LSD, which I was hearing about for the first time. By eleven o'clock my new bride was back in her dormitory bed, and I had returned the car to Hertz and was not charged for an extra day. I walked back from the Hertz place to the fraternity house in the middle of the night, about twenty blocks. You might not think so, but I was happy. I was married. I was in love. I was pretty well pleased with myself for the way things had turned out. Maybe this makes no sense, I can't analyze it even these many years later.

One thing, though, that I can see now, as I have already said, I did not see then. I had not had to get married. This fact simply never occurred to me. During the awful hours when Elizabeth slept and I waited, I did not *want* to get married, that much was pretty clear even then. And if I had had more sense I might also have figured out that oversleeping was Elizabeth's way of saying she wasn't so sure this was such a great idea herself.

Romance had set my course. Maybe that's the only answer. Herman had sold us the rings. The flowers were bought. The car was rented. The blood tests, the marriage license. We had talked so much about marriage. We had dreamed of small apartments together. We had talked about flowers on the breakfast table, about pets, and about children, especially about children. We said we would have a boy named Robert and we would call him Robin, after Christopher Robin. We would have a girl named Rebecca, and we would call her Becky. Elizabeth wrote a magical little children's play for one of her Elementary Education classes and named the two principal characters Robin and

Becky. This was our secret joke together when the play was produced on campus. We railroaded ourselves with romance.

Elizabeth and I had three children. There was never a Becky. One son we named Robin. Another we named Erik, and he recently became the father of my first grandchild. One died a few hours after his birth twenty-some years ago. Jesse was the baby's name. And Robin—well, never mind for right now what happened to Robin. What eventually happened to Elizabeth and me was pretty typical—the alcohol, the betrayals, the divorce— though God knows why lives are comprised of such events, the good or the evil. And who could ever have imagined, when I was buying a ring from Herman or choosing the wrong color flower or finessing the fifty-dollar deposit on an air-conditioned Lincoln Town Car, and otherwise sealing the lid on romance, that life would turn out in this way. I didn't see it coming. I still feel blindsided by my own innocence. So much depends on romance. Sometimes that point comes right home to me.

10

The Man I Killed

AT THE VERY BEGINNING of my plunge into romantic fantasy with Elizabeth, long before the wedding, I opened my eyes one day— morning, afternoon, I didn't know—and found myself in a hospital room and with no memory of how long I had been there or what had happened to me in the first place. This was Baptist Hospital in Jackson, the state capital. My mother was at my bedside, along with persons on the medical staff of the hospital.

A couple of days earlier, I learned eventually, I had been transported by ambulance the hundred miles or so from a small hospital in the Delta where I had landed after the car crash. I had been on my way to pick up Elizabeth for a date. The story was, I had collided head-on on a bridge with another car. My injuries were too grave to be treated in that smaller facility, so I had been brought here. My mother, who now sat anxiously gripping my hand, had ridden in the ambulance with me, as I was near death. She answered my questions as well as she could—where was I, what had happened? She detailed my injuries, broken leg, ribs, nose, collapsed lung, damaged spleen, head trauma, damaged kidney. The kidney was the most serious injury—my right kidney had been crushed by the passenger-side door handle of my father's Dodge Dart. I had been wearing no seat belt—this was before seat belts were commonplace—and so when the two cars collided I sailed across the front seat and into the door handle.

When I woke with these questions, these blank spots in my recent past, I had just come from the recovery room after an operation to remove the damaged kidney. I was going to be fine, I was assured. One more operation now—the broken femur would be set with an eighteen-inch diamond-shaped pin down its length—and then convalescence. Well, some physical therapy to get me walking again, but mostly just patience and the passage of time.

At the time of the crash I had been recently discharged from the navy, where I had served on an aircraft carrier in the Mediterranean. I had started back to college and had recently met Elizabeth. When the wreck occurred I was driving from Itta Bena to Leland, a town some forty miles away, to pick her up for a date. Briefly I felt some panic, for fear Elizabeth had been in the car with me, as I had no memory of the wreck. My mother assured me she had not been in the car, that Elizabeth was fine.

I lay in the hospital bed and settled into the difficult routine of pain and boredom. I was missing my semester. I was missing *J. B.*, a drama production on campus. Tubes went down my nose to drain my lungs, then they came out. I loved being a college student. I wanted to try out for a part in a play this semester. I had joined a fraternity.

I lay in traction for weeks. My mother hovered over me with tender care. My father appeared once or twice—he stayed in Itta Bena, going to work each day, regularizing our home in whatever ways he could in the face of my near death. I think, too, he could not bear the atmosphere of illness in a hospital, let alone my sorry condition.

My flat-of-my-back task was to recover strength after the one operation to prepare myself for the next. The pin was finally put in, and the pain increased. I became addicted to morphine and then to Demerol. I was weaned from these drugs with difficulty. Even after the pain had stopped I begged for the drugs, lied that my back hurt, anything to feel the ease of their narcotic. The craving slowly went away. Round-the-clock nurses sat by my bed night and day. They gave me regular massages. They rolled me over at intervals to prevent bed sores and pneumonia. I went to physical therapy, where I held myself between parallel bars and began to walk again. Eventually I learned to use crutches.

Elizabeth brought her homework from the college each day and sat in the hall outside my room and studied. I slept most of the time, but she never left except to go to class. She fed me, she wheeled me around in a huge old wooden wheelchair. Sometimes when we were alone we kissed. We managed to begin an invalid's sexual relationship during this time. Mainly she put her hand beneath the sheets for a few seconds, and then a nurse would come in with a pill or a thermometer and she'd hastily withdraw her hand and we'd giggle together and share this secret. When the nurse left she would try it again. Both of us were inexperienced.

You would think that at age twenty, just out of the navy, I would not have been so innocent. In the Mediterranean ports—Naples, Barcelona, Athens, Cannes, Istanbul—I had eyed the prostitutes in the bars, had longed for them, but I could never bring myself to go with one of them. The training films had warned of sexually transmitted diseases, of course, but that wasn't the problem. I just felt so sorry for the girls, the prostitutes. Their lives were ruined, didn't they know this? What would it say about me, and what would it do to them, if I affirmed their ruin with money, contributed to what must surely have been the death of their spirits? I know, I could have been more spontaneous, analyzed less, enjoyed myself more, but this was who I was, the almost-adult who emerged from Itta Bena somehow optimistic.

This sweet sex play of hands beneath the sheets was all Elizabeth and I wanted in any case. We were kids. We were making our way slowly, and together, into physical and spiritual regions as yet unvisited by us, and there was no great hurry.

The season changed, and I watched the time slide by from my window. The winter skies turned blue. The azaleas bloomed. I could see them from my bed, where I lay in traction. Slowly I began to mend. My kidney function was good, my femur was building up new bone around the break, my lungs were clear.

Then one day a woman I did not know came into my room. I had few visitors except for my mother and Elizabeth, so I was surprised to see anyone. A few times acquaintances from the college had stopped by, but I was a pale ghost, I was scarred and wheelchair bound, my weight had dropped to less than 120 pounds, and the sight of me was more than most college boys could tolerate. The day the woman stopped by, my mother had gone down to the cafeteria for lunch and Elizabeth had not finished with her morning classes yet. I wonder now whether this woman had not watched and waited for them to absent themselves before she made her appearance, which was slender and dark-haired and pretty. She told me her name, she shook my hand. She was small and even fragile looking, but her breasts were full and her voice was throaty and so I knew she was a woman, not a girl.

When our flesh touched, our palms, as we shook hands, I felt excited. The touch meant nothing, I knew, only a friendly touch. I was so innocent, so inexperienced. I felt guilty for my attraction to her. I felt as if I were cheating on Elizabeth, who had been so loyal as I had lain sleeping all those long days, weeks.

Somewhere in the conversation I learned that she was twenty-three years old, just a few years older than I was. That wasn't very much older. She seemed a lot older, maybe more "worldly" would be a better way to put it. There was something about the hard, tired look in her eyes, the carriage of her body that said we lived in different worlds. I wondered what she was doing here. I had been warned against speaking to insurance company people unless one of my parents was in the room. I knew this woman was no insurance company representative. She talked about the weather, asked me how I was feeling, exactly what my injuries were. She seemed interested in me. Two women, counting Elizabeth — one girl, one woman, I supposed — were interested in me at the same time. I had never dared to imagine such a luxury for myself. I wondered if I might ask her out sometime, when I got to feeling better. I didn't allow myself to think about Elizabeth just now. I allowed myself these guilty thoughts. I wondered if maybe she might be a little too old for me. Probably she was, probably she was just a nice person who liked visiting shut-ins and had no other interest in me.

She told me she was the wife of the man I had killed.

Those were the words she used: "the man you killed." This was information that had been kept from me. The man in the other car had died of his injuries.

SHE HAD THREE CHILDREN, all girls. She and the children were alone now, without a husband or father. Without anyone really. She had no family she could turn to. She was brought up in a whorehouse in Lafayette, Louisiana. Her mother had worked her whole life as a prostitute. As soon as she was old enough, around twelve she said, she started turning a few tricks to help out with expenses. That's the way her mother put the situation to her when she encouraged her to sleep with selected clientele, to "help out with expenses." Her mother told her she was putting away half of the money she earned in a college fund, so she could get herself an education later on, though she said she would always have tricking to fall back on in an emergency. There was never any college, of course. She said she supposed this was the emergency her mother had been talking about. It's funny how even a bad person like her mother could have some wisdom at times, she said. All of these things she told me with no obvious intent. She was not trying to get money out of me, not trying to sexually seduce me, not trying to make me feel guilty, nothing. She just wanted to see the man who killed her husband and left her with three children in a world that had never been all that friendly to her in the first place. I was an important person in her life. She wanted to lay eyes on me, that was all. She held no anger, felt no blame. She said, "If I ask Mum for help she'll just make me put the girls to work on their backs. The oldest one anyway. It's a solution, but it ain't a good one." I was surprised to hear that she used the word *ain't*. She said whoring out the kids was strictly a last resort. She said, "Well, it ain't even a last resort. I'll just kill them all first. I wouldn't never whore nobody out, not my worst enemy. Now me, it don't matter. I been doing this since I was twelve. I can lay there and close my eyes and I might be going to the opera in

New York City, for all I know. I might be sliding down some rocky river in Montana in a rubber raft, for all I know. I don't even know I got a dick in me. Kids though, it's different. You don't want a kid their age eating no dick. Yeah, I'll just kill them. I got me a gun, well Darnel's gun, the one he kept in the truck. That's the solution I'd go with, killing them. That would be the best thing all around. Oh, not that it's come to that yet, far from it. Ain't nobody getting killed today. We still got us a few options left open to us, I guess. Darnel had some insurance on the car, and a little bit of life—can you believe that? A life insurance policy! Ten thousand dollars. What a nice surprise. Ain't Darnel just the sweetest thing? That brightened up my day for sure, I can tell you. So I got a little bankroll from you killing him, so that's a break, a windfall, like they say. I'm doing okay. A big town like Jackson, you can earn some real money in just a short time. I'll parlay this setback into something good before long, get back on my feet again, every cloud's got a silver lining, like the poet said, get these girls into a nice school, get them some nice clothes." The girls were downstairs in the lobby, she said. "They don't let no kids come up on the regular floors, I don't know why. Ain't no diseases up here they couldn't catch in a whorehouse. You ought to see them sitting down there waiting for me in those big plastic chairs. I gave each one of them a magazine to thumb through. They act like they're reading, they are the cutest things. Their little feet stick out from the chairs, won't come close to the floor, of course, buckle-up shoes, white socks, I try to give them nice things. They're seven and three and the baby. Not so much of a baby anymore, eighteen months, started walking at nine months. Looks like she might have someplace to go, don't it? They're good girls, though. They'll sit right where I told them. They take care of that baby like it was their own.

They won't run off with no strangers or get into any trouble, you know. They are excellent little ladies and so I'm not going to worry about them, what's the point of worrying anyway? What tragedies were ever turned back by worrying about them? None to my personal knowledge." She had met her husband in the Lafayette whorehouse, she said. He was a long-haul trucker addicted to crystal meth. I had no idea what she was talking about. "He started off being addicted to just Benzedrine inhalers and then later on Dexedrine, them diet pills everybody is shedding so many ugly pounds with these days, but you know, they led him to the harder stuff, like the expression goes. If he could have just stayed addicted to that Dexedrine, he would have been fine. It kept him nice and slender, and he could drive damn near from Mississippi to California without stopping. But you know. You get something better and you got to try it. He said Dexedrine wasn't doing it for him so good anymore, plus being a little old-fashioned. He knew this pharmacist in Bakersfield who made the crystal himself, they was big pals, drinking buddies when he was out on the coast, so he had a lifetime supply, real cheap. I said even if Dexedrine still worked for him, he couldn't afford to be addicted to it when he could be addicted to crystal for half the price. God, I miss him. He was an idealist, you know what I'm saying? 'Idealist,' that's one of my favorite words, he taught it to me. Sometimes when everybody's asleep I just lay in bed at night and whisper 'idealist,' and the whole world seems a little bit better. Everything Darnel did he had somebody else's happiness in mind. The girls and me mainly, but everybody really. He was good to me. He was an excellent daddy to them girls, believe you me. He didn't once touch them, not a one of them, and as for putting them in a whorehouse, well forget about it, he was more of a fanatic on that subject than me myself and I. He'd kill your ass if he thought you were just thinking about it. I miss him. I don't know how I'm going to live without him. I'm not going to kill myself, I don't mean that. I got the girls to think about. And—this might seem like a pessimistic thing to be saying, but I mean, if worst comes to worst and the girls need to die, well, I mean, if I've already been selfish and took my own life, who's going to be around to kill them? It's complicated, I don't deny that. Sometimes I ought to think silent thoughts to myself and not say every single solitary word that pops into my head. Darnel used to say, 'If you think it, Peaches, it'll be popping out of your mouth in a minute.' He was so sweet. I can't believe he's dead. And damn near killed you, to boot. Sometimes on the crystal he'd just go off, like in a trance. He'd be awake and all, his eyes would be wide open, but brother he was gone. That's about what happened when he pulled into your lane that evening. That would be my educated guess. He never knew what hit him, or what he hit, I should say. He was just driving along staring out at the Delta probably, the rice paddies and the swamp, who knows what he was looking at. He loved nature. He could name all kinds of stuff, birds, trees, little wildflowers, shit. I guess I told you he saved me from the whorehouse. I talk so much I forget what I say. He parked the big-rig at the whorehouse and didn't even know it was a regular whorehouse. 'Imagine my surprise,' he told me later on after he married me, 'when I thought the place in Lafayette was a massage parlor and I pulled in there expecting to get a five-dollar handjob and here it turns out I'm in a full-scale whorehouse, whoo. I thought I died and went to heaven.' Oh he was a card, big talker, full of foolishness, on crystal you couldn't get him to shut up, in fact. You could tell he was flush, you know, rich. You can spot the ones who hold on to their money a mile off, if you've lived in a

whorehouse any time at all. He had bankroll written all over
him, innocent and pure as the drove snow, that's how my mama
looked at him, that's what she saw when she first looked at him
with his wide-open innocent eyes coming in through the front
door looking for a baby-oil massage and somebody to beat his
meat for him. Lord, he looked sweet. I was thirteen by that time
and I never had seen anybody as innocent and sweet as him.
Greed is what got me out of that place, my mama's greed, plus
of course the precious angel whose wings I flown out on. Mama
took one look at him and she stepped right up and said, 'Come
right on in my door. You look around, sugar, take your time, we
got lots of girls to choose from, but—' Here she pushed me from
behind so I had to step out in front of her in plain view. '—But
just for your information we have a special on today, a new girl
working for us, who might be somebody you'd be interested in
having a date with. Here she is, see what you think. Introduce
yourself to the nice man, honey, see if y'all don't like each other.'
Darnel took one look at me and said, 'How old is this girl?'
Mama said, 'You like them young, don't you?' He said to me,
'How old are you, sweetie?' Mama said, 'She's eighteen.' She
was backing off fast. She had seen something in him that she
didn't see right when he walked through the door. Her voice had
changed entirely now. She was hard and businesslike, not her
sweet-sugar voice anymore at all. She said, "Lots of girls, look
around, take your time.' She snatched me around by my shoulders and pushed me behind her so sudden I almost toppled over
a table. I slithered back around so I could see. I was already in
love. He was tall and slender and his eyes were so dark and far
back in his head from the road and the drugs he didn't look
quite human. Mama seemed to know this wasn't over yet. Darnel reached in his pocket and pulled out a roll of bills. I won't try

to impress you with how big it was, but it was big. It was four thousand dollars, it turned out. He dropped it on the floor right in front of Mama. He said, 'I'll take the girl. I'm leaving with her, if she wants to go. I'm taking her with me.' Mama looked at the money on the floor. 'This ain't no slave-trading outfit, this is a whorehouse,' my mother said, real indignant. She looked at the money some more. She said, 'You'll have to marry her.' Darnel looked at me. He said, 'I'm a real hard worker and a drug addict. I got my own big-rig and do coast-to-coast long-haul, so you'd have to travel. There's a sleeper in the cab-over, it ain't too uncomfortable. And I love you and you won't have to turn no tricks, not even for me if you don't want to. Want to take a chance?' I said, 'You bet.' Goddamn, he was a charming motherfucker, pardon my French. Is it any wonder I loved him so? Is it any wonder I can't quite believe it yet that he no longer walks this earth?"

BY THE TIME MY mother returned from the cafeteria the woman was gone. I felt like a stone. I wished I had been killed in the wreck and Darnel had survived. I wished I could marry the woman with the three little girls and be their father. I would live my life for them. I would be a better father than Darnel even. I wished their mother didn't use ungrammatical English. That was the only problem. I could overcome that. She could go back to school, learn grammar. I would love the girls and buy them nice clothes and take them to their daddy's grave. I would tell them my daddy died too, when I was young, the same age as the baby. I would say I didn't remember him. I would tell them all the things I did remember, show them the few pictures I had. I would encourage them to remember things about Darnel, I

would write them down for them. I would sit with a photo al-
bum, if there was one, and point out pictures of Darnel. I would
tell them about my stepfather, the man I called Daddy. I would
holler "I love you" down the hall to them at night, the way my
stepfather did. I wished I could bring the dead to life, all the
dead fathers. I wished I could kill the prostitute who whored her
baby out to help with expenses. Later I cried so hard I puked.
Elizabeth was there to hold the pan and cover it with a towel
and carry it away.

11

Loachapoka, Alabama

ONE AFTERNOON ELIZABETH BROUGHT a friend home to study for a Shakespeare test, a young woman I have to list as the first bona fide hippie I had ever met. We were living in a farmhouse in a little community in Alabama by this time, several miles from the university where I was enrolled in graduate school. Elizabeth had gone a little stir crazy staying home with our son, who was by now eighteen months old—we were calling the baby Robin, according to plan—and so she had begun taking a few university classes that appealed to her. She was happy, she was making friends of her own for the first time since we moved into the farmhouse. I was happy too, now that I was back in school and no longer tied to a job I wasn't well suited for. Right out of college we had lived in Florida for a while, where we had jobs in the publics schools, and I had been pretty unhappy.

I was immediately attracted to this girl who came home to study with Elizabeth, this hippie, whose name turned out to be Twyla, a strong painful attraction that is not really explained by her appearance.

Twyla was not a beauty by any standards. She had feverish, unhealthy-looking pale blue eyes and a weak chin. She had big feet and knobby knees. I didn't care. She was beautiful anyway. I couldn't take my eyes away from her. She was slender and barefoot, her straight blond hair hung down past her waist. It had never been cut. She wore no shoes or bra or other under-clothes—this was immediately apparent through her thin washed-out dress. Eventually I was able to look down the front of her dress when she bent over and I saw her small breasts and pale, pale nipples.

She was a California girl—seventh generation, she let slip easily into conversation—raised in Palo Alto and had taken her first lover when she was fourteen, "a dirty hippie," as her parents supposedly called the guy, who was himself twenty-two or twenty-three at the time, a graduate student at Stanford. It had been true love. They would have been married if her parents weren't so awful. He showed her how to smoke marijuana and seven times they had dropped acid together. I was strangely thrilled by this information.

Elizabeth said, "You're lucky you—"

I interrupted before Elizabeth could finish her sentence. "For heaven's sake, don't be so judgmental, Lizzie." This silenced her and I flushed with embarrassment that I had been obviously eager to hear Twyla's every word.

This guy shot Twyla up with heroine once, she said, because she needed to experience everything, even the bad stuff, but he wouldn't let her do it again because he loved her so much. Twyla said, "I dug it, man. He could do anything to me when I was high and I was just, like, *there.*" He had taught her to love the Rolling Stones, whose albums she wanted to have buried with her when she died.

Elizabeth tried to bring the conversation back around to Shakespeare, but Twyla loved to talk about herself. Her second lover was a forty-year-old black man with expensive suits and a big belly. He smoked big cigars. She told us all this in the most offhand sort of way, as she and Elizabeth began to make study plans. My head was spinning. She told us of many lovers. She said she had learned to pee standing up, that's why she didn't wear underwear, it was just so cool, you just spread your legs and let it fly, man, whew, you ought to try it sometime, Elizabeth.

Elizabeth said, "I'd get it all over myself."

Twyla said, "I can show you some techniques."

I left the room and they studied for a while. I pretended to be indifferent to their work, but I kept skulking through the kitchen trying to hear what they were saying. It was clear to me that Elizabeth was really just tutoring Twyla for the test. Twyla was picking her brain, Elizabeth didn't mind. Eventually I heard them stray from the subject of Shakespeare and on to personal matters. Later Elizabeth showed her around the house we lived in, the small white farmhouse beneath spreading oaks and pecans. "It's our dream house," she said, "but it's not as perfect as it looks." She told her that when we first moved in you could see right through the walls. The wind swept through these cracks like an arctic gale, and headlights from cars on the road at night blared in just as easily and woke us from sleep. During a bad cold spell the first winter, the water in the dog's waterbowl froze in the kitchen. We piled covers up sky high on our son Robin, and once or twice had to move the whole family out of the house and into someplace warm. Our fuel was stored in a propane tank in the backyard, and as there was no gauge on the tank to show the amount of fuel remaining, the tank sometimes ran out, leaving the house frigid and the stove unworkable. The

guy with the propane company refused to deliver fuel on weekends, so we had to exist for two, even three days at a time with
no heat or cooking fuel. Elizabeth referred to the bathroom as
the Black Hole of Calcutta—it was tiny and windowless and
dark, with no shower and barely any space to turn around. The
toilet depended on a shallow well with a defective pump for
water to flush. Not only would the pump "lose its prime" and
overheat and express its other many flaws, but sometimes the
water level in the well would fall so low that there was nothing
to draw up the pipes even if the pump was working. When the
levels fell this low, the water had to be tested for safety, and in-
variably the test proved the water to be unsafe. Elizabeth told all
this in a funny, appreciative way, not complaining, and I could
tell the description of the place had had its effect on Twyla.

At first I thought she was simply infatuated, happy for Elizabeth and envious in a friendly way. Much later I understood
that this was not true, that she was insanely jealous, pathologi-
cally maybe, and hated us for having what she could not and
would do anything to destroy what we had. None of this did I
suspect at the time, of course. I knew I should have left them
alone to work, but I could not. I came into the room where they
were studying. I had been looking after Robin, inside where I
was spying and also outdoors at the swing set and feeding lumps
of sugar through the fence to the goats.

"Okay if I come in for a while?"

Elizabeth said, "We're taking a break."

I stayed and stayed. I talked and talked. I became chatty and
charming, or so I imagined. I was a fool, I knew I was. I tried to
shut up, but I could not. I told every corny asinine thing I could
think of. Suddenly nothing that I had to tell seemed good
enough to bestow as a proper gift upon this amazing girl. I un-

derstood the paucity of my experience. I was a chucklehead, a hick, all things Southern seemed stupid and wan. All my innocent tales of a happy childhood were foolish and mean. I realized I had nothing to offer a hippie. I had outlived my time, my relevance on this earth. I had no social protests to report—I had been in the navy, for God's sake, lived in married student housing in college, had no other lovers than my wife. I had done no drugs outside those prescribed in the hospital, except alcohol of course. I had attended no sit-ins. I knew nothing. I was jealous of every man Twyla spoke of. And she was married too, Jeeziz! I hated her husband.

Later on I met him. He was slender and dark-eyed and dark-haired and gorgeous. He grew marijuana from seed and worked with the poor. His parents had been Christian Scientists, so if anybody said the word *spleen*, for example, he fainted. I thought even this was cool. He couldn't watch porno movies because somebody might speak of body parts in a clinical or mainly descriptive way. "Your testicles are tight and smooth," coming from the screen, would send him onto the floor. I thought even this idiotic phobia was cool. He had been jealous and suicidal when he first understood that Twyla believed in "free love" and that she planned always to take lovers, then he grew to understand it better. He began to see that there was always enough love to go around and that nothing could come between soul lovers, even other soul lovers—my poor head was reeling by this time—and so he began to take other lovers himself, including a high school girl down in Florida where they worked on a Vista project, a black girl he got pregnant. Now he had a child in Tallahassee named Robby. They were living in California when she had the affair with the black man who smoked cigars, and he, the husband, Frank was his name, took his morose self and a guitar and went all alone up in the woods on Big Sur and built a campfire and planned to sit there and strum the night away. Instead the wind caught the embers of the fire and blew them all over the dry forest and started a three-county forest fire that burned up a couple of small farms, including a dairy herd and all the barns. Frank was almost burned up himself and then had to spend some time in jail on suspicion of arson, but finally he got off.

Elizabeth said, "He had a *guitar* with him when he was arrested? That's hilarious!"

As if that were the point of the story. For my part, the guitar made the story. It's why they were cool and I was square. My entire history seemed trivial and worthless in the presence of this girl. She was only about nineteen, and I was maybe twenty-nine by this time. I found myself wondering whether I was too old for her, too middle-class, too Southern, too monogamous, too everything that I was. I was astonished to find that I had simply blanked out my marriage and the son I was holding in my arms as introductions were made. I was fantasizing sex with Twyla before I had known her ten minutes.

I checked Elizabeth's face to see whether she had noticed that I was making an ass of myself, and I thought she had not.

This woman, this girl, this Twyla, seemed to have brought with her into our home a completely new world, a world I had only barely heard of, California, the new sixties generation they talked about on TV. I envied it, her, everything that was not me, us. I wondered what she was thinking of our home, was it too "square," too older-generational? We had a couch—did hippies scorn couches? We had good rugs given to us by Elizabeth's parents, fuck. We had shelves filled with books. We were living in a farmhouse in Alabama at the time, growing all our own food, almost hippies ourselves, though we had not meant to be and didn't consider this a fact until much later. Twyla commented on the "cool lifestyle" we lived. I put this phrase in quotation marks to show how corny it seems now, almost a parody of itself, and yet it seemed absolutely authentic then, the finest most genuine compliment I had ever received. She loved the farm, the garden, the animals. Maybe I was a hippie after all.

She even said so: "You're kind of a hippie yourself, dude."

I almost swooned.

Elizabeth gave a curt laugh and said, "I don't think so."

I could have killed Elizabeth. I felt like I'd been "outed," to use an anachronistic expression. I wanted to be a hippie. Well, why not? A genuine long-haired free-loving acid-dropping hippie chick had proclaimed me one. Why deny what was mine by right? All my former dreams were hereby canceled. I didn't want anymore to be everything I'd ever dreamed of being. Husband, father, student, agrarian, forget about it. I was already thinking of growing a beard, finding out where love beads were sold, painting my car with flowers, burning a flag, a draft card, learning to talk differently, to say "dude" and "groovy" and "that's not my bag." "Lifestyle" I wasn't so sure about. I could say almost anything but "lifestyle." It was all coming back to me now, Johnny Carson, "happenings." What was a "happening"? Shit, I couldn't remember.

Elizabeth and I had seen hippies on the *Tonight Show,* and maybe in the news, but we had never met one, so I hadn't paid very close attention to what they were talking about. What were the chances I was ever going to meet one in my own house. They were supposed to be in Berkeley, I thought. Haight-Ashbury. It was coming back to me now. I was always a little embarrassed by them. They looked like fools for the most part. I hadn't realized how beautiful they could be. I was titillated and envious of their talk of "free love" and their casual politics of drugs, but mainly they seemed like a bunch of losers. I couldn't keep from thinking of James Dean who had it so totally made and didn't know it, what a whiner, well they all were. James Dean would have made a perfect hippie if he had lived.

"I love your pad, man," Twyla said. "I'd love to crash here sometime."

I should have been listening to Carson more carefully, I realized now. I would have to find out what "happening" meant before I saw this "chick" again. And now she wanted to crash here. In my pad. I had a crash pad.

Twyla said, "This is the kind of pad me and my old man want to get someday."

Jesus, I was living in a pad and hadn't realized it. Maybe I really was a hippie. Me and my old lady—Elizabeth and I, I meant—we had wanted this without knowing it was hip. Oh Christ. I wouldn't say it, I wasn't in love. Yes I was. Of course I was, oh fuck man, I was deeply in love. Out back we kept a big vegetable garden and ate what we grew, little else except some occasional meat that we bought in town.

Twyla loved that. "Oh man," she said, in her totally California way, "that is just so amazingly boss."

Fuck Shakespeare, fuck Elizabeth, fuck even Robin, God forgive me. I suggested a tour, didn't Twyla want to see the place? I showed her the pantry, where we kept the harvested garden, rows of Mason jars filled with vegetables green and red and purple, green beans and butterbeans and purple hull peas and okra and cucumber pickles and tomatoes, even potatoes. I showed her the freezer. We froze sweet corn and yellow squash and zucchini and mustard greens and kept them packed in cellophane packages in a chest-style freezer.

Twyla said, "Groovy Tuesday, bitches. Are you like, vegetarians?"

I said, "Yes."

Elizabeth said, "No."

At the same time.

We looked at each other. It was strange to have shared the same dreams as this girl who was so different from me, us. She dreamed of a farmhouse, a vegetable garden, all the things we had dreamed of. Why were Twyla's dreams hip and interesting and modern and ours so old-fashioned? We had promised ourselves, someday, a place where our dog could run free and chase rabbits and our son could grow up among slow cattle and a steady old horse and wide spaces. It was what we had, the house we were standing in. A little white-painted frame house shaded by huge trees, it stood within sight of only one other house, "the Big House" as that larger structure was called, a great antebellum home at the top of a hill, with a flock of wild peacocks living in the trees behind the place. Sometimes when I went out the backdoor in the early morning a cock and two or three peahens would be standing on the porch with puzzled faces and surprised eyes, as if trying to discover who the new people were. When the backdoor opened they would screech and take noisy flight, beating their loud wings like wild turkeys in the frantic, comic escape. They sailed ungainly through the air and into the trees.

I said, "Let's walk outdoors, I'll show you the place."

Twyla and Elizabeth put aside their books and study materials and went with me out the backdoor. A pasture with a couple of horses stretched across rolling hills to deep woods. I picked up Robin and shifted him onto my hip and felt the fine corn silk of his clean hair against my face. We went down the steps toward the pasture. A herd of nanny goats made their funny noises at us from across the fence and obeyed the gentle prompting of a huge, horned ram, who stood between them and the strangers beyond the fence. We walked out into the pasture and watched the comical goats fan away from us, their tails writing curlicues on the summer air.

I said, "Are you up for a long walk?"

I knew that Elizabeth was ready to walk, she loved this rolling land even more than I did. She pointed out huge gray mounds in the field, the beds of fire ants. She led Twyla to a patch of dewberries and picked a few for herself and a few more for Twyla. The berries melted on their tongues, and I felt proud of Elizabeth, even though I already knew I would throw her aside for one chance to make love to this magical person in our midst.

Through the woods ran a small river, where fish swam and where deer stood ankle deep on a sandbar and drank from the stream. We walked down onto a sandbar and I showed the others, including the child in my arms, the two-toed hoofprints of deer. "Look," I said, pointing at a certain pattern of tracks, "this was a doe and two fawns." Farther on I said, "Come over here, on the gravel spit, I'll show you where the raccoons come to wash their food." The farmhouse, and the land that stretched away from it, and all the animals, wild and caged, were a way of being in love. I loved Elizabeth in part because I loved this geography. Elizabeth and I, through some shared good instinct or intuition or mystery, had known this when we set out. In college, just as we had picked out our child's name, we envisioned this farmhouse, these wide skies. Now I was willing to offer it all to a nineteen-year-old nymphomaniac for sex. In the dizziness of testosterone and, I suppose, in fear of something I'll never be able to name, this fact did not seem in the least muddleheaded or dangerous or bizarre.

On the way back up through the pasture, as we headed back for the house, Twyla noticed a small, old, broad-backed horse that belonged to the owners of the property. She said, "Let's go for a ride."

This concerned me a little. I knew the owner and liked him. He was a bachelor, a gay guy, I suspected. We rented the farmhouse from him, in fact. He kept this little horse for his nieces, who were twelve and thirteen and who came twice a year to visit on the farm. He doted on these girls. He bought a blue bridle for them, and a little saddle, which he cinched onto the horse when they visited the farm. He would set them up on the horse and walk alongside as they rode. I knew he wouldn't want us pestering the horse. Nobody ever rode the horse until the nieces showed up at Christmas and in the summer.

I laughed at Twyla's suggestion that we go for a ride, as though she had intended it as a joke. The little horse was placid and calm, munching grass slowly. We walked up to it and I put my hand on its coarse hide. When I gave it a sharp friendly crack with my palm upon its flank it did not stir. The smell of horse rose up from the flesh with such poignancy that the odor seemed almost visible in the air above the place where my hand had struck. Robin reached out from my arms to touch the horse as well. He gathered hands full of its mane into his little fists. He is the exact age I was when my father died, I suddenly thought. If I died today, would he have no memory at all of this moment, of me or this horse's fragrant mane twisted in his fingers?

Twyla said, "I'm serious."

Elizabeth said, "No, absolutely not. This is private property."

I said, "Well—"

Twyla said, "I wouldn't get so uptight about some rich old fuck's private property."

She said the phrase "private property" as if it meant something filthy.

Elizabeth said, "Well, then, let's walk up to his house and ask him. He'll probably say yes. He'll probably put the saddle on for us."

Twyla said, "A saddle is like a really evil thing, man. It's like oppression, you know? Like the establishment always wants to oppress the masses and shit."

I said, "Really I don't think it would be a great idea." Twyla was beginning to scare me now. I felt some of my attraction for her waning. And yet I did not side with Elizabeth or common decency either.

Impulsively, I found myself in a diversionary tactic. I said, "But this young man might like to go for a ride. Want to, Robin? Want to ride the horse?"

Looking back through the veil of all these years this moment seems to have taken place in slow motion. I see the green pasture, a sky full of gathering clouds, the horse, the child, the two women. Myself, of course, grinning like a madman. Impulsive beyond even my own powers to imagine, I lifted Robin up and set him suddenly on the broad low back of the old horse. The place on the horse's back where I placed him seemed as wide and safe as a porch swing. The child was sitting there flat on his butt with his little legs stretched out in front of him. He smiled his crooked smile at me.

He was wearing corrective shoes then, I remember, with steel insteps and high tops, all laced up. His short pants were red, and his pullover shirt was white with a pattern of red clowns. I was about to say, "How do you like the horse, Robin," or some such ridiculous words, when the horse spooked. No sound, no sudden movement, nothing obvious to me, just the new small sudden weight of a toddler on his back, I suppose, with no warning at all. A rider, no matter how diminutive, was too much for the horse. It was an old horse, as I've said, and not a fast one by any means, but one moment it was there beside me and all of us were safe and smiling and happy, and the next moment it was moving, gone, running headlong away from us, and carrying my little son with him. For a long time the child did not fall. He stayed right in the middle of the broad back. The sudden acceleration toppled him over, of course, immediately, so the ride that he took on that mesalike table of horse's back was in a prone position. He was jiggling slightly with the horse's movement, but still he seemed to be lounging, stretched out, as on a porch glider. And yet the feeling for me was far more hideous than the image before my eyes. It was as if I had accidentally dropped him off a cliff, my hands were so empty, my son was falling away from me so fast. The horse galloped and galloped. It put such distance between us. It took Robin away from me. My hands were so empty! My eyes were riveted to the speck of red and white that his clothing made on my retina, but really by the time he fell I could not actually see the child himself at all, only the rags of bright clothing and some mass of familiar flesh that filled out those clothes, that gave them substance and meaning.

The bundle that fell from the horse to the ground seemed to bounce once, if bounce is really the proper word. Not a springy recovery or a leap upward that affirmed anything at all or seemed a metaphor for human resiliency or vivid resistance, but the earthbound necessity of movement that might occur with a sack of flour dropped from a height, more a simple jolt that changes the shape of the sack but really is no movement at all, a sudden shifting, redirection and settling, an unimaginative sudden conclusion.

THERE IS A GOOD deal more to tell here. It seems a great wonder we survived this day at all, these years later. Survive it we did. We went on living more or less happily, more or less normally, in the same little house for two or three years after this. Let me jump ahead to say that Robin was all right, he was unhurt. The accident could have been dangerous, even fatal, but thank God it was not. When the three of us reached him we found that he had had the breath knocked out of him and for a moment he made no sound at all, only cast his eyes wildly about for familiar imagery, only held his face in a terrible grimace, and then once he saw the three of us he expelled all that had been held in, his lungs reactivated. He needed to cry heartily for a few minutes to recover himself, to assure himself of the proper working of his internal organs, but he was not hurt, not in any serious way, he was fine, eyes wide open and amazed.

Among the adults there was a kind of hilarity in the moment, once we realized he was all right, that spared me much of the criticism for my idiotic behavior, which had placed him in danger. We laughed our heads off and comforted Robin and then became serious and recalled each detail of where we were at any given moment, what we saw, what we thought, and then someone would say some small thing, and off we would go with our laughter again. Briefly we became fearful he had fallen in one of the huge ant beds, which could have been more dangerous than a fall, fatal possibly, without immediate medical help.

When we had dusted him off and found this not to be the case, we laughed again.

I should go on to tell that in the days to come Elizabeth and Twyla studied together a number of other times and became friends, despite the too-sudden and disquieting beginning the three of us made together. Elizabeth did not hold my attraction against me, and we overlooked what seemed to have been an angry manipulation of us by Twyla that played a part in my bad judgment. Elizabeth liked her. They liked each other. They disagreed on almost everything and yet this was all right with both of them. I was happy for Elizabeth and yet I envied their friendship. The better we knew Twyla the less she talked in her caricatured hippie fashion, the less she bragged about her sexual promiscuity, and the more we saw what a lonely desperate girl she was, essentially raped and left by a graduate student when she was in junior high school, and now in love with a husband who had done the same thing to a teenager in Florida who lived in a shack in the swamp with a half dozen brothers and sisters who sat with scabby legs and snotty noses on a tumble-down old porch with a refrigerator on it, holding her new baby and trying to spell out a letter to this man in Alabama saying I love you, come get me, save me, oh God.

Finally I actually did "make love" to Twyla a couple of times. It was terrible, degrading for both of us, on a stinking mattress with no sheets in a storage room in the shack she and her husband lived in. She had long black hairs growing out of her pale nipples. By the time this happened, she and Elizabeth were not just first-time study partners but best friends, and so my betrayal was far greater than it might have been before they became close. Fucking Twyla was no great conquest, she was a nymphomaniac, plain and simple. Prozac and a twelve-step group could have probably prevented a lot of trouble if this had happened a few years later. Still, Elizabeth and I would stay married for fifteen more years, twenty in all.

But that's not the story I'm telling. I'm telling of the horse that was killed in the pasture that day as result of my setting Robin on its back and spooking it and sending it off with arthritic abandon. There is no great drama to it. After Robin slipped off the horse's back, the horse went on running for a while and finally stepped into one of the foot-deep holes left beneath one of the enormous ant hills, where the dirt had been burrowed out. Its leg was broken. We did not even realize this for a long time as we went on rejoicing that Robin was safe. We noticed that the old horse had stopped galloping in its slow comical way across the field, but it took us a while longer to catch on that something was wrong.

Twyla noticed first that the mare was limping. She said, "Look."

We looked in the direction she pointed. I said, "That old gal strained a gut." Nobody laughed though.

Elizabeth said, "I think she's hurt."

The horse stood still now, beneath a single cottonwood tree, as if for the shade. We walked across the field. Robin had stopped crying by this time and had lain his head on my shoulder, whimpering low as I carried him. We walked the twenty or so yards to where the horse stood and saw immediately that the ankle was broken. The swelling was already huge, and the fracture was compound, the bone had broken the skin of the ankle and there was a trickle of blood. I said, "Oh God." Or maybe all of us said this.

I left Robin with Elizabeth and Twyla and ran back up the

pasture to the Big House. Peahens bustled away from me as I crossed the yard and bounded up the porch steps. The old lady was there, the landlord's mother. She was smiling and gracious. She said, "Well, I should have been the one to come visit *you*." When I told her what happened she said, "I'll call Howell, he's at the office, he'll know what to do."

She left me standing on the porch while she used the telephone. When she came back, she said, "Howell asked if you'd kindly wait here at the house till the veterinarian comes. He called him. Then walk him out to where you left Sally."

I said, "I feel just awful about this. It's terrible."

The old lady said, "The girls will be crushed. Their father is a brutal man, their mother, my daughter, is a drunk. This farm is the only real life those girls have. They'll miss old Sally."

The vet decided right away that the horse needed to be "put down," but he decided to wait for the owner to arrive before he did anything final. He gave the old mare an injection of some kind, and after a while the horse became wobbly with the drug and knelt down slowly and rolled over onto her side. Her eyes were wide open and glassy but she was still awake.

The three of us were chastened and silent. In a short time we heard a small tractor making its way down the pasture and when we looked we saw it was driven by a black man and that the landlord was riding standing up beside him. I asked Elizabeth to take Robin back up to the house, and so she and Twyla were not there, thankfully, when the final shot was administered. The horse died quickly, and immediately it seemed a completely different creature from the one that had lain there two seconds before. It seemed not just to have died but never to have had life in it. The black man hitched the mare by its back feet to the tractor with a log chain and dragged it off into the woods where I supposed he would dump it into the deep ravine that separated the woods from the river. The landlord rode on the tractor with him, and so this left me to walk alone back through the pasture in the direction of my family and the rest of my life.

12

"Get a haircut"

I ANSWERED THE PHONE in the farmhouse kitchen one day and got the news that my father had just died. He was only sixty-one, and though he had slowed down some after a small heart attack the year before, the death seemed sudden and unreal. He had lain down in his room that afternoon for a nap and my mother had heard a sudden catch in his breath. When she came in from some other part of the house, "he was gone."

The call came in the late afternoon, and so the western sun was flooding into the kitchen windows from where it sat low on the horizon, beyond the pasture, big and fat and contented as a golden frog on a wide pale pond. Tacky as the farmhouse was, with its tin cabinets and sink and its piece-of-shit appliances, the kitchen seemed radiant with light. I loved the farmhouse more than ever. I loved Elizabeth more than ever—or so in my heart I felt, though by this time my betrayals had become enormous, as she was pregnant again and Twyla and I had begun our messy stew of sex and hippie bullshit on the dirty mattress in her storeroom. Our dog, a spaniel mutt, was standing in a kitchen chair

when the call came in, finishing off a few lunch scraps I had not
cleaned off the table. I kicked the chair and said "Shoo," and the
dog took a couple more bites and ran its tongue across the For-
mica for crumbs and salt grains and reluctantly got down.

I said, "Dead? Oh, really? When?"

This is the false voice I was affecting to take the place of any
true emotion that might accidentally creep into so important a
moment, rather than, say, my false hippie voice. I mean I could
as easily have exclaimed, "Dude! Far out!"

It occurred to me for the first time, even as I spoke, that I
had no voice of my own. I had no idea what I would sound like
if I sounded only like myself. It was a discomfiting insight, coming so unexpectedly. I had no idea who I would be, if my masks
were stripped away. Briefly I wondered how long this had been
going on, how long I had been a shell of a person. This thought
might have frightened me enough to cause me to reconsider the
direction of my life, if there had been any room for true feeling
in my heart, but as there was not, the insight passed behind my
eyes and flew away on the summer breeze. The news of my father's death did not penetrate any part of my real self, wherever
that self might reside. I did not connect it to the death of my
other-father, I scarcely need to add. I made no connections, felt
nothing at all, save only a puzzlement at seeing myself, as if from
a distance, standing neck deep in meaning and grief and feeling
nothing.

My thoughts would not cleave to the information I was re-
ceiving. I was thinking this was a perfect setting to hear about
your father's death, the afternoon sun through the windows, a
country kitchen, a pregnant wife, the no-count dog. The room
was glowing. Probably it was I who was glowing, as much as the
room. Daily drinking, even daily morning drinking, was com-

monplace to me now. I couldn't remember just when this came to be so, it was so gradual a thing. I was a little drunk, even so early in the day. I spoke of having "a drink" or "a toddy" or some other singular noun to describe my regular approach to unconsciousness. I was beginning to take a nap early in the day so that I might wake up refreshed and drink again in the evening. I could get drunk twice a day, once I got the nap system worked out, and still function pretty much normally. It was the perfect life, in a way. I worked hard, I studied Chaucer and Anglo-Saxon poetry, I farmed, I "made love," I took myself to strange comforts with alcohol. Despite the thoughtless cruelties and secrecy I perpetrated on Elizabeth and our slowly crumbling marriage, I thought of this as a perfect time in our lives together. It hadn't quite occurred to me yet just how long a distance I had traveled from Itta Bena. I didn't notice that I was becoming an entirely different person from the one I had wanted to be.

Since we met Twyla we were changing, I believed. Before we met her we had been too eager to grow up, I believed. We were dropping back, rediscovering our youth. Elizabeth and I were no longer simply persons who wanted a small farm with vegetables and animals; now we had become hippies together. She had grown her hair almost as long as Twyla's and she wore shapeless smocks and sandals and little owlish gold-rimmed glasses that she'd found in her great-grandmother's things and adapted with modern prescription lenses. I too had long hair, and now a colorful long beard, and I wore a headband needlepointed for me by Elizabeth and tied in back with a leather thong. I wore jeans patched in the rear with a small American flag and made up a funny story about being "busted" at a state fair in Montgomery for flag desecration. People I told this story to seemed to believe it. I almost believed it myself. "Oh man, I was bummed," I usually said in conclusion. I had learned a new language as well, it seemed. Not my own language, it turned out, but one I wore uncomfortably like the rest of my costumes as I surreptitiously checked metaphorical mirrors in hopes of catching an image of my true self. We had bought an old VW minibus and painted it all over with flowers and doodlebugs. The curtains we hung in the windows sported white "peace signs" on a blue background. It was hard to deny that I was a hip guy, dude, whatever. Who could deny that we lived the good life? How much hipper could you get? We sold vegetables to local markets and roadside stands. We hung around junk shops and bought a few things for the house, including a fine old pie safe that Elizabeth and I stripped of paint and sanded back to the beautiful wood. I had bought some tall slender drinking glasses of frosty-looking blown glass in a junk store, and I regularly filled them with crushed ice and gin and tonic, with a sprig of mint from the yard. Sometimes Elizabeth joined me for an afternoon drink, though not often and not at all for several months, as she was pregnant again, as I said. I smoked marijuana most days as well. I grew it on the back of the property and sold it in small amounts to students at the university. Frank, Twyla's husband, had helped me get high the first time.

The news of my father's death caught me at a particularly mellow moment. The gin, the setting sun. I felt bathed in sunshine, inside and out. My mother's brother was on the other end of the line, the man I'd fantasized having for my own father. For some impenetrable reason, I always tried to be especially blasé in his presence, and so when we spoke I was rarely myself at all, including this moment. I was busy putting on my show of being the perfect son, I suppose in case he was ever in a position to adopt. That's the way I acted in any case, as if I were on display at the orphanage. Under the circumstances, maybe I could be forgiven the charade at this time, as in a sense I was once again half an orphan, having just lost a second father. I withheld all genuine feeling of shock or grief when my uncle delivered this news, and in the process discovered I had no feelings of shock or grief, I had no feelings about my father's death at all.

"A couple of hours ago," my uncle was saying. Elizabeth came into the room. Robin was four by this time and we had recently enrolled him in Headstart, and she had just brought him home. He was complaining bitterly. I held my hand over the receiver and mouthed, "Dad died." Elizabeth raised her eyebrows and mouthed back, "Mine or yours?" "Mine, mine," I mouthed helpfully. She put on a quick, exaggerated sad face and ran a finger down her cheek to indicate a tear and then turned back to Robin's grouching. The barely nascent thought got through to me that neither Elizabeth nor I had any genuine reaction to this terrible news. He was dead. He died young, relatively speaking. We both loved him, and we were mouthing "boo hoo" and drawing cartoon tears.

Robin was in full complaint. He hated Headstart, he said, he had been smacked over the head with a plastic hammer and somebody stole his lunch and peed on it. He didn't like his teacher, she said "ain't" and ate a whole bag of cookies at lunch. He was saying he was never going back. Elizabeth was saying he most certainly was going back, those other children were underprivileged and didn't know any better than to pee on your lunch and did he ever think that his teacher might have been hungry and maybe grew up poor and didn't have enough to eat when she was small and he would just have to develop some tolerance for multiethnicity.

Robin looked at me like, "Huh?"

I wish I could say I saw the idiocy of this conversation at the time and that Robin had at least one parent with a brain in his head, but honestly I didn't see anything of the sort, I was in full agreement with Elizabeth.

I could hear my mother crying—no, wailing—in the background. My uncle, the man on the phone with me, was a doctor and so he was going through a brief history of heart disease in order to fill the impossible spaces that my mother's extravagant weeping and my utterly emotionless reaction to the news were creating.

"He would have been a good candidate for a transplant," my uncle went on—this was just after the procedure had become available. He admitted though that my father had never given such an operation any real consideration. "His heart was enlarged so that it filled his entire chest cavity."

It is a wonder I remember these words now, so little impression did they make on me then. Suddenly the screeching and crying in the background became louder, overwhelming almost, and so I understood that my mother was very near the phone. My uncle interrupted whatever he had been explaining to me about heart disease—childhood rheumatic fever, a weakened heart muscle, angina, the dearth of oxygen, on and on—to say, "Honey, your mama wants to talk to you."

Before I could even respond, she was on the telephone. She was saying something, but I had no idea what. Her tears, her sobbing, gasping, nose blowing were all I could make out. "I can't understand you, Mama," I said. "Try to get a grip on yourself."

Elizabeth held up the gin bottle and raised her eyebrows as if to say, "Want a drink?"

I smiled and mouthed, "Oh God yes."

She put new ice into the glass and more gin and a small amount of tonic. "Lime?" she mouthed.

I shook my head no and took the drink from her hand and pursed my lips and made exaggerated smooching motions in the air to thank her and then placed the rim of the glass to my lips and sucked the oily crystal fluid through the ice and between my teeth and breathed a fragrance of juniper berries into my lungs. I said, "I'm still here, take your time."

My mother finally got herself calmed down enough so that she could be understood. I couldn't imagine what she was going to say that my uncle hadn't already covered, in any case, more fully than anyone could have ever wanted. I just wanted her to get over it. Cut the crap. Say what you have to say.

This hard-hearted, wrong-headed picture of myself is painful to draw. But all this crying, this hoopla, seemed somehow hypocritical in any case. Whatever small threads of feeling were unraveling in me, relief was what came closest to seeming real. Didn't she feel any relief that he was dead? *I* was relieved. It was an odd thing to admit, but it was true. She loved him, okay, so did I, but hadn't he really been the problem all along? Hadn't all those nights of waiting for him to come home from Shiloh's, all those afternoons when she stretched across her bed and cried, been his fault? My father was a drunk, he was cold and indifferent to her, he was uneducated, racist, he was nothing like her perfect first husband, my other-father.

I drank more of the gin. I'm being unfair, I know. What I felt in the moment of hearing of my father's death had little to do with anything, I suppose, beyond my own unfelt grief. I was forgetting, as I had these thoughts, the man who invited Mitzi Hayworth into our house and saw the failure of his life in her diminutive stature and left my mother to face Mitzi alone. He and my mother had kept wedding vows in ways I was failing to do, and they had required of one another odd sacrifices, of which Mitzi Hayworth was only one, and one I feel sure the ancient authors of marriage vows never envisioned as applications.

I remembered the night I sat beneath fig trees with a loaded Enfield pistol and plotted my father's murder. Was that night for nothing, I wanted to demand of her. For what other reason would I ever have thought of such a thing except for her happiness? I could have killed him. My father. I almost did, would have done so if the revolver had not been a piece of shit and had fired the way it was supposed to. My own life came that near to ruin, for her.

So when she finally blurted out what she had taken the phone to say, I had built up a mighty reservoir of drunken resentment that outshone the darkness of my father's own alcoholic interiors. She said, "Get a haircut before you come to the funeral. Shave your beard."

The phone conversation was now over. In a way this request of hers, framed as a desperate plea, injected a sort of common-sense humanity into me that I had lacked until this point. The conversation ended amicably. She said no more, did not really even wait for an answer. I could have done anything I wanted to, it was simply a plea, a request. If my response had been, "No, I'm sorry, I can't do that," no bad results would have accrued. The truth is, I was happy to shave for the funeral. I knew what she meant. Itta Bena was a small town, they had seen few hippie types back then, they distrusted them. I would have looked like a fool, just as hippies on the *Tonight Show* looked like fools to me. To wear long hair and a beard to my father's funeral would have amounted to drawing all attention selfishly to myself and putting pressure of unforeseeable kinds on her. No, I didn't mind shaving, going to the barber. I hung up. I said to Elizabeth, "I can't believe he's dead."

Elizabeth sent Robin out the backdoor to play. She told him they would talk more later about quitting Headstart. Maybe quitting wouldn't be such a bad idea after all. She sat at the kitchen table and cried.

I stood behind her and put my hands on her shoulders and knew I loved her, and yet I felt nothing at all. I said, "I hope the barbershop is still open."

What happened at the barbershop was more memorable to me than the funeral, really. The funeral produced no dramatic moments. No scene was made. The service was quiet and dignified. I was clean shaven and short-haired, sitting with my mother in the chapel of a funeral home in Greenwood. Men who had known my father for many years greeted my mother and me quietly—"He was a good man," "I loved him like a brother." Some of them were the men from Shiloh's, sober and respectful. Many other people filled the chapel. They too spoke comforting words, and though I appreciated them, no feeling had yet touched me, no grief, not even a general sadness, and would not do so for many years, so such words seemed merely odd.

I sat in my seat exactly as I would have done at any other funeral, indeed at any other church service. I was not uncomfortable, I was glad that it would soon be over, that was the extent of what I felt. Though my mother had requested no flowers, the room was filled with flowers, for which I was also grateful, I'm not sure why. Funerals needed flowers, I suppose. A black man with whom my father had worked on the same paint crew for many years sat on the front row with my mother and me. In the eulogy the minister said of my father, "He brightened many a corner" and the man sitting with us whispered, "He did that."

This man cried before the service was over. I wondered how this could be so, a black man's tears for this father of mine whose television set risked pollution from the image of Sammy Davis, Jr., and for whom I had no tears.

My mother was finished with her crying. She had not cried since the day before, on the telephone. She sat stony-faced in the seat beside me until the service ended. I began to see that those tears over the telephone were preparation for this moment and for the years to come. She had been afraid she would never cry for his death if she did not do so immediately, so cry she had done, every tear a sudden death can muster, and now her obligation was finished.

SO THOUGH IT WAS sad, the funeral now strikes me as a sort of anticlimax to my promise on the phone that I would shave and get a haircut before I showed up in Itta Bena. I had hung up the receiver and finished off the drink in my hand. I had not used a barber for a couple of years or more, so I couldn't remember what time the shop closed.

I explained this to Elizabeth and said I was going to dash into town, some seven miles away, and try to catch the barbershop open. Otherwise I would have to wait until the next day to drive to Itta Bena, several hours distant. We agreed that I should go to Itta Bena alone, she was too close to her delivery date to risk the long drive, and there was no point in dragging Robin over all those miles for a funeral he was too young to attend. All this was decided as I was racing out the door, half drunk, to find a barber late on a Friday afternoon.

This was years before I began getting my hair cut in "salons" that employ a large task force of "stylists," and before ap-

pointments were necessary. The barber that I was looking for
was a direct descendant of Shorty Grable and the incredible Mr.
Shepherd, who by this time had already drunk himself to death
and would never rub another old man's nuts with a smooth river
rock.

The shop was a tiny two-chair operation in an old converted
Sinclair service station. A sign with a dinosaur still stood above
the overhang. I pulled into an empty space where the gas pumps
had once stood and leaped out of my car and tried the door. The
front door was locked tight. A sign said CLOSED. I knocked on
the glass, just in case. I waited and when there was no response,
I knocked again. I put my face to the glass and shaded the glare
with my hands cupped around my eyes. I could see the two
chairs, the mirrors behind them, bottles of tonic and bay rum,
brushes, combs soaking in a blue fluid. The barber was still in
there.

He was coming out of a back room carrying a whisk broom.
He stopped to sweep some hair on the floor into a long-handled
dust pan. I couldn't tell whether he had heard me or not. I
knocked again, rap rap rap rap rap very loud. He did not look
up, though obviously he had heard me. He kept about his small
tasks of cleaning up. He swept, he brushed, he picked up a
towel from the sink and tossed it in a bin. He walked into the
back room again and I was afraid this time he would not come
back out.

I began pounding on the door now with my open palm. It
sounded as if the place would come down, I was pounding so
hard. When the man came out of the back room again, I shouted
at the full strength of my voice, "Hey in there! Haircut! Haircut!" At least he looked at me this time. The look of annoyance
on his face told me I didn't have much hope of getting a haircut.

This barber was one of the most unattractive men I had ever seen. Indeed I would rank him as the most repulsive-looking fellow I had ever known to hold regular employment. I had never seen him before and wondered how on earth he had gotten a job of any kind, let alone as a barber. He was in his mid-thirties, I guessed. His hair was coal black and very greasy, quite long all over, well over his collar and somewhat down his back, but combed in what seemed to be a combination of two old-fashioned styles, a pompadour and a ducktail. He was wearing loud-colored plaid pants of several shades of offensive blue, with a red stripe. The pants were not clean, though they showed evidence of many washings. They were short for him and struck him well above the ankles. To compensate for the too-short pants, apparently, he was wearing boots rather than shoes—shoes, I supposed, would have revealed his white athletic socks. The boots had once been black but had never known the taste of shoe polish, and were filthy and the heels were run over. The coat he wore, double knit, had once been blue but now was limp and threadbare and had turned a vile shade of purple. His mustache had been carefully sculpted. Two firm lines of black hair grew down from his nostrils until they reached their nadir at his ample upper lip, where they turned outward in a pencil line and followed the lipline in separate directions.

He said, "Closed," indicating the sign.

The alcohol was pouring out of me as sweat. I was shaky and irritable. I shouted, "Please!" I was desperate. I knew of another barbershop near the university, but it would be closed too by now. This guy was my only hope until tomorrow morning. It hadn't occurred to me that in my long hair and beard I looked as freakish to him as he did to me.

I shouted, "My daddy died. I've got to look nice for the funeral." I was bellowing this at the top of my lungs.

He was bellowing by now as well, though his voice penetrated the thick glass door at barely a whisper. He bellowed, "Your daddy died?"

I bellowed, "Right. The funeral is tomorrow. In Mississippi."

"Your daddy died?"

"Right."

"That's terrible."

"Open the door, okay?"

"When did he die?"

"Just now. I just took the call."

"I'm sorry, man."

"It's strange," I heard myself bellowing in the golden glow of the setting sun, outside this old Sinclair station. "I don't feel a thing."

"You say you don't feel a thing?"

"Right."

"You're, like, numb with pain?"

"No, I'm more, like, indifferent." We were shouting at top volume in order to be heard through the thick door.

"Was he a sumbitch?" he shouted.

"No, gentle," I shouted back. "I loved him. He told me he loved me each night."

He shouted, "Got damn."

I hollered, "I can't feel anything, really. I don't think I love my wife. I'm having an affair and I don't love that one either."

He turned a key inside that he had left in the lock. I walked into the barbershop. The man cut my hair. It was a terrible haircut, almost as bad as Mr. Shepherd's cuts, a long time ago, but I didn't care. It was an obligation that had to be fulfilled, it didn't matter what my hair looked like. The barber was reluctant to shave my beard. He said it was a nice beard, it was just a little out of control. He wanted to trim it, shape it a little. He said, "I'm actually better with facial hair than head hair."

I said no, he'd better go on and cut it, take it all off, I promised my mama.

He told me about a disc jockey he knew who collected jokes. The disc jockey's name was Earl Temple, and he had clipped jokes from all kinds of places, especially *Reader's Digest,* and taped them to 3 × 5 cards and kept them in shoe boxes, tens of thousands of jokes.

I said, "Did you ever hear about a barber who used a big smooth river rock to rub old men's nuts? That was a story I heard as a child. There was a barber who claimed he rubbed old men's nuts with a smooth stone."

He said, "That sounds a little bit eccentric to me."

I said, "He was an alcoholic. He was probably lying."

He cut my beard with scissors first and then electric shears, and then he shaved me with a straight razor and cream from a soapy old shaving mug. He put steaming towels on my face.

13

Tell Me, Ramon Fernandez, If You Know

ONE DAY IN THE last month of Elizabeth's second pregnancy an old friend of ours from Florida showed up out of the blue at our door. Nothing could have been more unexpected, a-way out here on the farm. Elizabeth was by this time enormous and she suffered from backaches and leg cramps and every other symptom of late pregnancy, and yet she squealed like a teenage girl when she opened the door and saw him standing there with a small suitcase on the porch beside him. We really had been good friends during those hard years of first jobs and displacement after college.

I looked behind him for Margaret Ann, his wife, and suspected that something was wrong when I didn't see her. I had for a long time suspected she would not be able to tolerate certain eccentricities of his for much longer. We went way back with Ramon and Margaret Ann. We knew him first in college and then were best friends with both of them in Florida, where we went for our first jobs after graduation. Elizabeth and Margaret Ann had taught in the same elementary school, and Ramon and

I taught together in the junior high. On weekends we fished, we snorkeled, we played board games, we flirted innocently with one another's spouse, we followed a couple of big-league teams in their winter camps in Fort Lauderdale and Orlando. Our first children, both sons, were born in the same hospital, not a year apart.

I loved Ramon, and yet it was exhausting to be his friend. I always felt as if I were panting to keep up with him. It was everything, even the way he looked. He was the handsomest man I had ever known. Anyone would have told you the same thing. He could have been in the movies. I mean literally. The drama coach at Millsaps College had sent him to Hollywood for a screen test, which he did well on, but for complicated reasons declined to stay. Anyway, he was a terrific-looking guy. It was discouraging to meet new people in his presence, because they could never see me in the wash of his obliterating beauty.

He had had a hard life, a miserable childhood, his family had been poor and he had worked his way through two years of college catching chickens for Morton Foods, a filthy, brutal job that only the most desperate of persons would have taken, let alone stayed with for two years. Actually four years, if you count the part-time work he did after he received a full scholarship for his final two years of college. And yet his complaints always seemed mild relative to the nature of his deprivation. Chicken-catching involved walking into a massive commercial henhouse with a million, two million birds jammed into a small area. They were everywhere. You couldn't walk without stepping on them. You could hear their bones crush under your foot when you stepped, and hear them crack again when you caught them and stuffed them into crates, seven birds per crate. The heat was unimaginable. The stink incredible. The noise deafening and terrifying. You picked up seven chickens at a time, by the feet. Three birds in the left hand, four in the right. You held them upside down by the feet between the fingers of each hand, then stuffed them in a crate. The legs often snapped in your hand. The allergens in the air were so numerous and so toxic as to be literally fatal to some workers two three four times a year. Ramon himself had watched kids, grown-ups too, keel over with asthma, their lips and fingernails turning blue, their eyes rolled back in their heads, their bowels out of control and filling their pants, their lungs seized up. That's just the way it was in the chicken-catching business, according to Ramon. Once Ramon saved the lives of two men at once by dragging them into a head-to-head position on the floor of the chickenhouse and giving them alternating and simultaneous mouth-to-mouth resuscitation.

Ramon was heroic in this way, in many ways, really. He wasn't bragging when he told these stories. I never thought so in any case. As someone said in that book *Midnight in the Garden of Good and Evil*, "It ain't braggin' if you really did it." Not only did he send himself to college, he sent money home to his parents. His mother was a sweet and decent person, a simple woman, who had been overwhelmed by life and could do little to take care of herself. He had those three sisters, all much younger than himself, whom he doted on. They had little jobs too, the drugstore, places like that, but it was Ramon's money that put nice dresses on their backs for school and food on their table. His father was long gone, I was never sure where, maybe dead maybe only an escapee, and his older brother, who had been the sole support of the family for a time, had ended up in Whitfield, the state mental hospital.

My sorry complaints about my own relatively happy childhood seemed mean beyond thinking when compared to the generous and uncomplaining references he made to the snake pit from which he ascended. Even when he was still a child in that impossible home, he was a great success. Girls loved him. In college this had not changed. He was drop-dead handsome, as I said —square jaw, steely blue eyes, pale wispy hair, a raspy sexy voice with the slightest of Southern inflection, and the slender, near-hairless physique of an athlete. Indeed he was an athlete. He could do anything. He was quarterback of his high school football team, pitcher and clean-up hitter on the baseball team, guard on the basketball team. He could even skip rope, like a boxer in training, fast fast fast, left side right side left side right side go go go. In college he gave up athletics in favor of drama. He held all the male leads in plays for his four years of college. He played Brick in *Cat on a Hot Tin Roof,* Willy Loman in *Death of a Salesman,* Brutus in *Julius Caesar.* He brought down the house as Lord Byron in *Camino Real.* He had had the lead in *J. B.,* the play I missed when I was in the hospital after my car wreck. He'd had that screen test. After our brief careers as schoolteachers, he finished law school in two years, and in the meanwhile published an article in *American Literature* on Fitzgerald's *Tender Is the Night.*

He was a marvel of talent in so many fields. In a way it had been hard to be his friend. He was too smart for me, he wore me out. He never seemed to slow down, even when he was not working. He was always wanting to do things. Let's go here, let's go there, let's play Scrabble, Monopoly, let's Indian wrestle, shoot baskets for nickels, okay then pennies, okay then let's play H-O-R-S-E. He was in perpetual motion. He was rarely content to sit in his chair and get drunk, which I had been moving toward all along, I suppose, and which now had become my primary leisure activity. How like my father I had become, and yet I never on earth would have made this connection.

Ramon had been living in Washington, D.C., he told us, when his marriage fell apart. "She left me for a coach!" he wailed. "Not even a real coach. An assistant to an assistant defensive-line coach. I could have done that job straight out of high school. What a geek, what a fucking loser." He told us he tried living alone for a while, got an apartment, bought a little furniture, filled up the fridge with healthy food, got a roommate to save on expenses. The roommate used to be a croupier in Las Vegas and wore a toupee. "But it was a lie, Buddy, and I'm not a liar, as you well know, I may have faults but lying is not one of them, admit it, you know me better than that, you know that I'm no liar, I couldn't tell a lie if my life depended on it, I couldn't live like that."

Ramon was an enormous liar. He was the worst I had ever known. He would make a half dozen appointments—business, dinner, job interviews, dates, accountant, you name it—break every single one, not even try to get to them. Usually he slept through them. He might go to bed fifteen minutes before an appointment, saying, "I need to be especially alert for this meeting. I'm going to grab a couple of Zs to be sure I'm at the top of my form." Then he would sleep for two hours. This failure would leave him temporarily morose, almost suicidal. He would stumble through the apartment, groggy and stupid and wringing his hands slowly. Then he would have an idea. He would call, apologize, and reschedule. Sure, that's all he needed to do, it was simple. His face would brighten, his voice would become chipper and masculine and filled with humor and his throaty infectious laughter and good cheer and best intentions. "You name the time," he would insist into the phone, as he rescheduled a broken appointment. "The sooner the better. All I need to do is hop in the shower and I'll be there." The person on the other end of the line would be as charmed as anyone else in the world would have been by Ramon, and would suggest a new time, an hour or two later. Ramon would agree and then get back into bed and sleep through the new appointment. No one lied like Ramon, to himself as fully as to others.

I knew this, saw the same quality in myself, and could not translate these insights into a way of changing my own behavior. The lies around my affair with Twyla were slowly eating my insides out, and yet I had no idea this was happening. Ramon had had a zillion affairs. His wife had hung in longer than anyone could have reasonably expected. His wife was the one I had been attracted to in Florida, when Elizabeth and I lived down there. She flirted a little, maybe, but nothing more. He was the one who couldn't tell the truth. I never held such behavior against him, even before it became my own hideous behavior. In me it seemed a character flaw, in Ramon it was more an extension of his enormous energy, the wonderful male urge to compete, to reach great heights, that seemed to exude from his pores but as if from a depth.

Elizabeth and I brought him in the door with such joy, such sweet false memories nevertheless. He seemed to me an emissary from a former life, a better world, and to be in his presence recalled a time before my father had died, before I had lost control of my drinking, before I had a son of my own, a son who seemed increasingly afraid of me on account of the drinking, before I had slept with a woman outside my marriage—or with any woman other than Elizabeth at all. I could not have said these things, made this catalog of details from my past or present life, but their power surged through me nevertheless, I felt the electrical strength of hope blaze up from a few years distant and shut down some part of my present fear.

Or to say this simply, I suppose, when he walked through our door carrying his little suitcase, I began to focus on him, on Ramon's crumbling life and marriage and mind, and to ignore the decay in my own.

Elizabeth shared in the relief at having him present. She must have sensed that I was as lost to her as my father had been to my mother. She must have needed protection from this knowledge. She was even more unwilling to leave me than Margaret Ann had been to leave Ramon. Ramon's extravagant neurosis stood between our selves and our fears. He afforded us a shield from one another. In our joy at having him among us— between us, maybe—we were sharing truly for the first time in a long while. I mean this ironically, of course. Fully united were we in driving a wedge between ourselves. "Come in, Ramon, come in, we'll put you up on the sofa, old friend, how long can you stay, it's so good to have you, come in, don't leave, don't ever leave us alone." He was in our lives again, for better or worse.

Ramon set his suitcase down inside the door and took in the details of our home. In his mind, he was settling in. He looked around the farmhouse critically, as if to say, So this is it, this is the low place where I have landed.

Elizabeth showed him the sofa in the living room. "It's not bad, it's pretty comfortable," she said. She made it up with clean sheets and a light spread. She put two clean new pillows with white pillowcases at one end and turned on the light to show him how comfortable he could be, he could read, whatever he wanted.

We were both talking compulsively, we were so happy to

have company. We were telling him in a hundred ways how happy we were. We were the perfect family. To hear us tell it, we were the two happiest people on earth. I don't know why we felt compelled to paint our lives so ideally. With Ramon's marriage on the ropes it would have been a perfect opportunity to become honest about what was happening in our own. Nothing of the kind ever occurred to either of us. We were the world's happiest married couple, Ramon was the goat. We were taking him in to save him rather than, as would have made more sense, taking him in to learn from him, to hear his lies and self-lies and through them learn to say the truth about ourselves for once in our lives. Still I had felt nothing since my father's death, not for my father, not for anyone. Why didn't I tell him, and thereby myself, that I could no longer find the person that I had been when we were in college or when we lived near him and Margaret Ann in Florida?

I had started to scream at Elizabeth in drunken rages. I suppose if I had to name one feeling that I actually felt on a regular basis, it would have been rage. What I will tell about myself here occurred over a period of a couple of years, three years maybe, so my vicious treatment of my family was sporadic, not daily, but it was suddenly obvious that it was adding up to a pattern of abuse. Once I had smacked Robin in the face with a baseball cap, more than once I had spanked him with a belt, had snapped the belt like a whip to scare him, had squeezed Elizabeth's arm so hard she had my fingerprints in bruises on both arms. My remorse was huge, beyond melodrama, and yet the rage never really left. These secrets were tearing me apart. I kept comparing the mere neglect I had suffered as a child with the violence I inflicted. I compared the self that I had been with the self that I had become. I could have told Ramon these things. There were many other things about myself that stood in a long serpentine line ahead of "wife beater" that I was not admitting as well. I was a drunk, for instance. Compared to my own behavior my father's seemed saintlike and admirable. I was loud and abusive and violent. I was having an affair with a college girl, my wife's best friend.

I said nothing. Not now, not later. None of this did it ever occur to me to say. Ramon wouldn't have heard it, of course, he was entirely self-centered, but maybe I would have heard it. Maybe Elizabeth would have, and would have insisted that I do something to help myself, or left me and in that way helped herself. Elizabeth was a conspirator in the silence. She didn't say a word, and I knew she would not. She moved a small chest into the room for Ramon's clothes. "You can use the closet in Robin's room for anything you want to hang up," she said. She explained the limitations of the bathroom but said she felt sure that we could work out a way for all of us to use it without too much inconvenience.

That first night we stayed up half the night and talked. Mostly about old times, mostly about Ramon, since those were the safe topics for Elizabeth and me. I drank glass after glass of vodka, but Ramon had stopped drinking altogether he said, his nerves were bad, his stomach was bad, he had heard that drinking gave you hemorrhoids, and Elizabeth didn't drink on account of the pregnancy, so I had no drinking buddies. That was all right with me. Drinking alone didn't bother me at all.

We talked about the coach that Margaret Ann had run off with, an old poker buddy of Ramon's, a real lamebrain, a real chickenshit motherfucker too, he was probably a fag. This is the way Ramon talked, as his anger began to overflow into the conversation. One night Ramon had lost at poker and went into a rage and overturned the table, spilling cards and poker chips and whatever else was on the table, all over the floor. He said he pointed his finger in the coach's face and told him, "You get up from that chair, motherfucker, you so much as move, and you're dead." He said, "I told him I had a pistol out in my car, and that motherfucker knew I would do it, he was shaking in his chickenshit boots."

Elizabeth said, "A pistol! Really? You had a pistol?"

He said, "Not really, but coachie-boy didn't know that."

I thought he would laugh at this point, make a joke, but he did not. He kept on. Ramon was trembling with anger as he recalled the incident.

"And this coach, this faggot more like it, he just sits there, cards in his lap, poker chips, cigarette butts, potato chips, crackers and cheese, you know, he was scared to death, you could see fear written all over his ugly face. He was ugly too, I mean it. He was this bucktoothed motherfucker. No offense, Buddy, I like your overbite, really, it's distinctive, you know, you have a great smile, but this cocksucker was bucktoothed, flat out, you're much better looking than he was. The point is, he was nowhere near as good-looking as me.

"I tell you what I should have done. I should have finished off that motherfucker right then and there, while it was on my mind and easy to do. I didn't need a pistol. There was a poker in the fireplace, there was a tire iron in my truck. That's what I should have by God done."

I was pretty drunk by this time, so I did the unusual and said what came into my mind. I said, "Finished him off?"

He said, "Right."

I said, "*Killed* him?"

He said, "That's what I should have done."

I got up and fixed myself another drink. I thought he was probably exaggerating, but Lord who knew about such things, and he was so angry, just telling the story.

By the time I got back and started working on my new drink, the topic of conversation had changed, and I was grateful. Elizabeth and Ramon talked about when the children were born, the sweet little incompetent Indian River Hospital where twice the four of us had gathered to welcome our first-borns into the world. They recalled a nurse we all especially remembered, and even came up with her name, Darlene. They nicknamed their son Rabbit and we called ours Robin. We remembered all the late-night Monopoly and Scrabble games we had played, the bridge hands, the cookouts and overnight camping, the fishing and snorkeling, and it was easy to forget in the nostalgia that the games, all the activities, had been at Ramon's insistence, that he had approached them as cutthroat, not friendly, encounters, even fishing, and that having any fun at all had been difficult, particularly when Ramon lost, as rarely he did. We were far too happy to see Ramon to focus on his odd compulsions or the things about him that we did not understand or like. He was the same as always and at the same time he seemed different, reinvented I want to say.

This part of his complex soul was never easy to describe, but here it was again, this old friend I knew and loved, and also this guy I didn't know at all, this person who frankly frightened me a little when he got started on one of his wild riffs. He never seemed to lose his original character traits, but if you looked away for a moment, or for a few years in this case, and then looked back, well he had gained a few traits he'd not had before, and the addition of them made him seem almost unrecognizable. I ended that first evening earlier than the others. I was pretty drunk. I had managed to put Robin to bed before the worst of my drinking started. I said each of the one million nursery rhymes that were a part of our nightly ritual of going to bed. I sang a few songs from the fifties, Chuck Berry was his favorite, especially "Maybelline," read a short chapter of some book we were making our way through each night. I kissed him and told him I loved him and soon his breathing became sweet and regular with sleep, and I joined the others. I made it till about midnight, when I was slurring my words and staggering, and then Ramon and Elizabeth led me off to bed where I collapsed and apparently snored so loudly they closed Robin's door to keep me from waking him. The two of them stayed up and talked longer. Elizabeth couldn't have gone to sleep with me rattling the windows in any case.

IN THE DAYS THAT followed, our routine became more normal, more the same as before Ramon's arrival. Elizabeth stayed near the house, for the most part. She took care of Robin. When she needed to shop, Ramon drove her wherever she needed to go, and I had our car full-time. I went to the university, to my classes, I studied in the library most days, though a couple of days a week I only pretended to be there. Those days I drove out to Twyla's house when I knew Frank would not be there. Frank knew that Twyla and I were sleeping together, and this didn't seem to be a huge problem, or maybe no problem at all for him, but for my part, I couldn't stand to see him. I crept in and out of his house as if he had never heard of me. I wanted to fuck Twyla in their bed, but she said no, she wanted to keep the marriage bed "sacred." We did it on the flea-bag mattress in the storeroom, where a dog named Horse usually slept.

As much as I protested that I felt nothing—beyond of course the soul sickness of guilt, shame, envy, fear, self-loathing, rage, and all their cousins—there was inside me somewhere a silent alarm that throbbed its message constantly and destroyed every moment's comfort. The alarm signaled that there was still love on the premises. It was an odd message for someone who seemed to have lost the capacity for feeling, but there it was.

BY THE TIME RAMON had been on the sofa for a week, we were sick of him. In two weeks we were out of our minds. Locusts could not have descended upon a field of grain with more voracious energy than he brought to our home. He ate everything in sight. Anything we might put in the refrigerator for a later meal would turn up missing when we looked for it. He ate four avocados that Elizabeth had put in the refrigerator to have in salads. He ate all four at one sitting because, as he explained when Elizabeth discovered they were missing, "I was afraid they would spoil. You apparently don't know much about buying avocados. They were right on the brink of spoiling." He ate all the hamburger meat we had planned to use for spaghetti. He explained, "I noticed that Elizabeth has put on more weight during this pregnancy than seems healthy for her. I thought I'd help out by removing temptation. Hamburger meat is very fatty, you know. That's probably why she's gained all those unattractive pounds." He ate Robin's birthday cake, the whole thing. "Birthday cake!" he exclaimed in surprise. "There weren't any candles on it."

His constant conversation drove us to near despair. He talked constantly, compulsively, and every word was a complaint. He followed Elizabeth from room to room, as she worked, gardened, put Robin down for his nap, even as she tried to take a nap. He talked and talked and talked. Even I, self-ish beyond most human imagining, could not leave Elizabeth at home alone with him to absorb the full brunt of his deadly compulsive talking.

Ramon's egregious behavior came as near to turning me into a decent person as anything short of sobriety and years of therapy or spiritual conversion was likely to do. Something of compassion, if not love, surfaced in me. I stopped going to Twyla's house in order to stay home and protect Elizabeth. Never was a wife more grateful to a husband for so little.

Now Ramon complained to *me* on those days when I would have been with Twyla. I was dizzy with feelings of success. I wasn't fucking Twyla, I was protecting my wife, I was a good husband. I stopped going to classes altogether. Being a good husband appealed to me. It was addictive. I made excuses to my professors, who were generous. My telephoned excuses to my professors began to take on an eerie resemblance to Ramon's many excuses for broken appointments. Except for the fact that I was transmogrifying into a bizarre combination of Ramon and my father, I was almost heroic. So it seemed to Elizabeth, and frankly to myself as well. For the first time in a long while I began to think of myself as happily married.

Hindsight tells me I could have handled things differently, of course. I should have asked him to leave, at least to give me an approximate date when he might be leaving. At least I should have confronted the problem directly: "Ramon, listen, Elizabeth and I can put you up, but we need more privacy. We're not used to so much conversation. How about all of us just go about our business separately till dinnertime, then we'll talk all you want?" Something similar to that, at least.

These words were never spoken, of course. I didn't have the

guts, or for that matter the sanity to figure out that honesty would have been a good policy. I had told so many lies that the truth had faded away as an optional behavior. Unspoken lies were becoming my stock-in-trade. I only gritted my teeth, poured another drink, and offered my bitter, begrudging hospitality and let the complaining roll on. And maybe the truth is, I still needed him there. The complaints poured forth, and I went on swallowing them whole.

Ramon worried excessively about what he saw as an increasing bald spot on the top of his head. He read me long articles on "male-pattern baldness" and asked my opinion on dominant and recessive genes. Did wearing a baseball cap all through high school contribute to the problem, he wanted to know. He smeared his face each morning with Vaseline against the supposed ravages of the southern sun, the dangerous particulates that polluted the air around farms and farm animals. "They don't tell you about these things. You think you're safe in the country but you're not. The air in the country is filled with more dangerous toxins than the smog in most cities." In his suitcase he had brought several pairs of shoes, and he wore a different pair each day. Every pair was uncomfortable, and each in a different way, which he explored with me in detail. He told me the number of women he had had intercourse with during his lifetime—he even told me he had made a list of their names and offered to show me the list. He told me about a couple of three-way copulations he had engaged in, including two-women-one-man and two-men-one-woman. He assured me that he and the other man never touched one another. In the few weeks he stayed with us he had several suspected heart attacks—gas pains or muscle spasms I at first silently guessed. He scheduled two EKGs and wondered whether he shouldn't have X rays to determine whether a hidden tumor might be causing the discomfort. He took many different medications, some over-the-counter, some prescription. I never asked what they were for. They were for nothing. He suffered murderous migraines, the one complaint that seemed to have some actual basis in fact. Though I was grateful for those hours of silence during a migraine, I ached to be able to relieve his pain, it was so obvious and so real and it seemed so purely a metaphor for his soul's pain, which he never dealt with or even acknowledged.

I remembered now that even when we were living in Florida, he was always seeking help for some physical ailment. He was always, in fact, wanting to have an operation. An operation seemed to Ramon the one thing that could take away his suffering. Once he went so far as to check into a hospital and put on his pajamas and stay one night in a hospital bed at considerable expense, only to have the doctor tell him at the eleventh hour that he just couldn't justify operating on him, there was no point in it, there was nothing wrong with him.

My head reeled at this story. I said, "You were lucky you got an ethical doctor. This restores my faith in the medical profession."

He looked at me as if I had just stepped off a flying saucer. He said, "He was a quack, Buddy. Don't kid yourself, man. He could have found something to operate on if he had really tried."

He was afraid of everything. He was terrified that a mad gunman would shoot him from a highway overpass. He didn't know what to do with his life, he told me. He wanted to be a writer, but could not make himself sit down to write. He wanted to run for political office but feared being a politician would distance him further from being a writer. He wanted to find "the perfect woman." Never mind what he meant by this. He told me he sometimes rented a tuxedo and wore it in his house alone because it helped his self-esteem.

He complained that I made too much noise when I chewed my food. He refused to try a spinach salad I made one night for dinner because he suspected I had not washed the spinach leaves properly. He asked whether Elizabeth liked anal intercourse. He told me to stop using expressions like "this and that" and "that kind of thing" to fill in gaps in conversation. He corrected my pronunciation of several words including *harass* (emphasis on first syllable), *Thoreau* (emphasis on first syllable), and *prescience* (long *e,* two syllables), and became angry with me when dictionaries supported my pronunciation.

One day he asked me to meet him at a local bar. He had met a couple of women somewhere one afternoon and had invited both of them to have a drink. Then he called me in a panic and said he had no money and didn't know how he was going to pay for their drinks. I was working at the university that day, which was near the bar he mentioned, so I said I'd drop by and slip him twenty bucks and maybe have a drink with the three of them and then leave. His thanks were profuse, he could never repay me, et cetera. He said I was a real lifesaver because it depressed him immeasurably for someone else to have to pay his bar bill, it was a "thing" with him.

So I followed through on the plan. I got to the bar at about the same time the others did, introductions were made, drinks were ordered, double vodka no ice for me, piña coladas for the women he hoped to impress, a Pepsi for Ramon. Under the table I slipped him the twenty and he stuffed it in his pocket. He asked me to put some money in the jukebox, so I left the table and picked out a few songs I thought everybody would like. While I was away from the table the waitress brought the drinks and Ramon told her and the two women that he had no money but that his friend over at the jukebox would be happy to pay. When the waitress asked me for money for the bill, I thought Ramon must have paid for his and the women's drinks and that I was being asked to pay for my own, so I paid for one drink.

The women were immediately furious at me, for what I guess seemed to them an intolerable stinginess on my part. I could sense this, but I couldn't understand it at all. Ramon gave the waitress some sort of signal and she gave me an evil look and finally walked away from the table. I was still in the dark.

The three of us sat and sipped our drinks, the two women in an angry silence. Finally Ramon left the table and went to the waitress stand and paid the waitress for three drinks with the twenty dollars I had given him. The women slugged down their drinks angrily and quickly and left in a huff, because of my apparent cheapness. Ramon followed them to the door and apologized to them for my coarseness. He told them I had had a deprived childhood and was not to be blamed for being tight with my money. He told them he had borrowed twenty bucks from a complete stranger in the bar in order to pay for their drinks but that they shouldn't worry, he had taken the man's name and address and he would be sending him the money immediately.

When he returned to the table he said, "Well, you blew that one for me, thanks a lot."

It was at this point that I knew I had to kick Ramon out. The baby was almost due. Ramon had to go. He was too crazy even for me.

14

"It could be worse, it could be much worse"

I LEFT THE BAR and drove out the blacktop toward home. On my way, a couple of miles outside of town, as I was passing a pecan grove, a car came tearing around me at reckless hell-for-leather speed and left me in its dust. I recognized the car, it nearly ran me off the road. It was Ramon's little brown VW Rabbit, and before I knew it, he was far ahead of me, scooting right along, traveling at eighty or ninety miles an hour and rocking like a cradle on the irregularities of the macadam. I watched his car disappear over the next rise and around a bend in the road.

Despite his anger and my fear of what was ahead of me—the confrontation with Ramon that I expected—the appearance of the little car was so endearing and sweet, it was almost like a child's toy in its silly haste and defiant speed. I held on to the steering wheel in a ridiculous attempt to calm the chaos inside me by steadying the car in its lane. I was just passing a pecan grove at this moment, as I said. The afternoon sun had turned the leaves golden green. I looked out to my right and noticed that an intact three-story house was being moved on the huge bed of a tractor-trailer truck down a dirt road into the pecan grove where it would be placed on a new foundation. The tractor strained and heaved and diesel smoke blew straight out of an upright exhaust pipe, and the trailer leaned and creaked and the eighteen wheels peeled red mud up off the wet road and sloughed it off in wide strips from the tires. The house balanced precariously, but the truck and trailer and house eased into the clearing that would be its new foundation.

The house seemed alien and out of place in the grove now, but one day it would not. Hedges would grow around the front, a swing would creak on its chains in the back, beds of azaleas and perennials would be placed along a walk. A porch swing would move with the summer breeze. One day the house would seem always to have sat in that place. It would be someone's home. Dreams of happiness would have come true in this house, or hearts would have been broken. I wondered about the family moving the house. What hope was required, what possibilities were imagined by so drastic an operation as this house-moving! They were young, I was sure of that, they believed in the power of dreams to create realities. But what were their hopes, their dreams? The house was beautiful, a big wood-frame construction, a wraparound porch, a couple of gables, a chimney for a fireplace. An enormous yellow crane already sat in place in the grove ready to help the house into its new place, where lives would take root or wither. To raise children in a pecan grove? Is that the detail they sought in hope of perfect happiness? To grow children as hearty and ageless and straight as the big trees? In twenty years the trees, if there was no drought, no unexpected disease, would be taller and straighter even than now, their dark trunks more black with good health. What would their lives be like, the people who invested so much hope in moving this house? Would those children's father one day come home and lie down on the bed and say to their mother, Yeah I'm home a little early, I'm not feeling so good today, a little indigestion I think, but go on to your meeting, sure, I'll just lie here till I feel a little better, really just a touch of indigestion, that's all, go on to your meeting, honey, and then would that loving wife be interrupted at the meeting with the news that her husband, the man she had just left at home with indigestion, was dead? Would the woman have an eighteen-month-old child? Would she sit without tears and stare out the window of the house, which was now leaning and creaking and moving slowly across wet red clay to its foundation, into a green glade of pecan? Would her heart be broken? How would her child turn out? Would she someday say, You mean I burned up all my money and love to move this house here only to have him die? Only to raise a child who is a drunk and an adulterer?

THESE WERE BITTER THOUGHTS, I realize. Probably they are not the thoughts I actually entertained in the moment I drove past the pecan grove. They couldn't have been. Maybe they are not even the thoughts of the person I am today.

In the famous poem "Among School Children," Yeats asks if a young mother with her baby in her lap could look into the future and see that child as a sixty-year-old man or woman, would the young mother think the labor and pain of childbirth had been worth the effort. The implication is that the certainty of time's production of loss is so great that the only answer is that the pain would not have been worth it.

I don't believe this, not really. It's a romantic, whiny question, I realize, and not one I want to tie myself to forever. And yet there is something in it, now that I am near sixty myself, that seems worth asking. It's a question that certainly occurs to me.

I shake my head when such thoughts come into my head. I fling them away from me like water being shaken from a dog's back. I watch them sail away like silver coins flung from a pouch. Live for this day, I tell myself. Seize the day. Such lies are scarcely better than Yeats's question, the other side of the same poetic coin, I suppose. It's all about death, in one way or another. That house in the pecan grove is as much about death as about hope. As I drove home to consult with Elizabeth about our lives, which were collapsing into alcohol and abuse and lost love, I was still innocent. I was incapable of thinking such a thought, let alone cleaving to it. Most days now I am still incapable of such thinking.

I STEPPED ON THE gas pedal. I knew I would not catch up with Ramon in his speedy little brown Rabbit, but I wanted to get home as soon after him as I could. I imagined several scenarios. In one he was remorseful and suicidal and apologetic and would do anything to stay in our favor. In another he was logical and calm and could explain to both our satisfaction that actually we benefited from his lies and that he had somehow done us a favor. In another scenario he would bust up our house and beat my ass. The last of these would have been my preference, as it would have been the one easiest to finish with our original resolve to kick him out. It's impossible to explain fully the kind of hypnotic pull this troubled man's personality held over us, his old friends. I considered not going home at all. I could have simply left the problem for Elizabeth to deal with. I could have turned down the gravel road to Twyla's house. I could have gone back to the bar and finished the double vodka I had uncharacteristically left behind. I did neither of these things. That was the extent of Ramon's positive influence on me. I actually thought of someone else before myself. I couldn't bear the thought of Elizabeth having to bear the brunt of Ramon's anger and wild story of the drinks I didn't pay for.

I wondered whether the amazing drunkard Mr. Shepherd, the barber in Itta Bena, ever experienced a moment of grace before his death, as I was experiencing now. Had he ever been so fortunate as to have a person in his house crazier than himself by whom he was transformed, however briefly, into a caring and thoughtful man? I hoped that he had. Very briefly I believed I caught a glimpse of the person that truly represented me. There were no masks, tricks, drugs, lies, women. I was a good man. I loved my wife. I loved my son. I was the person I had been in Itta Bena. I was the person who had thrown pebbles at my sleeping bride's window in Franklin Hall at Millsaps.

It was only a glimpse but it lasted long enough anyway to get me into a parking place out by my old garage and in time to see Ramon fling his suitcase and several pairs of shoes into the trunk of his Rabbit and tell Elizabeth that he had never been so humiliated in his life. He was gone. He would not even look at me. He got into his car and slammed the door and gunned the engine so hard that when it started up, a cloud of dust blew up out of the gravel drive behind his tailpipe. He started the car in reverse, and the wheels were spinning so furiously in the dirt that it seemed take forever to find sufficient purchase to actually begin moving. When the car did move, it blasted backward, and Ramon cut the steering wheel sharply and caused the little car to spin around so hard that for a moment I thought Ramon had lost control and might go flying out through the pasture fence.

This did not happen. He braked fiercely, shifted gears, and slung gravel all over the side of the old garage. Rocks hit the propane tank with such force the sound was like bells in a carillon. And then he was truly gone. He flew out the gate and on to the road and as suddenly as in a dream, he was out of our lives.

Elizabeth and I stood and looked at one another in astonishment. She was still standing on the back porch, I was standing beside my car in the yard. You might think we would have laughed, but we didn't. Robin was not at home, thank goodness. He was down at the Big House, playing with the landlord's nieces, who had come for their summer visit. He could have been run over by Ramon's car, in that final extravagant exit, if he had been playing in the yard. I said to Elizabeth, "Are you all right?" She looked at me strangely.

She said, "You seem different." I knew what she meant.

I said, "I love you."

She looked at me carefully, studying me as if there were a puzzle to be solved.

YOU MIGHT NOT THINK a single day in a life would continue for so many years as an urgent vivid memory, as this one has done, but it is true, I remember every nuance, the way the light refracted through the windows and fell upon the water in the dog's bowl, the rattle of the pecan tree leaves against the breeze, a rumble of distant thunder and the fragrance of rain in the clouds, a chatter of squirrels in the trees, and especially the comical bleating of goats in the pasture. I remember this day because it represented an oasis in the wide arid desert of my emotions, the miraculous rebirth of feeling. I felt love. I felt it, and I was aware of the importance of feeling in the instant of its appearance. I will see this day forever as palm shade and deep clear pools and coconut milk. I loved my wife.

To have been without feeling for so long and now to be suffused with it made me giddy, as giddy and happy as once, a long time ago it seemed, alcohol could make me. I was giddy in love, but more than that, giddy with the newness of life, for that is what I equated with my renewed capacity to feel. What a beautiful day it was, how memorable in each detail. I believed I owed this revelation and all its joys to poor Ramon. Without him, his inexplicable neuroses, I could never have reached this—I blush to exclaim—*transcendent* plane. The capacity to feel was not permanent, I am sorry to say. Soon enough I was deadened again, as if a thousand miles from the events of my life. But for now, I was a sentient creature, ripe with possibilities that had for so long been lost to me.

A car pulled into the front yard then, and for a split second I feared that Ramon had come back. But it wasn't Ramon, it was Mrs. Salter, in her ancient Cadillac, bringing Robin home. Elizabeth stuck her head out the door and hollered, "Thank you!" Mrs. Salter hit her car horn two deafening blasts to say hello/good-bye. Robin ran into the house saying, "Can I go back tomorrow?"

Robin was almost five by this time. His hair was very blond, so late in the summer. He was tan from the sun, but the sun had also brought out the freckles across his nose. The previous Christmas Santa had left him a platform-style rocking chair, just his size, under the tree. He came into the house and immediately plopped down into the chair and started to rock himself. The chair was in the shape of a bear. By sitting in the chair, Robin seemed to be sitting in the bear's lap. The tall back of the chair was the bear's comical head and face, with big funny eyes that rolled when the chair rocked, and bright red lips painted on a white face. At first he was only the same happy Robin who came in from play each day. He checked us out then, as always he did.

I never knew what he was looking for. In my worst moments of fear of the damage I might have done him with the drinking and yelling and hitting, I thought he was checking the safety of his home. Other times he seemed only a bright inquisitive boy interested in the world around him, and only because it was the world. Now, though, he checked me twice over. Something was different in me, his look seemed to say. I had felt this difference, Elizabeth had sensed it, and now even he seemed aware of a difference in me. Suddenly, with a face illuminated as from within, he said, "Daddy, I love you!" and turned around in the bear chair he was sitting in, and kissed the bear flush on the red lips. I knew that he was kissing me. I knew so many things. I said, "I love you, Robin."

I TELL THIS PART of my day in such detail in order to define the person I was in the next hours of that day. At dinner that night I looked at my wife across the kitchen table and saw her face turn querulous, then maybe fearful. I said, "Lizzie?" She stood up from her chair.

She said, "I think my water just broke."

Her due date had not arrived, she was two maybe three weeks early, so I felt some concern, not much, but there it was. I was grateful to feel anything. Concern was not so bad.

I said, "I'll grab a few things."

She said, "The bag is mostly packed, just get some—" She named something I should get from the bathroom, but I didn't hear her. Her water had not broken. The back of her skirt was splotched with bright red blood.

She twisted her skirt around and saw this. She said, "Uh-oh."

I grabbed up Robin from his chair at the table. I saw disaster in our future, I saw unhappiness and pain, I saw the death of a child who, even before he was born, I understood I loved, I saw the loss of other parts of me, my interior self, that had been loosened but not sloughed off fully yet. A day earlier, an hour earlier possibly, I would have felt nothing. I said, "Get in the car. Let's go. Now, Lizzie, in the car."

We saw the baby once, after the birth by cesarean section. He weighed not quite five pounds and was lying in an incubator with his little chest heaving like a bellows. The nurse standing so grimly beside the incubator knew, as we should have known I suppose, that Jesse Robert was dying. As Elizabeth and I looked in through the big picture window—my wife sat pale in a wheelchair—we thought we were watching the first breaths of a long life, when in fact we were watching the last breaths of a short one. After a minute or two the nurse closed the curtain, and after a total of seven hours, the child was dead. Elizabeth came near death herself. Placenta previa was the problem, a dangerous condition for both mother and child. Many people told us how lucky we were that Elizabeth had pulled through.

The hospital room where Elizabeth lay was streamlined and bare, white walls, brilliant sheets, an IV stand with clunky bottles of fluids that were changed periodically, a rolling table for meal trays. Elizabeth's face had scarcely more color than the sheets she lay on. Even her lips were white, she had lost so much blood. Her voice was subdued with the drugs and the trauma and loss of blood, but she smiled anyway, talked easily, enjoyed holding my hand. Many visitors came. The Episcopal priest at the church we attended, fellow students at the university, women and men Elizabeth had taught school with before she took maternity leave. Twyla and Frank even stopped by and stayed for a short time. They did not look at me or speak to me for the entire visit except to say hello and good-bye but rather spoke directly to Elizabeth.

Sometimes the room was empty, only Elizabeth and me. I wished that I could be the same comfort to her as she had been to me when I lay in the hospital in Jackson. Not sex, of course. I mean, I wish that by my presence I could have assured her that our world would continue to turn, that she could be weak because I would be strong enough for the two of us, that I would always be present to her and true to her, as by her faithful attendance she had seemed to promise to me in those earlier days.

My presence seemed, to me anyway, to promise the opposite of all this. Hadn't Twyla just left us? Didn't that prove the hopelessness of expecting me to provide any kind of protection? I could scarcely tolerate standing in my own skin, let alone being strong. I paced the room and moaned. I pounded the wall with my fist. I cursed God. I cursed the doctors, the hospital, myself. Elizabeth ended up comforting me.

Once when Elizabeth was napping, her mother and I happened to end up alone in the room at the same time, and her mother told me something she had never told anyone before. Of all the people on earth only she and Elizabeth's father knew this. It was something they had sworn never to tell. She worked up to the information. It was difficult for her, indeed impossible, to come to a moment so intimate without the preface of useful or otherwise irrelevant information. She began by telling me long-winded stories of her childhood and upbringing in Virginia—Tidewater, as she always insisted on specifying. The theme of these tales was always the same, that her family was one of "quality" and some wealth, that she dated no one who did not know that the proper way to kiss a woman's hand was to bend to the hand, not to raise the hand to the lips.

I squirmed in my chair.

She talked on and on, Tidewater this, Tidewater that. Soon she began talking about having fallen in love with Elizabeth's father. He was not like the others, she said. His parents were Pennsylvania Dutch, they were poor, they worked in a concrete plant, spoke mostly German in the home.

I had never known her to be so frank or personal.

His parents were good people, she allowed, but limited and filled with prejudices. His father ended each day white as a ghost from cement dust. In his ears, his eyelashes, everywhere. "Oh, Walter had good prospects," she said, speaking of her husband. He developed an idea about the making of cement blocks and then developed the patent on it. That's how he made all his money.

The story was losing its interest for me and becoming more typical of the type of thing she more commonly told. I started to think of excusing myself. I felt a little claustrophobic. I looked at Elizabeth and saw that she was sleeping very hard. She was propped up in bed against her pillows. Her mouth had fallen open and she was snoring lightly. Her mother kept up the slow drone of her voice, with its soft Virginia accent. I was beginning to feel a little sleepy myself. Then the tone shifted again, and I found myself waking again, listening carefully, in fact. This is where she began to tell what no one had ever heard before.

Elizabeth, she told me, was not really an only child, as everyone believed. "Oh in a way she was, of course. We raised no other children. She was all we ever truly had." But, she said, there had been another pregnancy, a couple of years before Elizabeth was born.

"Another pregnancy?" I said.

"Yes, Elizabeth had an older brother." She told me the date of his birth. The date was a year or more after the date of her marriage, so I knew this was not a "love child" that had been put up for adoption. "He weighed eight pounds, a little more," she went on. "A beautiful child, apparently, with blond hair and blue eyes. I suppose all babies' eyes are blue when they are born, but you understand. A perfect child, fingers and toes, all that. The thing is, though, he needed lots of special attention, they told me. They didn't bring the baby into the room, because the hospital wanted to give him all this special treatment. Walter told me this himself. He was the one who kept me up to date on how our baby was doing. I had had twilight sleep, they called it, some mild drug to ease the pain, and so I remembered the birth, sort of, but not very much. I said, 'But Walter, can't they just bring our baby in the room for one little minute? Can that do any harm?'

" 'Oh no,' Walter explained. 'There is a new theory these days about that.' And he would go on to explain technical, scientific things that I was too tired to understand.

"Women were treated like children then, of course. Doctors, husbands—they knew what was best for us. That's why I'm telling you this. You're not like that, Buddy. It was good that you cried. It was good that Elizabeth had to take care of you. I wish Walter could have cried. Anyway, the baby grew, Walter reported how many ounces of milk it was taking, how long it was growing, how much weight it was gaining. They had to cut his fingernails, they grew so long! We went over lists of names together, oh it was so hard to decide. There were so many beautiful names. Six whole weeks passed, that's how long I lay in that hospital without seeing my baby. I said, 'Walter, this is getting ridiculous. I'm fine, the baby's fine. I want to hold that sweet baby.' I mean I put my foot down, you can understand that. Six long weeks. I had started thinking I'd better sew a christening dress. No, there was an ancient christening dress in a cedar trunk at home somewhere, I remembered it finally. It was the dress my grandmother had made for my mother. I wore it after her. I didn't know what kind of shape it was in. I begged Walter to go open up that old trunk and see if he couldn't find that dress, which would have been ideal. That's when Walter finally broke down and told me the truth. The baby was dead. The baby was born dead. That's it. That's the end of the story. Elizabeth's father and the doctors lied to me for six weeks. They told me small details of my child's supposed life. A child that lived inside me and grew large but never breathed the air of the outside world. My husband lied to me. For my own good, he said. That's what he said. He lied to me so I would not feel sad. You're lucky, Buddy. You're in pain, and Elizabeth is in pain, you're both disappointed, and you'll never really ever get over this. But it could be worse. You don't think so maybe. It could be much worse."

15

Hair of the Dog

ELIZABETH WOKE ME ONE morning after one of our terrible fights and said, "I should never speak to you again, but look at this." I was wrapped in the bed sheets, which were twisted and sweat-soaked from a night of drunken sleep. My mouth was dry, the pain in my head and limbs was so intense that when I opened my eyes the images of my surroundings, even Elizabeth herself, seemed to flicker in the manner of old silent movies. Elizabeth flung a local newspaper onto the bed beside me. In the paper was a news story that she knew would appeal to me. It told about a corpse in Prescott, Arkansas, that had been embalmed and left standing in the mortuary broom closet for sixty-four years. It might provide "material" for a piece of fiction, she believed. It was just the kind of thing I would be interested in writing, she believed, and she was right.

We had moved again by this time and were living in a college town in the amazing Arkansas Ozarks. The skies were blue and clear, the lakes and streams brimmed with water pure enough to drink. And now we also had another child, a boy named Erik who was born just a year after Jesse Robert's death. Erik was like an angel, he was so beautiful. His skin glowed, literally, sparkled like snow in sunshine; his hair was snow white and fine as corn silk and seemed to float about his head like a halo. Later, when he was grown, Erik would regret that he had been what he called "a replacement baby" for the brother who had died, but to Elizabeth and me he was heaven's messenger, and never had there been born on this earth anyone so fully anticipated and loved, and to us he replaced no one, for no one had ever been even remotely similar to him.

Robin, who was six years old by now, sat beside the baby's cradle and marvelled openly at his new brother's ethereal beauty. The dark shroud of Jesse Robert's death still covered us all—the space he had so briefly occupied could not have been filled by even this glowing child—but we thought of ourselves as a happy family, perhaps at long last.

Among the many changes in our lives was my decision to leave teaching and begin to try to write fiction. Elizabeth had agreed to support the family—she got a job in a local elementary school—and my job would be to stay at home with the children, and in that way find hours in the day to learn to write. It was the most impractical of plans, and yet by slow torturous steps it began to work—to seem to work, in any case—in almost every way. I earned nothing, I published nothing, what I wrote was execrable, and yet to look at me and to listen to me speak, one could hardly deny that I was a writer. Every moment that was not devoted to the children, I spent before my Smith-Corona portable electric typewriter. If writing was what made a person a writer, I had passed the test. Clickety-clack, clickety-clack, I moved my fingers over the keys, I turned out the pages. I was thirty-five years old, unemployed, and hungry to write whatever it was I was meant to write. This alone should have qualified me for the appellation of writer.

Writing was my constant focus, to the exclusion of almost everything else. I wrote, or I talked about writing, 100 percent of the time. No conversation was complete without some reference to me as a writer. Never mind that I had published nothing, never mind that I took a writing course at the university and made a C. I was a writer, and if you didn't believe it, just ask me. Suddenly everyone I knew or cared about was a writer. To hear me tell it, anyway. I pretended to be friends with writers I had never met. I went to readings and heard writers read, and the next thing you knew I was best friends with them, had "spent a weekend" with them. No lie was too preposterous to identify me as a writer among writers. I was a writer, really, no kidding, I insisted, with every word and gesture.

Elizabeth colluded with me in this fiction, if fiction is what my new identity really was. She not only said this, she actually believed that I was a writer. Her believing this so thoroughly, despite most of the evidence, probably contributed to my actually becoming a writer at some point later on.

Calling me a writer was a part of a larger plan. Elizabeth and I had agreed, without words, that my being a writer would take away the sting of our grief for Jesse Robert's death. Where we got this notion I don't know, but this was the plan. Other people go to therapy or buy season's tickets to the opera or football, or they have affairs or get involved in community service or a motorcycle gang. We took parts in the farce that I was a writer. Why we should have chosen this route, or metaphor, or whatever it was, as our escape hatch, I have never understood. I only know grief was why I became a writer, plain and simple. There was no better reason for the decision than this. Not to express the grief or to "deal" with it, but to flee from it, to blot it out and deny the truth of it.

Drinking did this too, of course, circumvented the unbearable pain that I felt for this child I had not really known, and in my mind the two were related, writing and drinking. Hard drinking was part of the romance of writerly suffering. I sincerely believed this part. When I finally quit drinking years later, I believed that I had also quit writing, the two were so intricately woven into a single fabric in my imagination. As I had imagined my situation in the beginning, I was standing in the rear of a long queue of writers headed by Faulkner and Hemingway and other notable drunks. I had taken my humble place among the masters, and I would not give up my place in that line even if it meant I had to drink myself to death.

Becoming a writer was not Step One in our denial, of course. The process began immediately. When Jesse Robert died, neither Elizabeth nor I could admit that he had ever lived. Our denial was so extreme it reminds me of those people on daytime TV shows who have exhibited behavior so pathetic and bizarre that the audience can't quite believe what they're hearing. When my mother called and asked whether she should wear a hat to the funeral, I said, "Funeral?"

She said, "The baby's funeral."

I said, "Baby?"

When the priest came and asked about "arrangements," neither Elizabeth nor I knew what he was talking about. The closest I came to any such admission was to say that Elizabeth had "miscarried," though she was only a week or two from full term when the baby was born. So far did my denial extend that, in fact, no funeral was held.

So it was no accident that Elizabeth woke me to send me in

search of this corpse-in-the-closet that she had read about in the paper and thought I would be interested in checking into. Old Mike was the name the locals had given the corpse that I would set out in search of. I could make jokes, I could pretend that Flannery O'Connor's spirit still lived somehow in me, but I was looking, without hope or direction, for my son's unburied body —and maybe my first-father's grave—at least to lay eyes on them, or their representation, to confirm their substantiality, to undo the emptiness I had invented through denial. Not burying my son was a replication of that first unreal death, a love I fantasized but never really knew. For all my life I had been a fatherless child, and now suddenly I was the childless father. This I could not accept, it was intolerable.

Moving to Arkansas had been another form of the same escape plan: Keep moving and you will feel nothing. So we believed, in any case. We might have been tumbleweeds blown by the winds of grief. I enrolled as a writing student briefly, but by the time of the drunken fight and blackout that Elizabeth and I had just suffered, I had dropped out of the writing school and had become a hanger-on in the writing community, very much the same as I had been when I was "manager" of the Itta Bena football team. I liked thinking of myself as a writer. Mainly, of course, in addition to avoiding grief, putting on my writer act circumvented my thinking of myself as a drunk and a freeloader. I had no regular employment, Elizabeth was supporting us, I stayed at home all day and brooded, as I imagined writers around the world were doing.

I'm very hard on myself when I remember those difficult days. I admit I was not completely worthless. Robin was in junior high, playing soccer, clarinet in the school band; and now, as I said, we also had another child as well, Erik, with whom I spent all my hours. Erik had been an unexpectedly bright light in my life. I could not take my eyes off him. Even when he was a baby, his laughter could fill a room. I managed to stay sober during the daylight hours usually, and so I was helpful with both the children. I sent them off to school, I took them to the doctor when they were sick, I gave them a snack when they came in from school in the afternoon, I sang rock 'n' roll songs from the fifties to them. In the winter we rode sleds, and in the summer we swam. I built playground equipment in the backyard, a tetherball set, a playhouse, and a gizmo on a cable that Robin could sail through the air on, from the back porch, across the yard, and into the high branches of a tree. I tried this device once myself and flew with force straight into the tree trunk.

I put in a garden in the spring, and when tomatoes ripened in the late summer, the boys and I gave each tomato its own name. The first tomato each year was always named Elvis, and the second was always Priscilla. I planted fruit trees and eventually harvested the fruit and made apple jelly and peach preserves. I sat upstairs at the Smith-Corona for a few hours a day and wrote stories that had nothing to do with me, of violinists and tightrope walkers and ballet dancers who lived in European countries. I sent them out to the *New Yorker* and felt forlorn when they came zooming home. Tolerated as I was as a hanger-on in the writing community, I could not tolerate myself, not even long enough to write an honest story.

But the beauty of my situation, complete unemployment, was that I could stay up as late as I wanted and drink as much as I needed every day. It was relatively inexpensive, the way I went about it. I hung out in as few bars as possible and so engaged mainly in solitary drinking, which has the drunkard's advantage of very low overhead. I could get a liter of scrofulous vodka for three dollars and change at a dreary, damp hole-in-the-wall called The Party Store, and so this is what I did, day after day, waiting as long as I could each day to begin drinking. The clerk at The Party Store was a pathetic creature with Elephant Man's disease, hideously misshapen, toothless, and impossible to understand when he spoke. He never bathed. Still, this was my favorite store, and I was a loyal customer. I felt at home here. My attendance at the package store was almost perfect, the Elephant Man knew my name, and though I was never sure what he was talking about, he always had the kerosene-smelling vodka already bagged by the time I made my way through the door. I was such a regular customer I might as well have been delivering the mail.

There was one bar that I frequented when I wanted stimulating adult conversation, a place called Leonard's. It was out of town and filled with dangerous men and women, some rednecks, some Mexicans, some Indians from Oklahoma. I fit in well enough. Happy Hour was at seven o'clock in the morning. There I learned a trick with a bar towel that came in handy when my hands were shaking too badly to bring a drink to my mouth. You drape the towel around your neck, holding it by either end with your hands. You pull the towel down slowly across the back of your neck toward the table with one hand—this stabilizes your hands so you can grasp the shot glass—and then and you pull slowly and firmly on the towel with the other hand so that it draws the hand with the drink in it steadily up to your mouth. The first shot of vodka rises slowly to your face and no matter how shaky your hands, the drink is controlled and stabilized by the towel. You don't spill a drop.

Some nights, in warm weather, I'd walk to a nearby park,

fragrant and green—sometimes Robin and Erik would go with me—to watch a softball league at play. I was living the good life.

I was telling, though, about the morning that Elizabeth woke me with the strange news story of the dead man in the broom closet. I said, "I'm sorry" to Elizabeth—these were the first words out of my mouth. I barely remembered my bad behavior from the night before but was certain that some form of apology was necessary, as was becoming true virtually every day by this time. I was never well in the morning, and so it was this morning. I was nauseated and feverish from alcohol poisoning. I was sweating, my hands were shaking, and the sheets were soaked. Happy hour was already over, and I was too sick to drive there anyway. I could not look at the newspaper Elizabeth had thrown onto the bed with me until I had bolted from the room and sat for a while with my head in the toilet. The porcelain toilet was cool. Driving the porcelain bus, this practice is called in the South. This was my routine each day. I found a part of a flat beer sitting on the kitchen counter and took tentative sips, testing my stomach, and found that it stayed down. It was almost refreshing. I drank it all—hair of the dog—and was happy to see that my hands had stopped shaking so violently, though there was still a tremor.

When I was able to read the news story that had interested Elizabeth, I learned about this broom closet–based corpse. Prescott was a town a few hours south of Fayetteville, I learned. Old Mike had been a beggar and pencil salesman long ago, and was found dead sitting upright against a tree trunk one evening on the weekend of the county fair. The year was 1911. I imagined him sitting with his feet stretched out, his one hand still upon his knee holding a tin cup, the other hand still clutching a small bouquet of yellow No. 2 Ticonderoga pencils for sale, penny apiece. The body had been taken to the local funeral home and embalmed and set aside for the time when a relative or friend might think to claim the body for burial. No one ever came. The body was never claimed. Over time the owners of the funeral parlor passed along the business to younger relatives and often they spoke of going ahead and burying Old Mike at their own expense, but somehow it never happened. Old Mike was moved from table to table, room to room, additions were added to the original funeral home, Old Mike never quite fit in, and for a long time the late pencil salesman was lost in the dark recesses of the property and of memory. The embalming process, back in the old days, was not sophisticated, and so the body was preserved much more permanently than modern practices allow. One result of such permanent embalming was that the flesh was made as hard as oak by the fluids. Old Mike had turned to leather, stiffer than any board on earth, stiffer indeed than saddle leather, and the same color, as the harsh embalming liquids had given him a permanent tan. Somewhere along the way—no one I later interviewed remembered when, or who was responsible— the body had been rediscovered, on a gurney perhaps, in a rear hallway. The person who found him had a sense of humor of sorts. Old Mike was dressed in a starched shirt and tuxedo. Big white eyes were painted where real eyes had once been, and the body had been fitted with gold-rimmed spectacles. He was a kind of landmark, a legend that would "put Prescott, Arkansas, on the map," as a local resident later told me. Old Mike no longer was relegated to back rooms and obscure gurneys but was now placed prominently, in his new duds, in a front hall closet, where all anyone need do to visit with him was to open the door and look in. And view him many did. More than a mere curiosity, Old Mike became a tourist attraction. At first local classes from the elementary school filed by the broom closet on field trips. Later, church groups did the same, for exactly what lesson I was never able to determine, though there were allusions to taxidermy and the Resurrection. The phenomenon did not remain local. Soon tour buses from other town, other states, made Prescott one of their stops. A legend grew up around Old Mike. The gold work in his teeth, I was told when I visited the funeral home, was intricate and sophisticated, far more advanced than any such work being done in the United States before the year 1911. Many believed the work to be Italian. The conclusion was inevitable: Old Mike was descended from royalty, an Italian count, most supposed. The morning of my terrible hangover and introduction to all this material—in its bare-bones form, you might say—was the summer of 1976. The state of Arkansas had passed a law making it illegal to display a corpse. For this reason news of Old Mike had hit the papers. Old Mike was about to be buried. Time was of the essence, Elizabeth was telling me on that morning. If I wanted to meet Old Mike, or at least attend the funeral, I had better sober up quick and get my butt down to Prescott. It had to be something as urgent as this to thaw her heart sufficiently to allow her to speak to me at all, after the things I had said the night before. I said, "Elizabeth, I'm sorry. I don't know what gets into me."

The day I arrived in Prescott, Arkansas, in search of Old Mike was steamy and hot, following a brief, unpleasant rain. I was sweaty and miserable, I was tired from driving these several hours, my van was old and not air-conditioned, and the muffler had a hole in it. The alcohol from the night before leaked full-strength from my pores. I looked hopefully for the familiar orange roof of a Howard Johnson's or maybe a Holiday Inn or the cheery sunburst of a Quality Inn. I imagined a cool shower, or maybe a soaking bath, a bucket of ice from the ice machine, the air-conditioner thermostat cranked to the limit, cool white pillows to prop my aching head. I drove along the perimeter of the little town for a while, this way and that way, noticing car dealerships, farm-implement companies, and signs to Delight, Arkansas, Home of Glen Campbell, but found no such comfortable accommodations as I had imagined. In the dead center of the dying little town, however, stood an ancient two-story hotel, a white-painted wood structure with porches and gables. I parked the van and resigned myself to this resting place for the night, before I began interviewing undertakers the following day.

When I entered the tiled lobby I saw its enormous fireplace and carved woodwork and brass spittoons and thronelike shoe-shine stand and closet-sized little elevator, but whatever grace or elegance the lobby might once have known was by the time of my visit long gone. The whole place had fallen into a sad decay. The tiles were filthy, the elevator had a sign on its door announcing VATOR BROKE, the bellhop was sleepy and aged and reminded me uncomfortably of . . . well, you know who he reminded me of. For many reasons a depression flopped over my shoulders like a heavy, dusty bird on a too-small roost.

It was not that I didn't like the people who managed the hotel, I did like them. The bellhop was not the monkeylike caricature in New York; he wore no brass-buttoned suit, no pillbox hat, he was not drunk or dirty or deformed. Indeed he was a kindly gentleman in slick blue gabardine trousers and a faded but clean red smock. He was well-spoken and intelligent and not at all ashamed or embittered by his station in life. The white-haired woman who stood behind the high mahogany counter and rented me a room—three dollars a night—and gave me my key, and her sister, also white-haired and wearing a red waitress uniform (she waited tables in the adjoining cafe), were equally likable and kind.

It was the specialness with which they treated me that caused my confusion. The moment he saw me the bellhop came to life. There were, apparently, a few steady customers of the hotel, traveling salesmen, but no one who approximated as closely as I did the image of a genuine "tourist." Tourist status seemed very high among the staff here, and already I felt inadequate to live up to their expectations of me in this role. The lively bellhop fairly twittered around me with small talk. The sisters were no less aflutter at the sight of me. What had brought me to Precott, they wanted to know; would I be staying long, what was the weather like north of here, where would I be headed tomorrow? I could not reveal to them that I had come to town to view a corpse, the indignity to them seemed somehow too great, even personal, though now that I think of it, what harm could such a revelation have done, as the corpse was in a sense famous and not at all a novelty to the locals of Prescott and, therefore, not the comic humiliation I had projected it to be. In any case, I kept my mission vague but tried to answer all other questions as truthfully as I could. Briefly the key ring could not be found, a moment of keen embarrassment to the three of them, and once it was found there was a short, whispered discussion, a little frantic, about which room might be "made up." When these details were settled and I was set to go to my room, I thought for a moment that all three of them together would usher me upstairs as a kind of delegation to ensure my comfort. At last the sisters honored the bellhop's prerogative and stood aside, their hands folded nervously at their waists, and we left them and headed up the stairs to my room.

Already I knew I could not stay the night.

These good people wanted me to love this rattletrap old place as they loved it, and I knew that I was too far beyond feeling of almost any kind to pretend successfully that I was not appalled by the accommodations. Complaining would have been as monstrous as it was pointless, and hiding my disappointment was impossible.

The bellhop inserted the key for me and opened the door to my room. With pride he directed me into it. He showed me the bathroom, the clean towels; he turned on the water to prove that it ran hot. He pushed his hand on the bed and caused the springs to creak and assured me of the high quality of the mattress. He flicked the bedside lamp on and off to show me that it worked. He told me that if the room felt too warm, the window could be raised to let in a cool breeze. I tipped him lavishly and he was gone.

The room was, in a manner of speaking, spotless. But such a long time had passed since it had been put in this condition that an even topsoil of dust had settled on everything—the plastic chair, the deal dresser, the mirror, the bedspread and window sill. More even than I had in the room in New York, I thought of the fictional room in which Homer Barron met his untimely end at the hands of Miss Emily Grierson in Faulkner's "A Rose for Emily," and the dread of splendid decay became all the more intolerable to me.

The window opened with ease, as the truthful bellhop had promised. I held my canvas bag out and dropped it into the alleyway below. I had no notion of ever coming back. I stooped and stepped out of the window onto a line of jutting bricks that formed a ledge about twice the width of my foot. With difficulty I squatted and maneuvered myself until I could hang from this ledge by my fingertips. I dropped to the ground and felt sharp pains blaze through my feet and calves.

When I could stand again, it was a simple matter to slip around the edge of buildings and emerge from the shadows at some distance from the hotel. When I could return to my van without being seen, I drove to the edge of town and slept the night in a town park, scrunched on the backseat.

Next morning I woke early, washed my face in the park's birdbath, combed my hair with my fingers. I went to the funeral home and conducted my interviews, saw the facilities, saw photographs of Old Mike, though as I have said, Old Mike's funeral had taken place earlier in the week. At the end of the day, as I pointed the van north and began to drive away from Prescott toward my home, something like despair overcame me, suddenly, unexpectedly. I stopped at a DX station and got a Coke from the machine and washed out my mouth. It was typical of the exaggeration and imbalance of my emotions that I imagined that the taste I was unable to wash from my mouth was that of betrayal.

I drove back to the hotel to make whatever amends I could, though as soon as I arrived there, I knew that the simple truth was now an ideal beyond my poor powers of conduct. I circled the block a few times, uncertain what to do. At last I approached the old hotel from the rear and eased the van down the narrow alleyway and parked beneath the window from which I had jumped the night before. By standing on top of my van, I found sufficient handhold and foothold in the old brick wall to pull myself, with effort, back onto the ledge and through the window again.

Once in the room, I turned back the covers of the bed and rumpled the sheets. I squashed down the feather pillow with my hands. In the bathroom I stripped the wrapper off a new bar of soap, washed my face and hands and threw the towel on the floor. I urinated and considered leaving the toilet unflushed, but could not go quite so far in leaving my mark. What kind of guest would fail to flush the toilet?

Everyone was happy to see me when I emerged. They greeted me with warm smiles as I made my way down the stairs. They were waiting for me at the bottom. The sisters wanted to know whether I had slept well, whether the bed was all right, whether the water was hot enough, whether I might makes suggestions for improvements to make future tourists more comfortable. I praised the accommodations. I commented on the excellence of the mattress, the heat of the water, the cool of the breeze that blew the night through my easily opened window.

The bellhop was there as well. He said, with first-thing-in-the-morning hop-to-it-iveness, "I'll just run up and get your bag."

This was a problem. I didn't have a bag, of course. My bag was in my van. I was so taken aback by the oversight that for a moment I could not speak. I stood before them with my mouth open. The sisters' bright countenances darkened suddenly and horribly. I had been found out, this seemed an inescapable fact. I stammered, "I—I—"

The elder sister, out of her darkness, said, "Mr. Nordan did not have a bag."

The bellhop looked at her, into that hard darkness, and their eyes locked. After a few seconds he said, "I forgot about that. That's right."

We said our good-byes, we spoke of the weather and of roads and directions. We said another round of good-byes, strained of course, but polite. I walked several blocks out of my way before backtracking by a different route to my van in the alley. I had been twenty-four hours without alcohol and was beginning to feel shaky. I was on the lookout for a place to pick up a six-pack. I was already writing the article in my head, and as yet had no idea why I had developed this sudden intense interest in unburied corpses. I drove away from Prescott, Arkansas, forever.

My trip to Prescott yielded little more information than I have already told about Old Mike and those who owned him, if *owned* is the proper word for a man who once was some mother's child. By the time I arrived, Old Mike had already been buried in a pauper's grave, as he should have been decades earlier. I saw a cartoonish photograph of him, no more. His chemical-darkened flesh and painted eyes made him look like Al Jolson. I was directed to the closet where he had stood for so long and only felt a little sad as I stood and looked and longed for a kind of hilarity. I met the grandson of the man who embalmed him; the grandson now owned the funeral parlor. He knew little, said little, though he did give me an interesting lecture on modern embalming techniques, which I was able to use in an article I later wrote on the subject. My interviews with the locals were, I'm sorry to say, condescending on my part, and I treated them as freakish rubes, and joined with them in failing to acknowledge the humanity of the dead man we were calling Old Mike.

Old Mike was not the last unburied corpse I would pursue. Before I became aware that my pursuit was a form of "acting out" on feelings I had chosen not to feel, unburied bodies became my vocation and quest. I visited Big Jim's Elegant Junk, a store in Knoxville, Tennessee, that featured a corpse in a wedding dress in an open coffin. I went to California to see a cowboy corpse used as a promotional dummy in a traveling Wild West show. I went to a suburb of St. Louis, where the Mississippi

River had flooded and unearthed dozens of graves and left the bodies and caskets scattered helter-skelter across the landscape. I went to Cruger, Mississippi, where the perfectly preserved corpse of a beautiful young woman was accidentally disinterred by backhoe putting in a sewer line. She lay submerged in alcohol inside a glass-topped coffin. She had auburn hair and a red velvet dress and delicate high-top shoes with leather bottoms and a silk boot. Her head lay on a pillow of striped ticking. I published articles on the subject of unburied corpses across America. I researched them, I traveled far and wide, I laid eyes on every one.

THREE

16

"I had that cat for seventeen years"

The story of Robin's death has been hard to write. I wanted readers to feel some of the loss I felt on that bad day. I wanted them to know him as I knew him. You'd think—or I thought anyway—I could quickly sketch out a context of our home life, happy some days, not so happy other days, maybe some homey details, meals for example. Robin would eat his baked potato and then hide whatever food he didn't want to eat, liver, say, or green beans, down in the potato shell. That was the kind of thing I thought might tell a reader who Robin was, what he was to me. Or before that maybe a physical description, his sidelong crooked smile, his gray-green eyes, his delicate hands, his energetic laughter. I would write about the family dog, big and woolly-white as a sheep, the hilarious newspaper fights between me and Robin and Erik at night on the couch, the game Robin invented called Bowling for Cats, maybe some of the sadder things too, regrettable things, like the divorce from their mother. Robin was especially hurt by the divorce. For a while he spent most of his time at his best friend's house, and even started to call his friend's parents Mom and Dad. Robin never got to know Annie, the woman I'm now married to, and this strikes me as another sad thing I might write about.

In writing terms, the divorce might have become an effective foreshadowing sadness that would prefigure the deeper grief of Robin's death. I'd planned to write about how well Robin was doing in college at the University of Arkansas, I'd planned say he had a good part-time job in a biology lab. Then I'd planned to tell how Robin's friends suddenly realized that no one had seen Robin for a few days and that Elizabeth realized this too and got worried and called the police and then called me, up in Pittsburgh. I was already living with Annie by this time. I had wanted to sketch out not just how worried we all were, but how we had to keep on with the ordinary details of jobs and dirty dishes and bank loans, as if the days when we didn't know where he was were like any other days of our lives. I thought about making a comparison with that Auden poem "Musée des Beaux Arts," about Brueghels's painting of Icarus, who falls to his death as the rest of the world goes on about its business. As I had imagined the structure of the piece, I figured I would finally come to the place where Robin's car is found in the Arkansas wilderness with Robin's decomposed body inside. I worked and worked on this, but I never could get it to come together. I couldn't make my son's life seem real, or important, I couldn't communicate a sense of what it meant to confront that empty space in all our lives that his dying left. I had lost a son before, the baby Jesse Robert, who I had not really known, but even all these years later, when I set out to write, I was tongue-tied and inarticulate.

I can imagine one of Robin's college friends one day writing such an essay successfully. In fact, I like to imagine such a thing.

It would be a great essay, the one this friend would write. I can imagine him writing of going to Robin's room in the fraternity house and finding the grieving mother removing clothes from the closet, picking up his smelly sneakers, gathering up a stack of vocabulary cards from a study session for the German test, putting his desk lamp into a cardboard box. Or I can imagine a girlfriend standing on a corner of campus, waiting for a bus back to the dorms, and seeing Robin's car slide by, the silver Prelude being hauled along behind a tow truck from a local service station, and noticing that the Prelude is all covered in flies. I can imagine how puzzled she would have been. I imagine her getting on the bus and telling the driver which dorm to take her to and thinking, "I swear, that car was covered in flies." All this might be in somebody else's essay. I can imagine the smaller crevices of that girlfriend's life being illuminated by the shocking memory. I can imagine her remembering a small gift Robin had given her, an insect locked in amber, and seeing this moment in her life as a similarly vivid silence. Maybe by the time the essay is written, the girlfriend is married to somebody else and not very happy and wondering how her life would have turned out if Robin had made another decision and lives had been allowed to go along their original paths. Maybe the fraternity guy who walks in on the mom and the smelly sneakers has some other kind of life and some other dreamy fantasy. I wish someone would write those essays.

But what can a father say? I find myself silenced by the magnitude of how much there is to say, by the inadequacy of words. Words are sufficient for a father's death, a lover's, but not for a son's. That's the wall I keep coming up against.

My son's death was a suicide. He was obsessed with the thought of death, tortured by it. The first time he thought of suicide was in seventh grade, after a small disappointment in the middle school marching band formation. He asked his Oiuja Board when he would die. The obsession continued. In high school he started to drink. With alcohol he drank himself into deathlike stupors, he threw a chair through a plateglass window in a fraternity house because he saw his reflection in it. Who is at fault in my son's death? Isn't someone to blame for this horror besides the boy himself? I am. What is a responsible context for the writer to put that piece of information into? Even random murder would seem simpler to write about, somehow. Still— No matter how much I have grown spiritually over the years since Robin died, no matter how much therapy I've had, no matter how much more I know about depression than I did then, still there are days when the only context that seems reasonable is that I was an inadequate father, that if hadn't lost my temper that time, if I hadn't succumbed to alcoholism—in short, that my son's death was my fault. The self-blame book is not the book I want to write, and not one I suspect anyone wants to read. Indeed it's not the life I can afford to live. Self-blame is usually a way of avoiding something more hideous anyway, something you're willing to be punished for but unwilling to change, or even something terrible in the imperfect structure of the universe. What I am left with is this lengthy complaint that I don't know how to talk about my son.

MANY PEOPLE TRIED TO comfort me at the time, of course. Some relied on the old tried and true "I'm sorry for your loss" remark, which shows they're up to date and know that nothing really helps anyway so they might as well say this lame old thing, but at the same time pretty much prove themselves to be idiots who can't think of anything more personal or creative to say. Others misapply what they learned in therapy or church and tell you this will make you a stronger person.

"What don't kill you makes you stronger," one guy said.

"God never gives us more than we can handle," countless others have said.

Others want to help you to curse God, which ironically is no more comforting than the admonition that your boy's death is part of God's larger mysterious plan or that your son was too good for this earth and God needed him in heaven. Others related deaths that they had suffered to prove they knew exactly what I was going through.

One of these deaths was a ninety-six-year-old grandparent in a nursing home—"When that good lady died, why I—."

And another woman—I swear to God, this sounds like a lie, but it's not—related my loss to the death of her seventeen-year-old cat. "I know just how you feel," she said. She went on and on about the cat. I ended up comforting her. "I had that cat for seventeen years!" she wept.

After about a year, another woman told me, "Get over it, you can't grieve forever."

Others avoided me altogether. These are not hateful people. In fact, they're my friends, some of them people I love, including the lady whose cat died. They too are limited by the enormity of a son's suicide.

The persons who came closest to being helpful—and there were a great many of these—were the ones who said, "Nothing could be worse than losing a child." It didn't help, because nothing helps, but you had to admire the attempt. Momentarily they submerged all their losses in favor of mine. It is an elegant gesture, and the elegance is helpful. They were acknowledging that in the grief event of life's Olympics, I had taken the gold and they, the losers, would present me the medal. In some cases even this turned out to be a selfish act, I suppose. Sometimes such people were simply and suddenly scared shitless that their own children were capable of the same act and would die, and so by their generosity to me they might win a reprieve. Or maybe not, maybe they only had caught a glimmer of a clue.

It's not quite true that nothing helped. One guy helped. I have to admit, this one old guy in Pittsburgh made an impression on me. His words were not really any different from a lot of other people's. He put his face in his hands and shook his head back and forth and said, "Oh my God. Nothing could be worse." The difference was, when this guy was seventeen years old he was imprisoned in Bergen-Belsen and was forced to watch as his whole family was murdered by the Nazis. So what he said about my place in the hierarchy of grief carried some authority. This helped. Maybe one other person helped as well. When Robin's body had been autopsied and then cremated, it took a while for the ashes to be sent from Little Rock to Fayetteville to be interred. During the time when we were waiting for them to come, I was walking around the church grounds with the Episcopal priest, a big guy who had once been a college football star. I liked him. We stood by a pool of goldfish and chatted. He explained that "ashes" were not really what we were waiting for; what was left over after cremation was actually bone fragments. We talked about a lot of different things. There had been a lot in the news recently about the ineffectiveness of the U.S. Mail service. There was a joke that four more numbers were being added to the zip code because too much mail had been getting through.

I said, "I hate to think of Robin having to travel by U.S. Mail."

We looked at one another and laughed. We walked a little longer on the ground, we fed the fish. This priest was about six-five, so it's hard to picture him with an impish grin, maybe. He said, "You know, he could end up in the Dead Letter Office." We laughed our damn heads off.

17

The Amazing Technicolor Effing Machine

I HAD BEEN LIVING with Annie in Pittsburgh when the news came that Robin was missing. I had begun my new life, is the way I thought of my situation at the time.

The divorce from Elizabeth was long since complete. The two of us had moved quickly to bring the marriage to an end. Both Elizabeth and I had claimed we were ready to make an ending, a quick clean break, to move on with our lives, though once the divorce proceedings were initiated, I felt as if I had suddenly waked up and discovered that I was hanging from a bridge by my fingertips.

When the divorce actually went through I felt as if I had just let go of the bridge. I left Arkansas and drove 1,000 miles north where I drove through the Fort Pitt tunnel and saw the Three Rivers Stadium, and the fifty-foot spray of the fountain on the Point, and the confluence of wide rivers, the sweet ease of coal barges and paddle wheelers along the bright water, and silvery bridges as far as you could see, and I cried for what I had lost and for what I was afraid to find.

I had almost nothing. I had so recently quit drinking that my hands still shook slightly. I was lonely. I was frightened. I had cashed in an insurance policy and got money for the used car I was driving. Everything else that I had taken from my twenty-year marriage to Elizabeth was crammed into the backseat of that car. I had what was left from the insurance policy as a small bankroll until my job started four months hence. I was unsure what I would do until then. Then, when nothing else in my life seemed to be working out—I found Annie.

I loved her immediately, at first sight, as the saying goes—literally the first second I saw her. Falling in love with her was the first truly sane response I had made to my environment in a long time. When we met, I was still unemployed and staying for free with a strange couple I had met in a Laundromat (a step up from the YMCA barracks where I had stayed for my first month in town), so I had plenty of time to strengthen my tottering sobriety. I was going to meeting after meeting, a self-help group for alcoholics, partly to get away from the people I was living with, partly just to have something to do with all the hours. The first time I saw Annie, I was at a meeting in a church basement in the Shadyside section of Pittsburgh, along with a lot of other people who were trying to quit drinking. She was sitting at another table, across the room, through the cigarette smoke, and I knew right away that I loved her, it was as simple as that. I'd heard of love at first sight, but I had never before experienced it myself.

I loved the way she looked, of course. Her hair was dark and soft, her eyes wide-set, her mouth a generous invitation to conversation and kisses. Her laughter could break my heart. It did break my heart. She was sitting with other women, and occasionally she leaned this way or that to speak or listen to one of them, she smiled, she laughed, and my heart ached to hear each syllable from her mouth.

Throughout the meeting, I watched her and only her, and when it came her turn to speak I thrilled at the husky timbre of her voice. I wanted to kick myself for forgetting to listen to what she said, but already I was stupid with love and could only gaze upon her, drink in the music of her voice, if not the meaning of the words. I had no idea what the topic of the meeting might be, in any case, so listening more closely would have scarcely helped. If alcohol had dulled my mind, the intoxication of her presence made me a complete fool.

We met eventually, we talked, things went pretty well. She was less sure of me than I was of her, obviously. It didn't take a genius to figure out that I was not much of a catch. I was poorly dressed, my hands still exhibited a slight tremor, I laughed too loud at small things, I was fidgety and nervous, I was unwilling to say much about where I was living at the time. I was what re-covering alcoholics call a "low bottom" drunk. This means I had done significant damage to myself before I began to work at quitting. This must have been obvious. I couldn't invite anyone to "my place," since that place would have been, for my first month in town, the YMCA or, later, the home of a couple of the strangest persons in Pittsburgh. "Low bottom" was not an ap-pellation that inspires women to date a man.

It was clear to Annie, as to anyone who noticed me at all, that I was not merely a recently hopeless drunk, but a displaced person as well. I was a country boy, it was clear. My Southern accent set me apart. I still had shotguns in the backseat of my car from my hunting days. I had no idea who the Steelers were. And in any case, I looked completely forlorn all the time. Tears came to my eyes each time I spoke of Robin or Erik, how much I missed them. To tell the truth I was still crying some for Elizabeth too. It says something of Annie's own instability that she found anything at all in me to hold her interest.

Still we found things to talk about, we struggled some, but we found things—our hopes, our dreams, which truly were about all I had to call my own, unless you count my regrets. I dreamed of writing a good book, I confessed to her—a great book, I went so far as to say. I dreamed of finding peace of mind. Of all impossible dreams, this seemed least achievable. The only people I knew in Pittsburgh were people I met in church basements at what I was then calling my Don't Drink meetings. This was a joke I made to soften the sting of the truth of my life, that I was an alcoholic, a drunk, exactly like my father, or probably worse.

I knew a few other people, actually, including the couple from the Laundromat in Highland Park. The wife was a big-boned Iowa-farm-girl-looking person, except that farms were not what you thought of when you looked at this woman. She spoke with a strange foreign accent, not exactly Germanic. It was the same accent Meryl Streep uses in her accent-movies. She was six feet tall, with blond hair in a GI-style buzz cut, and steel-blue eyes. I don't think I had ever seen such a woman. She had an excellently shaped head, I noticed. She looked like someone who might be cast in a World War II movie as a German prison guard. And yet—this is the truly odd thing about her— she wore girlish clothing, frilly dresses with sashes and patent-leather shoes, or she wore poodle skirts and starched blouses and bobby sox and saddle oxfords. She was soft-spoken and had a pretty smile.

Her husband was short, merry, roly-poly, with a big belly and a big, ready laugh and a generous heart and a huge gray

beard. His eyes twinkled with a merry sort of mischief. He wad-
dled slightly when he walked. He seemed to be several years
older than his wife, and I couldn't look at him without thinking
of Santa's elves. I mean this in a good way. His cheeks were rosy
and merry. In an odd way, he made me think of good family men
from my childhood—or rather, he resembled my fantasies of
such men, grandfathers in storybooks and other sturdy, jolly
souls. He made me long for a normal existence. He gave me a
thoughtful gift, a nice plastic laundry basket so I wouldn't have
to stuff my clean clothes into a pillowcase. It was the first gift I
received as I began my new life in Pittsburgh.

We washed clothes at the same time every weekend, at this
Laundromat, the three of us. Even now when I smell the fragrance of laundry detergent and bleach and hot water, I think of
this couple—though, as I will explain, not necessarily in a fond
way—and I suppose because my life was so empty, I missed
them like family for the whole week that we were apart between
wash days. Washing laundry became something I looked forward to, the highlight of my week. I believed I could learn from
them. Dorris and Helga were their names. I longed for a life as
normal and comfortable as theirs seemed.

When I met Dorris and Helga I had been living for a while at
the YMCA downtown, as I said. Pittsburgh has an excellent Y,
and it offers a couple of levels of comfort for people who make a
temporary home there. People who can afford it can get a pretty
nice room, private in fact, with a tiny private bath. I was watching my funds carefully, though, so I had settled for the Y's less
luxurious accommodations by opting for a lower tier of sleeping
arrangements. I rented a bunk in a huge gymnasium-like hall for
three dollars a night. The sheets were fresh, there was a clean
wool blanket, and as I was usually exhausted from doing noth-

ing except attending Don't Drink meetings all day, I slept pretty well. I walked miles and miles during the course of a day to save on gas. I had a locker (with a combination lock) where I stored a few things, including my portable Smith-Corona, and so I even managed to type a few lines of fiction in the YMCA "library" from time to time. The library was a dingy room with a library table, a couple of filthy overstuffed chairs and a handful of mystery and western paperbacks on a shelf, and yet it did provide a certain feeling of normalcy in my chaotic emotional life. A black-and-white TV set with a rolling picture and two viewable channels sat on a wire stand at one end of the room. I have to hand it to myself that I never stopped working at writing stories during this time, through the worst of my drinking and through those terrifying days and months of early sobriety. I had no trouble working or writing letters with the television playing, I was lucky in that way, so in a sense I had already begun to settle into my new life with a certain ease.

The real trick to living at the Y was waiting until late enough, or rising early enough, to use the showers when relatively few other men were in there. I've always been modest, I won't apologize for that. The Y was where I lived, I hadn't known what else to do when I arrived in Pittsburgh, this was my home, my "reality," "life on life's terms," as folks at the Don't Drink meetings were fond of saying. Much later when I was first getting acquainted with Annie, she said, "If one more person in these meetings tells me 'When life gives you lemons, make lemonade,' I'm going to smack them." That was my first genuine laugh in a long time. Well, I was so much in love.

I had looked at a few terrible apartments—in East Liberty and Greenfield and Polish Hill and even the Hill District—but my bankroll would have been gone in a month, and I could have died of rat bites or been killed by gunfire in those neighbor-hoods. The YMCA was pretty bad in some respects, but heaven compared to the next nearest thing I could afford. I was squeez-ing that insurance money for all it was worth. I had looked for interim jobs half-heartedly. I found a newspaper in the Y library and looked through the classifieds for part-time work, maybe, but I didn't really want to find anything. Maybe I was ashamed to work at McDonald's, I don't know, I really don't know what kept me from taking something, some small employment to make life a little easier.

The space I eventually rented, as I was saying, was a few feet of concrete floor with an army cot in a huge room—barracks style—with a hundred other guys as pathetic as myself. The place was noisy, my God. Even after lights out at ten o'clock it was pretty noisy, the coughing, the snoring, the sudden screams from a nightmare. I hung out in diners with other ex-drinkers knocking back cup after cup of bitter coffee until finally there was nothing else to do but go "home."

I tried not to feel sorry for myself, I tried to take "an attitude of gratitude," as the people at the meetings advised me to do. I took all advice seriously, even advice that rhymed. I made a grat-itude list and tried not to think how pathetic I seemed even to my-self. I took out a ballpoint and a small pad and began to write, sitting on the edge of my bunk. I haven't had a drink today, I wrote on my list. That was always my first item. Okay, and my health was returning, I continued. That was two things I was grateful for. Three, the YMCA sheets were clean each night. There were big fans; they were noisy as an airport runway, it was true, but they kept the place cool enough. So that was an-other thing to be grateful for.

I wasn't really grateful, or if I was, only for short periods. That fucking fan was a stretch for even the most liberal gratitude list. This was summertime in Pittsburgh, a sauna of a town, trapped in a naturally heated cauldron between three boiling rivers, the Allegheny, the Monongahela, and I think the third one is the Styx. And who cared if the Y met some minimum health standards, Jesus. Somebody ought to record the snoring in that fucking place. It's one of the Wonders of the World.

Back to my list. I was never hungry, that was another thing I could write down. I ate well enough, and could pinch pennies at the same time. You could get a hot meal at the Y for fifty cents, usually soup or macaroni and cheese, and a hunk of bread and butter and usually Kool-Aid. So yeah, I was grateful for the food. I could write this part without feeling resentful. The food really wasn't bad, especially on those days when the crowd was down and I could find a quiet bench at one of the long tables where I didn't have to sit beside some soup-slurping motherfucker wielding his spoon and crust of bread like weapons against the enemy. The chicken soup was excellent, the vegetable beef had barley in it, which I didn't like so much, but it was okay too.

I finished the list. It was a pretty good gratitude list for somebody who was essentially down and out in Pittsburgh. As an afterthought I added Catholic hospitals to my list. Mercy Hospital, in the Uptown section, especially. If you're ever really hungry, you can always go to a Catholic hospital and they'll feed you. Catholic hospitals can be counted on to be decent places when the rest of the world is going to hell. You won't hear me complaining about the Catholics, ever.

These gratitude lists were a way of reminding myself that

things could have been worse. Things had been worse, in fact, very recently. I finished my list. I felt better. I was grateful. What the hell.

ONE WEEKEND AS DORRIS and Helga and I were sitting together at the Laundromat, something happened that sparked a change in my living circumstances. Dorris and Helga were big readers, and so, as we always did, we were all sitting there in the Highland Park Laundromat reading novels, side by side. The machines were going, the chairs were pretty uncomfortable, but in fact I was feeling happy in the company of my new friends. I was reading *A Fan's Notes* and considering my next gratitude list. I was grateful I wasn't as bad off as the poor drunk in the book, that was something to be grateful for, and I was also thinking I would include Dorris and Helga in my next list. I was truly grateful for the time we spent together. The fact that they were literary people was a part of what appealed to me, though their tastes were old-fashioned and frankly a little odd. Dorris read Tolstoy almost exclusively—"The sweep, the panorama!" he would suddenly exclaim, "the fragile single hearts!"—and Helga always had clutched in her huge prison-guard hands some delicate volume of poetry, Rilke or Lord knows what else. Sometimes she would look up from her reading and her face would be beatific, it's the only word that really describe her. She might read a line or two aloud to the two of us, something about the springtime greenness of the trees coming into leaf being a form of grief, and her voice would catch, her eyes would become moist, and then she would fall silent again, and look again deep into her book as if into deep clear water. Such comfortable, sweet moments occurred to the accompaniment of the coin changer as it dispensed silver in a casinolike bursts of generosity, and to the easy evensong of the dryers, the abrupt gush of water in the Fill cycle, the dogged and determined chuffing of Wash, or the reckless centrifugal abandon of Spin.

One day in the midst of this music, the elfin Dorris and his strapping wife asked whether I would like to share supper with them that night in their home. This was the first time either had suggested broadening the range of our relationship, and it came to me like an incredible gift. A home, a real home, like the one I had lost.

"Yes," I said, "oh yes, yes, yes, thank you, yes." Later, after a fragrant lamb stew that Helga had prepared in their little kitchen, with its red-checkered cafe curtains, the three of us sat in their den and took off our shoes and put up our feet and chatted quietly until we were all talked out, sleepy and scarcely able to move from our chairs with a drowsy pleasant lethargy. Dorris and Helga sat together on an ancient leather sofa and I took the matching easy chair.

Their next offer was an answered prayer. They invited me to move out of the YMCA and into their spare room. The room had no furniture, they warned, not even a bed, and I would be obliged to sleep on the floor, but without a moment's hesitation I said yes, again, yes, yes, oh God yes, thank you, yes.

Need I bother to say that I overlooked many signals that might have clued me that this would turn out to be a bad idea? The most obvious of these was that to prepare the stew Helga had worn a sort of costume. While Dorris and I sat in the den and chatted, Helga busied herself in the kitchen and indeed cooked the entire meal while wearing stiletto heels and the frilly apron, and the fishnet stockings and the dustcap of a French maid in a farce. This was all she wore while she cooked. The daintiness of the costume emphasized the manly height and bulk of her stature. I had seen this, taken mental note of the lunatic oddity of it, and yet the instant the offer came, I agreed to move in to their spare room.

It did not occur to me to use this information to help me make a decision about staying the night, or indeed moving in with this strange couple. There being no bed for me did not even register with me as an unusual detail. I can't explain this satisfactorily except to say that in a sense Helga was always in costume, her clothing never suited her enormous physical presence in any space she occupied. The French maid costume was certainly her most extravagant offering, but not essentially different from her many other fashion choices. I had overlooked much already; this was merely one more thing.

Or maybe the only explanation that anyone needs is that anything on earth would have seemed more normal than an army cot at the Y. Even an attitude of gratitude could not cancel the YMCA barracks and what it told me about how far I had fallen. I would have overlooked anything to escape my current reality, the "life on life's terms." Dorris and Helga, eccentric though they might have been, were the lemons life was dealing me to make lemonade.

That really must have been what I told myself, if I told myself anything at all. Or maybe—this of course is in terrible hindsight—I was preparing for that most abnormal state of all, which I was soon to enter, to be a parent at the graveside of his child. That, however, is another story, one that I have already told as well as I know how.

Helga provided me with a pillow and a blanket, and so there on the hardwood floor for the first time I rested my grateful bones and soon I was asleep. No mattress had ever seemed so comfortable as that solid slab of wood. I scarcely turned over during the night. I woke rested and well. Dorris and Helga were still asleep behind the closed door of their bedroom. I folded my blanket and put it with my pillow in a corner of the room. I dressed and left the house and made my way downtown to the Y, where I unloaded my locker into a duffel bag and stood at the corner near Market Square and grabbed a PAT bus and moved fully into my new digs. I had a new home, a real home in a real house.

I saw little of Dorris and Helga during the day, it turned out. For various reasons, some of my own doing, we saw each other only slightly more often than before I moved in. For one thing, I didn't want to become a Ramon-style boarder. Mornings they came from their room, but they said little and only moved slowly about the house. I followed their lead and was a silent shadow in their midst. There was a crude, cold-water shower and toilet and a big shard of mirror in the cellar where I made my morning ablutions, and this was fine with me. We began to coexist. I felt very free to take my turn in the real bathroom of this house, but I preferred cold water and privacy for now to almost any other comforts of home. This new arrangement was so far superior to my recent communal showers at the Y as to leave me giddy with gratitude.

My usual routine was to rise early and to walk to a regular early meeting in a church basement nearby. First Things First was the name of the 7 A.M. meeting that I liked. The same people usually showed up, only a few early risers, so it was an especially comfortable place to have my morning coffee. Dorris and Helga were usually still asleep when I left the house. After the meeting I went with a few other guys, "recovering alcoholics," as we called ourselves, to Ritter's Diner for eggs. Wednesday mornings there was a meeting right there in the diner, in a back room, where the diner supplied the coffee and you could order breakfast. This section of Pittsburgh is full of shady streets and flowering gardens and small home-owned businesses and friendly faces. It was within walking distance of my new home. By the time I had finished breakfast, the day had begun to heat up and I had said good-bye to my breakfast companions and was sitting in my nicely ventilated room at Dorris and Helga's place, cross-legged on the floor in front of my Smith-Corona with a sheet of paper rolled in, and life was good.

Oh life was very good. I had my own key, so I came and went freely. Dorris and Helga were out, usually, by this time. They both had jobs. What could have been more fine? I made a point of taking all my meals outside the house, so as not to impose upon my hosts' hospitality, and this arrangement worked very well. Evenings when Helga and Dorris were home, together the three of us sat and watched the evening news and chatted quietly, and then usually we turned off the TV and sat and read in silence until bedtime. Helga's costumes were never so extreme again as when she prepared dinner that first night, but usually she did seem more or less outlandishly attired. She had an outfit I thought of as her milkmaid costume, with a bonnet and apron and wooden pail, and another I am not sure how to characterize but possibly Mennonite, or maybe only a country librarian. It was hard to say. I was shy to question her about this game of dress-up that she seemed always to be playing, though I often complimented the way she looked, and always she thanked me. Once or twice she said something like, "I hope this doesn't just seem silly to you" or "You don't think this one goes a little too far, do you," and always I would assure her, "No, absolutely not, not at all."

After I had lived in this home thus serenely for perhaps three weeks, Dorris took me aside one day and showed me an expensive toy of sorts that apparently he had owned for some time. This was the first time their eccentricity took on what might have been an unhealthy, or possibly dangerous, quality. Helga was not in the house when this initial conversation occurred, as Dorris had made certain, for this little talk, Dorris's body language seemed to say, was just between us men. He invited me into his and Helga's bedroom, where at the foot of their big bed stood an old-fashioned steamer trunk, with wooden bands and leather straps and a big brass lock. He closed the bedroom door discreetly behind us and went immediately to the trunk, which he unlocked, a little mysteriously I have to say.

"Helga has a key, too, of course," he assured me, unnecessarily.

Out of the trunk he lifted, when the great lid was open, what seemed to be a dark metal box about three feet square. Extending from the box, attached to it somehow, octopuslike, were several dangling flexible "arms," flopping this way and that, chaotically, as he transferred the box from the steamer trunk to the made-up bed, where he placed it on the quilt that covered the bed. The box reminded me strongly of the robot on the old *Lost in Space* TV show, the one that was forever flopping its arms about and saying, "Danger, Will Robinson. Danger!" In fact, from somewhere deep inside me I thought I heard a similar warning, equally urgent, "Danger, Buddy Nordan. Danger!" There was also, I noticed, a cord and plug dangling down, so that the box could be plugged into an electrical socket in the wall. This was some kind of machine, I was beginning to realize.

"I don't show many people this baby," Dorris confided to me.

I could think of nothing to say, nothing at all. I spent my days talking to people who were trying to make sense of their alcohol-shattered lives. In meetings and over coffee we spoke of God's grace and of service to others and making amends for the wreckage of our past. We "worked steps" that we believed, on faith and on observation of others like us, would lead not merely to a sober life but to spiritual awakenings in our drug-deadened selves. In my most peaceful hours I breathed the damp air of church basements. I visited Veterans Administration hospitals and prisons and halfway houses and rehabs and detox units in hopes of offering comfort to someone like myself and thereby acquiring one more day's sobriety for myself. I ate doughnuts and drank coffee and prayed on my knees to stay sober one day at a time. None of what I did during a day prepared me for this moment. Indeed, in my solitary hours I wrote stories about a boy who longs for his alcoholic father's love in Mississippi. I identified as much with the father as the son. Weekends I stood in a phone booth on a corner and talked to my own sons, whose hearts I feared I had broken. What did I know of black boxes drawn from a steamer trunk? What, in fact, was I doing in Pittsburgh, where I was less than merely a new person, I was an alien being?

I looked at the box on the bed. The flexible arms of the mechanical octopus—the robot, whatever it was—were fitted with one of two types of devices at the end. One was a funnel-shaped affair, and the other was a smaller connecting attachment. I could make no sense of any of it. Dorris plugged the box into the wall socket and left it on the bed and went back to the steamer trunk. He bent down and this time he pulled out of the trunk, like a rabbit from a magician's hat, a large, flat, black leather case of a certain kind, a sort of portfolio-like affair, that he laid out on the bed and then flung open with a flourish.

I'd seen a couple of movies and TV shows in which big-city

black-market gunrunners displayed their samples of handguns in much the same way, in a similar case. When the leather case was open fully, it could be seen to be fitted on the inside with clear plastic pockets, just like the cases the black-marketeers used to display their wares, but whatever it was I was looking at in these pockets, they were not firearms. I couldn't tell what they were, at the time. My eyes took in the images but my mind would not translate what I saw.

There were nine clear plastic pockets, three across, three up and three down. Each pocket held a single solid brick-red-colored cylinder of some kind, each exactly alike except in size. Each cylinder, from left to right, grew progressively diminished in size. The first cylinder in the first pocket was a foot long, approximately, and nine or ten inches in diameter. The others were smaller, down to the ninth pocket, which held a cylinder only two or three inches long and thin as a pencil. Dorris removed the first of these, the largest, from its pocket and showed it to me.

Realization came to me with dizzying force. Perfectly and realistically shaped artificial penises in nine sizes, brick-red in color, as I said. Big red cocks, nine of them, on display, count them for yourself.

Dorris unsnapped the first pocket in the case, as I said, and brought out the largest dildo and held it in his open palm. He proffered it to me. I stood with my hands at my side, unable to move just yet. He squeezed it and opened his palm again. He kept holding it out, in my direction.

"Take a look at this baby," he said, extending it to me. "Go ahead, take it, give it a squeeze."

As if I were a robot myself instead of a man who prayed each morning and each night and spoke of a Power Greater Than Myself and believed, however clumsily, that God's grace had taken away my self-destructive compulsion to drink alcohol, I took the foot-long cock into my own hand, I held it, I tested its heft and bulk, I gave it a squeeze. I offer no explanation or apology. The dildo was made of high quality hard red rubber. It was firm and well-veined and the head was large and well-shaped with a small opening in the tip. I looked at the big cock there in my hand. I squeezed it again.

I said, "Yeah, that's something, all right."

Dorris took the rubber cock from me and confidently attached it to the end of one of the octopus arms fitted with a connecting device, not a funnel. It snapped securely into place. He held it up briefly for me to see, as much as to say "Voila." He reached then for a switch on the fucking machine—for this is the name I learned to call it by, this black box—and clicked it into the On position, and immediately a sound issued from the box that was both unnerving and self-explanatory. I knew it for what it was, I knew this gasp and grunt to be the sound of an air compressor, plain and simple. Inside the black box a motor was operating a small compressor and pump that, in turn, operated the octopus arms of the machine, and therefore the dildo attachment. The sound that it made was at once a sigh and a groan, slow and as filled with sexual resignation and guilty desire as a sound from human lungs and throat.

Dorris said, "I like to think of it as the Amazing Technicolor Fucking Machine." I managed not even a smile at this joke, though some sort of sound did issue from my mouth, something low and indescribable. Now when he handed the foot-long rubber cock back to me I had to hold on tight, for compressed air pumping through the flexible arm in short bursts caused the dildo to take life. The machine gasped and sighed, the cock in my hand squirmed and pulsed, it took up a regular stroking motion, and I had to hold it tight in my hand to keep it from jumping away from me.

Dorris may have noticed my discomfort, for he took the dildo from me and tossed it lightly onto the quilt on the bed, where the huge red cock pulsed and squirmed and stroked empty air, seeming almost to crawl across the covers of the bed in search of something.

We said nothing, either of us, for what seemed to me a very long time. We only stood and watched the dildo, and listened to the disturbing sounds of the machine that drove it.

At last he did speak. He said, "Some day, when you feel comfortable of course, not a minute before, I hope you'll slip one of these cocks into Helga. She'd like that very much, you know."

I couldn't speak. I could only stand and watch the slow strokes of the dildo across the covers of the bed. By my silence I must have seemed to give my assent. Dorris went on talking about the machine. He told me everything. You could fuck eight people at a time on the machine, he wanted me to know. Four women and four men. The funnel-shaped devices at the ends of four of the arms were for men to put their cocks into. Through those hoses a suction was created, so the machine would suck you off. "Theoretically it will suck you off," he added, a little ruefully. "In practice it's a little more complicated."

He explained that although women could just eyeball the size dildo they preferred at a given time, a special sleeve had to be fitted and designed especially for each individual real penis that wanted to use the fucking machine. The machine came with special instructions for how to measure an erect penis—the instructions warned that the most common mistake was to exaggerate the size of the penis—and then a sleeve would be made and immediately shipped to the customer. Only an exact fit would insure the vacuum necessary to the sucking motion of the machine. One mistake was allowed per cock, but after that an extra charge would be levied.

"If you're at all interested . . ." he said.

Still I could not speak and so he deftly dropped the subject.

He and Helga had taken the fucking machine to a Swingers Club meeting once, he told me, and one woman agreed to try it out, but "All in all, I'd have to say it didn't go over particularly well."

THIS WAS THE LIFE I was living when I met Annie and fell in love. On weekends I would fuck Helga, first with the Amazing Technicolor Fucking Machine, and then with my own cock. After she had come, her large body would sprawl so fully across the bed and take up so much room that only she could lie there. I would be edged off onto the floor, or more commonly, I would simply rise guiltily and shamefully and go into the shower and cry and throw up and leave her there. Dorris never joined us in the bed, thank God, though he was the sole operator of the machine itself, which had several speeds, it turned out, and so either Helga or I would, from time to time, say something like, "Let's kick it up to seven, see what that looks like," or words to that effect.

I may have stopped drinking, I may have learned to speak seriously of spiritual growth and to pray each day, but my life seemed still far from within my own poor powers to manage, and so it was mainly a fantasy, I suppose, that Annie's beauty and her ability to draw laughter from my broken spirit would be enough to heal all that was sick inside me.

Nevertheless, it was true love, this much I knew to be true,

that first time I saw Annie in a smoky room in a church basement, I'll never waver in that belief, and it was immediate, love
at first sight, as I've said, and it required that I take control of
my life on a level beyond just "not drinking." It meant I had to
move out, I knew this. Dorris and Helga—I would pray for
them. Now the YMCA as an item on my gratitude list seemed altogether just and appropriate. The raucous cacophony of snores
no longer irritated me, it filled me with laughter and joy.

I was no great catch, I admit. Annie was manna from
heaven, and with miracles I was not inclined to argue.

18

The First Annual Pittsburgh Marathon

THERE IS A PHOTOGRAPH of me, which I look at from time to time because it reminds me of those days when Annie and I first began to make a life together. The snapshot was taken as I was standing in a crowd of people watching runners pass by in the first annual Pittsburgh Marathon. A few of the runners are visible within the frame, with shorts and tank tops and large white placards with their registration numbers pinned to their shirts. You can sense the holiday atmosphere. The sun is shining, spectators are smiling, cheering, holding out paper cups of Gatorade, couples stand together arm in arm, some have baby strollers nearby, others have dogs on leashes. If you could see just outside the frame of the picture you'd see Mellon Park, green and fragrant, enclosed in a high iron fence. You'd see big hardwoods with new greenery, the last of the late tulips. You'd see children playing on a green hillside, you'd see dogs chasing Frisbees, picnickers opening lunches on the marble remains of the old Mellon estate. Farther outside the frame, you'd see a circling news helicopter, and graceful, elegant hot-air balloons floating far above the crowd in many colors and stripes and shapes. One balloon looks like a gigantic can of I.C. Light beer. Police motorcycles are also parked nearby. If you used your imagination you could hear the crackle of their two-way radios, you could hear the cheers of the crowd, the blast of the hot-air torches beneath the balloons, a car engine revving up, the barking of a dog. Far away from the frame, the Kenyans are winning the marathon, taking first and second. No one can see them, they are so far ahead of the pack.

Though my image is at the center of the photograph, I am the one thing in the scene that does not seem to fit—it looks like I've been cut out and pasted into a second picture as a joke. I am a glum figure, the only person dressed in a jacket and tie. I seem to be watching the race, but with no pleasure. Perhaps I am only waiting to cross the street. Or more likely I belong in some other picture altogether and am looking at something else entirely. Actually, the camera had captured me walking home from church on the only day that year I was in attendance. At church I had been praying, as well as I knew how, for my son Robin, who had not been seen for three days. Elizabeth had called from Arkansas to give me the bad news that he had dropped out of sight.

The photograph cannot hold the days that follow. The time went by so slowly it seemed as if an entire summer were passing, though it was less than this. The loan came through for the house Annie and I wanted to buy. We went to the closing, we signed the papers. The house was old and in bad shape, so we borrowed a few more dollars and had a guy put up some dry-wall. He was a jack-of-all-trades, so we had him install a small bathroom upstairs as well. We went on living in a rented house in the same neighborhood while the remodeling was being done. Annie's children didn't want to move, they told us. They said they wouldn't go, they would live full-time with their father. She and I got into fights about money. We got into fights with each other and with the children about many things. We stuffed clothes into bags and stored them in the new house. The same with a few pieces of furniture. Everything we owned looked tawdry. The roof sagged, we now noticed. We didn't have enough money for new carpeting, so we borrowed more money at 22 percent interest. Annie lost her job and went on unemployment. I talked to Robin's mother and brother daily. We used phrases like "Missing Persons Reports" and "All Points Bulletins." Rumors emerged about Robin's whereabouts. Somebody thought they'd seen him riding in a blue car. His own car was a silver Prelude. Silver might be called blue, so maybe it really was Robin. I felt hopeful.

One day the mailman rang the doorbell and told us there was water running out the front door of the house we had just bought three blocks away. It was true. Water was flooding out the door. A pipe in the new second floor jury-rigged bathroom had broken. The ceiling had collapsed onto the new drywall downstairs. The furniture and clothing we had stored there were drenched. The carpeting that we couldn't afford was ruined, along with the electrical fixtures. Nothing was insured. I found the water cutoff. We swept water out the door. We sopped up water with towels, turned fans on the soggy carpeting. We went back to our rented house. We worried about money. The phone rang. It was Elizabeth, down in Arkansas. Robin's body had been found by hikers in the deep woods. A green plastic garden hose ran from the exhaust pipe of his car, in through the window. The crack in the window was sealed with a coat that he had stuffed there. A note had decomposed along with the body. Dental records were used in the identification. That's what happened.

BEFORE ROBIN WAS BORN Elizabeth and I moved into a spanking new subdivision in Indian River, Florida, where we had taken jobs right out of college. The house was built of concrete blocks, there were oleander bushes in the front yard and a little lemon tree behind the kitchen. The house across the street was a mirror image of our own.

The main thing was, the house had a small bedroom on the front that would be perfect for a nursery. The plans we had begun making in college were still our favorite avocation. A crib would fit there on this wall, we agreed, a small chest of drawers on an adjacent wall, a changing table and Bathinette here and here. We would get a rug, a rocking chair, a diaper pail.

The room was well furnished in our minds long before we bought a single piece of furniture, or for that matter long before Elizabeth was pregnant. The room was airy and light, the windows were on the west side of the house, so the morning sun would not wake the baby rudely or too early. Curtains, of course. Elizabeth would make curtains for the room herself. We would pick out the fabric together. This would be perfect for the baby, who, of course, we had already named Robin. Should we buy a camera? We made plans with this degree of certainty. The romance of marriage and children that we had begun in college had encountered its bumps, its imperfections, since our drive to Livingston, Alabama, in the Lincoln Town Car that day in April, but reality had not as yet made the slightest inroads on that romance.

Sometimes when I think of the two of us then, Elizabeth and me, I almost forget to grieve for Robin, and think only of those two kids that we were, so hopeful in love. We lived then in our dreams, only there. The scraggly little lemon tree in our backyard, the new-sodded yard, the white-washed concrete block.

Good lord, my old heart breaks for us. If this sounds like retro-active self-pity, well, so be it. I love those kids we were.

The room I was describing—the baby's room, we already called it—was our life then. No other space in the house inter-ested us so much as this. Indeed no other part of the house in-terested us at all. Not once when we were looking to buy did we consider the size of the rooms, the convenience or inconvenience of the kitchen arrangement, the completely stupid placement of the "bath and a half" right next to each other. Not when we walked through the "model home," not when we drew out of the bank the five hundred dollars we had borrowed from Eliza-beth's father, not when we signed the mortgage papers. Having a baby—living up to the terms of the romance on which we had made the most important decisions of our lives—that was all we were thinking of.

I want to divert their tragedy, these hopeful kids, the erosion of their dream, the loss of illusion, the devices of habitual love that will break their romantic backs. They believed that by dreaming beautifully, they were safe. They didn't know yet that dreaming well, and even living well, are insufficient protection. I wish I could take them aside and tell them. They would do nothing differently, I know. Even if they could see the future, I suspect they would go on with their hopes intact. Who could have believed a vision of a future world that did not include their happiness and the beauty and health of their child?

I can't imagine the world without Robin—or rather, I can well imagine the world without him, since he is not here and will never be here, but I cannot imagine a world that never held him, heard his silver laugh, beheld his pickerel smile.

19

The Family Oven

THERE USED TO BE a place on Negley Avenue in Pittsburgh called the Family Oven. It's gone now, but around the time of Robin's death, it was prominent. A lot of working-class families went there for a meal. It was a greasy-spoon sort of place, not bad— liver and onions, meat loaf with gravy, chicken potpie, breakfast any time of day, unlimited coffee refills, that sort of thing. I chose the Family Oven as a spot to break up with Susan. Susan was a girl I slept with a few times after Robin died. The Family Oven was the kind of place I knew she would like to break up in.

Let me just say, I'm not proud of this affair I was having with Susan. Annie was badly hurt when she found out. It's a miserable thing to have to tell about yourself. I had lots of good excuses at the time for needing to have this affair, I'm sure. I don't really remember what my excuses were, to tell the truth, except that I blamed Annie. Susan was the same age as my poor dead son, a fact I scarcely took notice of at the time. I was consumed with guilt and knew that finally I had to do the right thing and break up with her.

We had done this before. Susan was young and hippified and homesick for her alcoholic father in Delaware, and so in a perverse romantic way places like the Family Oven seemed "homey" to her, they simulated happy homes. Once we broke up in Ritter's Diner over homemade apple cobbler, and another time in Market Square at a place called Diamond's, which had cafe curtains and a waitress with a black eye.

The Family Oven had tiled floors and high-backed booths and wood-grain paneling on the walls. Lonely old men in shirtsleeves sat at the counter over heavy cups of steaming coffee. A disfigured waitress served them with a smile, a flirtatious remark. The manager, maybe the owner, of the place was short and barrel-chested and heavy-eyebrowed. He patrolled the tables and booths and spoke in a kindly way to everyone. There was (always, it seemed) a sad struggling family trying to secure a baby in a high chair. There were lantern-style chandeliers hanging over each booth. So it might have seemed like a home to anyone as lost and youthful as Susan. At the time Susan was twenty and I was forty-eight, and of course I had not been married for very long to Annie, my new dark-eyed, dark-haired wife, who could only watch from a sort of faraway sideline as I played out the black game of my desperation.

Susan and I sat at one of the tables by the window. She knew what was coming. Across Negley Avenue, where we looked out the window, there was a squat whitewashed building with BABY-LAND painted in large letters across the front. From where we sat we could look into Babyland's show window and see bassinets and bath tables and baby furniture.

It was time for the right words, words that would make me a good man, a faithful husband once again. I said, "Susan, I want you to know how much you have meant to me over these past eight or nine months."

Susan had ordered coffee and filled the cup with sugar and milk until it overflowed into the saucer. She lifted the cup and placed a paper napkin into the overflow and I watched it become stained and soggy with the milk-white coffee.

I said, "Here, I'll throw that wet napkin away."

She said, "No, it's okay," and set the cup down on the napkin. She stirred the coffee and left the spoon in the cup and drank around the spoon.

I said, "I don't know what I would have done without you during these months."

She said, "You're giving me the ax again, aren't you?" She was looking out the window at Babyland. She put her cup down on the soggy napkin again, and I reached over and took the spoon out and put it on the table beside her cup.

I said, "Susan, I wish you wouldn't use that expression, 'giving me the ax,' okay?"

She said, "I don't care if you give me the ax. You can give me the ax a million times and I'll still love you."

The coffee mess was too much for me. I picked up the saucer and the wet napkin and walked from our table to the counter and asked the waitress for a clean saucer. Not the disfigured waitress, the younger one. She didn't change expression, only swooped up the saucer and shoved it beneath the counter with a clatter and placed a clean saucer before me. I thanked her and walked back to the table where Susan was waiting.

I resolved to start over, gain firmer purchase on my intentions. I said, "Susan, darling—"

She said, "I like it when you give me the ax." She was serious. She said, "Giving me the ax always makes you feel better about yourself. All I ever wanted was for you to be happy."

I said, "Please respect my wishes in this, Susan, and stop using that expression, please."

She said, "The number of times you give me the ax is the measure of your love for Annie. I love you for loving Annie enough to give me the ax so many times."

I said, "Jesus, Susan. It makes me feel terrible to give you the ax. Really, terrible."

Susan cried for a short time, deeply but without much sound. She said, "I've never loved anyone so much in my life as I love you."

I knew that Susan was not entirely sane—maybe it is more accurate to say she had no balance in her life—and it was impossible not to want to hold her and tell her I loved her, even though I didn't.

I said, "I love you, Susan."

In a few minutes she had finished crying. She blew her nose on a napkin and smiled a small smile. She said, "You don't love me." There was no bitterness in her voice, only sweetness and sacrifice. She said, "You love the way you feel when you are with me. You love to be adored."

I looked at Susan and thought that I did love her. She was tall and slender and green-eyed and flat-chested and her hair was cut very short. She cut her hair herself—chopped at it with shears—and she called it her mongoloid idiot cut. For all her beauty, she did look a little moronic. Her earrings were blue plastic replicas of the Empire State Building, and her clothes were all purchased at Goodwill. Some days she asked me to call her Ruby or Myrtle and to pretend that she was a beauty-parlor operator in McKees Rocks. Other days she was Tish or Twinky and pretended to have lost her virginity to a boy named Shep at the Yacht Club dance—(I don't claim to understand this)—and to have twin sons named St. Elmo and Sharky.

I said, "No, I do love you."

I did love her, in a way, and I wanted to stop cheating on Annie.

We went on drinking our coffee. The waitress had filled Susan's cup again, and Susan overflowed it again with milk. Another soggy, stained napkin soaked up liquid in her saucer. She was still drinking around her spoon.

I asked Susan if she wanted something to eat. She said no, no thank you, and then after a few seconds, as if she had thought of an alternative to food, she said, "I want to have a baby."

I knew she had been looking at Babyland, and at the family with the baby in a high chair, and at the rest of the pathetic, sentimental hominess of the Family Oven, and I knew that all of it must have been working on her, but I was a little frightened anyway.

I said, "Honey, you're, uh, you're not pregnant, are you?"

She looked up at me around her spoon and finished taking another slurp of coffee and then said, "Like fun I am."

She was so *young*.

She said, "Don't I wish."

I had to end this affair. I had known before I came here that it had to be done, and now I was even more certain. Susan would go on with it forever if I didn't end it, she would hang on until it killed her.

I said, "There has to be some kind of closure." I had been in therapy for a while and had learned to talk this way.

She said, "I know."

I said, "I want to put closure on this by telling you I love you."

She said, "I know, I love you too."

I said, "You gave me what no one else could have. You held me when my need was boundless." I was beginning to enjoy the sound of my voice. I said—added unnecessarily and untruthfully—"Our minds and bodies are perfect together."

Susan did not speak. She knew the value of silences. The waitress filled up her cup again, and again Susan overflowed it and piled another soggy napkin into the soggy mess in her saucer. It was the napkin she had blown her nose into.

I tested my voice again. I said, "You were my mother and my wife and my sister and my friend." I began to feel light-headed. I believed I was wonderful with closure.

Susan knew what to do. She said, "Our lives are a single line in time. We grew up together as children." She was good at this too. She said, "I have lived your whole life in quietness."

In that moment I loved Susan, I knew I did, and I wanted the words to go on forever, no matter how preposterous. The words were their own truth. I said, "It's beyond sex, our love is more than sex."

We held hands across the table.

I said, "Our tragedy is our comedy." What the hell was I talking about? I had gone too far now. I knew I had lost control, that I was making no sense, but I couldn't shut up. I said, "You'll always reside in the sunniest, most joyful hemisphere of my soul."

I didn't care what I meant. Even in the awareness of the meaninglessness of these words, I could believe them, their cadence and sound if not their content and meaning. The words were an event that would substitute for the event in front of me, this adulterous affair with a girl-woman less than half my age.

I said, in the hope of calming down some, but still possessed by the voice-demon in my throat, "Let's leave here, Susan. We will kiss once, and that will be our good-bye." I stood up and she stood to follow me. I said, "We will never see each other again. We won't call, we won't write. We will be completed in spirit, forever alive in one another."

She said, helpfully, "No words."

I said, "None."

She said, "No sex."

I said, "There will be no need."

She said, "I love you."

I said, "Oh, Susan, I love you, I love you so purely, so passionately, so innocently, so much like loving a perfection of myself."

We were walking to the cash register where the bushy-eyebrowed little owner/manager was standing, as if he were waiting only for us, as if we fulfilled some sweet fantasy of a father and daughter appropriate to the dreams he had once dreamed of this homey, sweet place of business. To see him stand there, expectant and beautiful, decent and hopeful, made me love him and made me love the Family Oven, as if it really were the home he had tried to simulate, the home Susan was forever falling in love with in its many Pittsburgh incarnations, Ritter's and Diamond's and God knows what other places of homecooking and disfigurement. It made me wish there was a God, it made me hope with such desperation that there was one that I believed in this moment heart and soul that I was capable of being touched, in touch with such a spirit, one with the power to lift even the burden of grief. I remembered, once after Susan

and I had made love on the mattress on the floor of her apartment (in an uncanny déjà vu of Twyla's dreadful mattress)—
Susan's incredible apartment, by the way, her filthy, messy, upside-
down dump of an apartment, with its unnatural-looking, frilly,
gauzy-pink curtains at the window, its utter absence of furniture save only the bare mattress and a discarded, broken bathroom sink, which Susan seriously referred to as her "sink
sculpture"—we were lying there and Susan was examining, lovingly, my naked, middle-aged body, spent from the exertion of
sex and more frail than I had imagined I would be at forty-eight,
"I look at you and think you are Christ."

At the time I had been embarrassed and appalled, and yet
now, suddenly, as I was about to pay the check at the Family
Oven cash register, I found that I did feel Christ-like. I started to
tell Susan that loving her was like loving God. I didn't say this.
Not yet.

As I had this thought, I turned from the smiling little man
who was about to take my money and whose eyes were filled
with love and approval for me and the girl he must have mis-
taken for my daughter, and I grabbed Susan's hand and, in an instant, on an impulse, I turned from the counter and the cash
register and the foil-wrapped mints and cheap cigars and the
newspaper rack, and I pulled Susan with me into the Pine Sol ef-
fulgence of the men's room, and shut and locked the door.

I don't know what I meant by this impulsive gesture. In many
ways the things I did, both large and small, seemed entirely out
of my control during this time. I found myself frequently, as in
this moment, an amazed spectator at my own actions. I wanted
to hide away from the world, I suppose, lock myself in. Susan
was simply a hostage, as she had been from the beginning.

Almost immediately someone was knocking on the door.

Knock knock knock knock knock. Rapid, frantic, insistent knocking. I was not safe at all but simply trapped. I looked at Susan, to say I'm sorry, to make some sufficient apology by dragging her into this mess, but her eyes told me she needed no apology at all, she was having a wonderful time, she thought our locking ourselves in a public men's room was a fine adventure, appropriate in every way.

Knock knock knock knock. The knocking was even more persistent than before, louder and maybe angry. Knock knock knock knock knock. Blam blam blam blam blam. It was loud and fierce now. I was paralyzed with fear and shame. Susan said, "Lock it, man. That sucker'll never get us in here."

Knock knock knock knock knock.

Very briefly I believed the visitor at the door might be someone who loved me. I believed it might be Robin.

As soon as this though entered my head, the knocking stopped. Completely stopped, the way the winds are supposed to fall still in the eye of a hurricane. The no-knocking was louder, far angrier sounding than the knocking had been. Nothing. And then nothing nothing nothing nothing nothing.

The pain of grief had never been worse than in this moment. Fully half of me believed that Robin was standing outside the door, ready to say, "It's all been a mistake. I'm alive." The other half of me—

I said, "I hate to open that door."

Susan said, "Yeah, this is fun."

I said, "No, I mean I hate to face whoever is out there."

She said, "They went away."

I unlocked the door and opened it.

Robin was not there, of course. He was dead and would never return. This bad fact was more clear to me than it had ever been. There lay the restaurant. There the glass-topped counter, its foil-wrapped mints, its cigars and cash register. There was the disfigured waitress, there the chandeliers above the booths.

Susan was right in one sense, anyway. No one was waiting to admonish me or arrest me or be repelled by me. There sat the asthmatic old men and their coffee, there the families, across Negley Avenue gleamed Babyland and a world of hope and fertility. Susan was right about that too. Babies should be born into the world, innocence should multiply. There was no one outside the fearsome door! No one beyond the smells of Pine Sol and Clorox and the Double-Buddy toilet-paper holder. It was a miracle, the grace of Susan's innocent optimism, proof of the goodness and loving kindness at the core of the dark, hurtful world so filled with evil surprise.

I walked out of the rest room and took my wallet from my pocket and put money on the counter for our coffee. The disfigured waitress took my money but did not smile at me, did not look at me. I looked down the line of old men for one who might be my dead son in disguise. No one looked at me. No one did I recognize.

I took my change from the disfigurement—she was surly and inhospitable—and I looked past her just in time to see the manager of the restaurant come through the kitchen door.

He was furious. And somehow shorter and heavier-browed than before. He had been the knocker at the bathroom door—there was no denying this fact any longer—and now he was back.

The dear man was speechless with revulsion and disbelief. And then, somehow, it was over. Susan and I were out of the restaurant, in the parking lot, in the noise of traffic, in the early spring humidity and haze, in my car with the doors slammed shut and the windows rolled up—my terrible car, an orange Pinto, fifteen years old and probably explosive.

And then we were backing out of the parking lot. Susan was driving and I was in the seat beside her, staring straight ahead and numb with strange pain—and then turning on to Negley, and for a moment I knew I was lost and I believed I would have to die of this failure, this preposterous fantasy of innocence that was, after all, only the same sick, selfish unmanageability of my long unmanageable life raised to yet another exponential power and disguised as something as decent as a family's business and a family's decent pride in it.

We left the Family Oven behind us and finally out of sight. We drove across the East End of Pittsburgh, and for a long time neither of us spoke, only drove without direction or destination. I wondered how my life on earth could have started with such hope and now have come to so little as this. Could I have really been that child in a Superman costume the day the television set arrived? How had my life come from there to here?

I said all this to Susan.

She said, "It was funny."

I said, "It was not funny, Susan."

She said, "I was laughing, man. Whoo. I thought it was funny."

She believed that such a moment was an indication of the spontaneity and unexpectedness of love, that for us to have done such a thing was a good and hopeful sign for the world of lovers.

When she told me this, I said, "It would have been all you say—but only if I had done it with Annie and not with you."

She drove in silence for a minute. She said, "It is anyway. It's funny, and it's good."

I had hurt her, and I didn't care.

I said, "No it isn't. It would only be a good thing if I had done it with Annie."

She said, "Do it with Annie, then. I'll still love you."

I said, "Yes, you love me, and you are also out of your mind. Annie would never do such an insane damn thing."

Susan was truly stricken now, but she said anyway, "I don't care. I still think it was funny."

I said, "That tells me something about you."

She said, "And I still love you, even if you hurt me so bad I want to die."

We were almost to her apartment now. She drove and looked straight ahead, and I looked straight ahead too. We wound through the little neighborhoods of Pittsburgh, Morningside, and Friendship, and East Liberty, and Point Breeze—the potholes, the Busway, the traffic, the tall old brick houses with stained glass in the third-floor windows. Big yellow footprints, faded from a year of rain, marked the path of the Pittsburgh Marathon. We heard the two o'clock train whistle as the Amtrak clattered through Shadyside on its way to West Virginia.

Susan slowed the car and parked on the street in front of her apartment. We sat for a few minutes without speaking, and then she said, "You could come in for a while if you want to."

I said, "I'm sorry for saying those things to you."

She said, "It would probably make you feel worse to make love, but if you want to—I mean, if it would help—"

I said, "No, you're right, I'd probably feel worse."

She said, "Well—"

I said, "I'd better get on home. Annie will be getting off work."

She said, "Do you think I'm a geek?"

I said, "No. No, I don't think you're a geek, Susan." I said, "Do you think I'm a bad person?"

She leaned over and kissed me on the cheek and then opened the door of the orange car and stepped out. I slipped over into the driver's seat. I watched her go inside her dumpy little apartment, with its sink sculpture and frilly pink curtains.

I tried to see Susan through the front window but could see nothing but reflections. Often when I left, she would stand and watch me until I was gone. This time she was not there.

I thought she might be lying on her mattress. The afternoon sunlight might be slanting through her bedroom window. She might imagine—though it would be unlike her—that the sunlight was the secret, unilluminating light of madness. She might be remembering her father in Delaware, her mother's kitchen table.

20

We Are All Alone

THE PINTO MADE ITS rat-a-tat-tat valve noise beneath the hood, and the warm wind blew through my long hair as I drove home. The neighborhood in Pittsburgh where Annie and I lived held no beautiful houses—indeed ours was the homeliest on the street. They were solid shot-and-a-beer structures of various shades of red or yellow brick, a few wood houses, no-nonsense dwellings where lives got lived. Since Robin's death, Annie and I fought constantly. Annie never smiled. She didn't talk to me. She was distant.

"What did you do today?" I would say, goading her to speech.

"Nothing."

"Well, you must have done something."

"I went to work. Why are you grilling me?"

"I'm not grilling you, I'm trying to have a normal conversation. What happened at work?"

"Nothing. I worked."

"What did you see from the car on your way to work?"

"Would you please just shut up?"

"'Would you please just shut up?'"

"Don't mock me, Buddy."

"'Don't mock me, Buddy.'"

Shouting, recriminations, door-slamming, tears This was the new life we were living. I knew I was defective, an intolerable wretch with a dead son

I was seeing a therapist at the time who said I should communicate better. I knew this already. It's the reason I was always trying to initiate small talk, as a place to begin at least. I vowed to try harder. Not the affair, but other stuff. I didn't want to communicate myself right out onto the street. This therapist's ears were covered with hair, incidentally, over the tops of his ears. His hairy ears drove me crazy. I didn't communicate this either.

I read in *Glamour* magazine that sharing sexual fantasies was something women liked to do, so this was the way I decided we might communicate. I gave it a shot. I said, "I've got an idea. Let's share sexual fantasies. You go first." We were in bed, Annie was reading the newspaper. She wouldn't do it.

"I'm not good at fantasies."

"Oh, sure you are," I insisted.

"Can't I just read the newspaper?"

"It'll be fun."

She put down the newspaper. She told me a fantasy involving a couple of our friends she was attracted to. I was so shocked and hurt I was ready to jump off a bridge. I didn't let her know this. I kept on with the fantasies strategy. During lovemaking I pretended we were a gorgeous couple in a porno movie. I described us as the actors, I told about the director, the camera operator, the movie set, the plot. I spoke in movie-making lingo—"Cut, that's a take," whatever I could come up with. Other times I pretended that we were in bed with another couple, or that friends were watching us or encouraging us. I filled up our bedroom with talk.

I became utterly focused on sex. I brought up the idea of sex in the middle of anything else Annie might be talking about. Once I interrupted her when she was talking about the death of her mother. I said, "Whaddaya say we go to one of those sex motels sometime, you know, with all the videos and sex toys."

I won't try to describe the glare she fixed upon me. She said, "Do you even know what you just did?"

I said, "Huh?"

"What you did just then."

"What? I just thought it would be something fun we could do together." A mother's death seemed an affront to me, I couldn't tolerate hearing about anyone's death but my son's.

The house that we lived in was an old, old structure, but it had been remodeled so often and so poorly for the past hundred years that nothing of its original self was discernible. Apparently it had once been a small caretaker's house, when Pittsburgh was young, but now it was larger, and oh my God. The character and style that you normally associate with old houses was completely missing in this one. There was no Victorian symmetry, no gables or dormers or shuttered windows, no gingerbread or stained glass or tower. The color scheme seemed to have been chosen by a psychotic person. The largest portion of the exterior was covered in white shingles, another part in green shingles, and a large section containing the kitchen was aluminum siding painted red. The roof was shingled in two colors as well, green and black, and the square brick columns that held up the front porch roof were yellow brick. The porch had been added as an afterthought and with inferior materials. The porch roof, which slanted steeply, was the most visible feature of the house. It was made of metal and had rusted in large patches all over and so presented itself as a ghastly reddish brown.

THE HOUSE LAY AHEAD of me. I pulled the Pinto into the driveway, and felt its specter cast a pall over my whole life. Everything I had ever lost or feared losing rose up before me. The sordidness of my affair with Susan was shockingly apparent, maybe for the first time in its fullness. I was stricken to think of her terrible, self-destructive idealism. I wanted my son back, alive. I wanted my own life back. I wanted the freight train in my head to stop its terrible noise. I imagined Annie in the house now. I imagined her at the sink, cleaning a kitchen that could not be cleaned. I imagined her hands in a sinkful of soapy water. I imagined a yellow box of SOS pads, a bottle of Murphy's Oil Soap, these hopeless images. I took a deep breath. I strengthened my resolve. I would go inside that house and make our lives right. I would become a different person. I already was a different person, hadn't my axing Susan proved that already? I would become the perfect man. I would give up all lechery. I would withdraw all demands. Sex would become an earned part of respect and intimacy. I would be truthful, I would learn to communicate, I would learn to wear Birkenstocks and ratty sweaters. While my body sat behind the wheel and did not yet move, my heart, my prayerful soul, my best self, flew on ambiguous wings out of the explosive Pinto and through the Sears vinyl windows and into the house to my wife's heart, where it rested for one golden moment in peace.

During my reverie, Annie had been inside hard at more practical work. I stepped just inside the front door and watched her as she finished up. It was work I think she enjoyed. She went about it efficiently, methodically. Not the soapy mundanity I had imagined for her, a wifely toiling at the kitchen sink, making clean the uncleanable, but a work of the heart. She was kicking me out.

It was not easy work either, it was labor that required dedication and commitment and physical strength. It required many trips up and down the stairs, top floor to basement. She was ripping to shreds every card I had ever written to her, tearing apart, breaking into pieces, cutting up with the scissors every gift I had ever given her, throwing these things and all my belongings, shoes, shirts, jeans, books, long-lost items I was interested to see she had found, into the basement, helter-skelter in a pile, where they would not pollute her line of vision, every stitch of clothing, every crossword puzzle, anything that reminded her of me, indeed all evidence of my existence. My wife had built a golden pile of shredded metaphors at the bottom of the basement steps, while I had only contemplated them as abstractions from the ivory tower of the Pinto. She made trip after trip past me. I watched my life pass in front of me, all exterior manifestations of it, anyway.

On one of her passes through, I said, "Can we talk?"

At first there was no response, but then eventually I learned a few things.

Susan, it turned out, had given Annie a call before I got home. Susan had explained everything to her. I don't say "related" everything or "spilled the beans" or even confessed or unburdened herself or ratted on me. She just called to make things clear. Susan was a genuine idealist. In her wacky way she believed in the sanctity of love, she believed in marriage and commitment and even communication and truth-telling. She believed in *my* marriage. She wanted the best for me. She had called to assure Annie of these things and to assure her that though she loved me and wanted to bear my child, that I did not love her, that I loved only my wife. "Oh, sure, he said he loved me plenty of times," she explained, "but that was only to make me feel better." She explained the many times I had "axed" her and how these were evidence of my commitment to my marriage. She told Annie, as I pieced things together later, some nutty version of the incident in the Family Oven rest room. Which is to say, she told it pretty much as it in fact happened. She told her she hoped to have a baby someday. She told her about the baby furniture we had seen in Babyland.

Annie was almost finished with her hauling and ripping and breaking to bits. There were no hysterics, no screaming. Annie's face was a blank slate. She seemed more rested than she had been for a long time.

21

The Underworld

FOR ALL ITS FAILINGS in the upper spaces where our marriage was disintegrating, the house had beneath its floors a large dry basement. This was to be my new home. This was a compromise arrangement. I had wanted to communicate and work things out. Annie wanted me to move to another state. Even she, in her pain of betrayal, could see that hers was an idea no more feasible than mine. There was nowhere for me to go. Money was a constant problem. I had no money, and neither did Annie. We were barely making the mortgage each month as it was, and keeping the kids in decent school clothes. How could we ever hope to maintain this house as well as an apartment for me, or even a rented room somewhere? I would have gone, I wasn't holding on to any false hopes. It just couldn't be done. A decision for me to live in the basement required little discussion. I would get out of her life, just not today. It would take time, no matter how loathsome my presence. I never tried to deny Susan's story, incidentally. If you knew Susan you would recognize before two words were out of her mouth that she was incapable of any falsehood. Annie had sense enough to know this and so did I. Susan was in the weirdest way the purest person I have ever known.

A few basement-style windows dotted the upper walls of the space that now I descended into, and let in a ghostly light that did not seem to move outward into the room beyond the windows themselves but only to hold there in their emptiness and throb softly as a pulse. The windows glowed in their cavities like alien things. They breathed like paper lungs. The dim room beyond them seemed scarcely affected by their metallic pulse and alien wheeze.

All of my material possessions lay waiting for me there, at the foot of the stairs. My pants, my shirts, twisted together, sprawled about, looked like a tragic accident. I thought I saw bodies, lifeless and random. I remembered a fatal car crash I'd seen as a boy. I thought of my son in his car. I went down the stairs. Annie's footsteps now I could hear above me. I reached into a pile of clothing. I began to pick through the tangle. I separated one thing from another. I even named them: shirt, jeans, shoe. To make sense of the jumble, to find clothes to wear, places to put them, required hours. Steady and slow, I did what needed to be done. My work now was as necessary and deliberate and strange as Annie's had seemed as she expelled these possessions of mine from the space where she would begin to make her life above stairs without me. As I worked, I found that I was crying.

This surprised me, though I had cried bitter and guilty tears since Robin's death. There was a difference in these tears, this crying. As I said, it took me a while to notice that I was crying at all. I didn't know what I was crying for. If I say for "lost innocence," well, even I roll my eyes. What I cried for seemed ancient, not traceable to its source, like a long and mysterious

river. I didn't have to think about this crying, I didn't have to
suffer it, I didn't have to curtail any activity in order to engage in
it or alter my steps or my thinking in any way. It was a form of
breathing.

The large room of the basement was dark and cool as a cave,
of course, since it was in fact a cavern of sorts. There was no
proper ceiling through most of the space, only low overhead
pipes and tangles of wires in rafters, and above them the under-
side of the kitchen floor, where again I heard Annie's footsteps.
In other places the rafters and pipes had been hidden above the
flimsy boards of a ceiling. At one end of the large room sat the
washer and dryer that Annie's father had given us when we married. At the other stood the enormous old furnace and boiler.
Off to the side a couple of grim, poisonous-looking little storage
rooms were walled into the hillside, where we had shoved certain detritus of furnishings, suitcases, an old single-bed mattress
from one of the boys' rooms, items too miserable even to fit into
the hopeless spaces above ground.

These auxiliary rooms—which were called "cold rooms"
and were supposedly once used for storing canned goods and
sacks of potatoes and turnips and whatever—were true caves,
with one wall of bare cold earth, not even covered with plastic.
Spiders of many poisonous varieties resided here, I was sure. My
life in the underworld of our home had begun.

I have omitted saying that there was one area of the basement that already I had some familiarity with, even some small
affection for, unlike my feelings for the rest of the house. It was
an enclosed space—not exactly a room that you could call a
proper office, since it was narrow and small, only about six feet
across, ten feet long, and there was no door, and the floors and
three walls were constructed of rough concrete, and the furnace

and boiler, as big as a Volkswagen, sat bubbling and flaming and sucking air at one end. A person six feet tall would not have been able to stand up straight beneath the pipes in the ceiling. This space was the cubbyhole where I kept a desk—an old library table that Annie had paid ten dollars for before I met her—and my Smith-Corona portable electric typewriter. I had taped a large poster of Shakespeare on the only wall that would hold a poster. I had a favorite straight-back chair, painted red, that I sat in. I had pieced together a bookcase from a few cinder blocks and a couple of planks I found in the garage. I wish I remembered which books. A collegiate dictionary, a one-volume Columbia encyclopedia, the compact OED, I remember those at least. So in a sense this was my space already, however inadequate in most regards. I had written one book here, in fact, upon this library table and with this very Smith-Corona. So although I wasn't exactly coming home, as I moved into my new quarters, I was grateful beyond even my own expectations to have gained at least a reprieve before I had to begin life in alien surroundings.

I worked on through the afternoon, sorting through the mess, and noticed that the dim basement had become almost completely dark. I turned on a small lamp on the desk and kept working. I felt hungry but did not stop to eat, in part because I did not want to encounter Annie in the kitchen.

I had never owned many clothes, really only jeans and shirts and a sports jacket, so finding space for my things was easy. They hung on overhead pipes from wire hangers at the furnace end of the room, shirts first, jeans next, jackets after that. I rolled my underwear and T-shirts and socks military style, so as to use the least space, and lined them neatly on the bare boards of my makeshift bookcase, which I had extended by hauling in a couple more cinder blocks and planks. I listened for Annie's footsteps, and when I heard nothing for a while, I crept back up the cellar stairs into the kitchen and grabbed the broom before she came back downstairs, and took it down to sweep out my new quarters. The last thing I did was to go into one of the execrable "cold rooms" and drag out the single-bed mattress we had put there when we got a new one for one of the boys. On a regular bed it had been saggy and worthless. On a concrete floor, it might be just the thing. Mattresses and bare floors had somehow become a major theme in my life.

Rid of Susan and her idiotic idealism at last, the last of my lies fully exposed and therefore no longer a burden to me, and assured of never having Annie's love again, I began to feel a strange and unwonted exhilaration. I was exhausted that night from the emotional crisis as well as from the work of outfitting my apartment and making it habitable, so once I collapsed onto my new bed, I slept better and longer than I had in months. I did not dream of my son, I did not worry about hiding my secrets, for there were no secrets, my snoring kept no one awake. For once in my life I was utterly undistracted from my soul's center. In my new digs I knew who I was. I was a writer, that alone, almost. I was a bohemian. Anyone who laid eyes upon my living space would have agreed. I had lost everything and was therefore free, like Bobby McGee. I had to be the luckiest man on earth. I had never really felt this even when my two children were alive. If I could figure out a way of knowing exactly who I am at all hours of the day, as I did in this moment, I would have it made. This was the way I was thinking then, in the first moments of relief I had experienced since the night we learned of Robin's death. To celebrate, the next day, I walked into Shadyside to the hardware store and bought a cheap floor lamp to set beside my writing table. I carried it home in a long box, over my shoulder, whistling as I walked.

This became my life, a writer's solitary life in a basement cell. Living alone in the basement on a bare mattress on a concrete floor, cooking no meals, taking my meals at cheap diners— the Blue Plate Special, slabs of sweet potato pie for dessert, hard-edged waitresses with a ready pot of coffee—watching no television, reading as late as I wanted, listening to NPR in the morning and the Grateful Dead radio broadcast on Sunday nights, taking the bus wherever I went (I didn't want to get into a scuffle with Annie about who needed the car), visiting with her children when they came down to my little cell to see me—who could have asked for a better life? I realized I wanted from life exactly the opposite of what Susan had wanted. She chose places like the Family Oven to simulate homes, happy homes, I suspected, of the type she herself did not have. I chose a monk's life.

I chose eating establishments for the anonymity, for solitude. I wanted no car, which families inhabit, but buses, which surround you with strangers. I wanted no television, but the disembodied voices of radios. I wanted no sex partner but myself, so that I would not forget that though I might actually have been cursed to fall in love, nothing changed the fact that I, like everyone else on this earth, was all alone.

And yet during this time I grew immeasurably closer to my son Erik, who by now was an Army Scout serving in the Persian Gulf. I wrote long letters, he sent me handsome photographs of himself in uniform.

TIME PASSED. THE NOISY tornado inside my head continued to roar, but once in a while there was a lull, a moment that I could reasonably call true peace. Spring became summer. I watched this happen, as if through a glass darkly, by observing a few natural details outside the high cloudy basement window. I rarely went out of my cell, except to meet the two classes I taught at the university, but I could see that the rain fell less frequently against the pane. The lightning flashed less frequently. More light pushed its way in through the window, some days it did, anyway.

Then one night the sewer backed up and flooded my room as I lay sleeping, and I woke to find myself stewing unironically in a roomful of shit, which once again was an easy metaphor to apply. I was surprised to discover that this made me laugh rather than descend into despair. I spent a day with a shovel and mop and pail. I scrubbed clean what could be cleaned and threw away what could not. The mattress was ruined, so I hauled it out to the trash heap. A plumber Roto-Rootered the sewer pipes. A rug guy smoothed my rough floor and laid indoor-outdoor over it. I bought a narrow European-style bed from Ikea, the cheap Swedish furniture store in the mall. I set up the bed next to the furnace. The small room was crowded, there was scarcely an inch of floor space, but still I was comfortable. I bought new sheets and pulled out my old L.L. Bean blanket and made up the bed. I went about my solitary days. I read, I wrote at my typewriter, I listened to the radio. I had a telephone installed in my room. I bought a bright-colored rug from Ikea to spread on my new neutral-colored carpeting. I painted all the overhead pipes with red enamel, to match the rug. Then I painted the bookshelves red. Annie came down to do the laundry one day and noticed what I had done. She surprised me by hanging simple red curtains on curtain rods on the basement window. Over time, more posters went up on the walls. I sold a piece of writing and with the check I bought my first computer, a Mac Plus with no hard drive and one meg of RAM.

I began to love the deplorable house. One day, I'm not sure when, the house was no longer an atrocity to me, a color scheme from hell, a Cyclops from the street, a kitchen without cabinets where you clunked your head on the overhead light fixture. it was a house, a home. I know this sounds silly. I don't care. I loved my home, this small space of it that I occupied so comfortably, and tentatively, with trepidation, and all the rest of it as well. Seeing it from beneath, from underground, beneath its stairs, I saw it entirely differently. The warmth of the red rug and red bookcase and red curtains and L.L. Bean blanket lent warmth to the upper floors as well as to the basement, straight up through floorboards and all the way to the ceiling. What was good in the depths, in the dingiest corners, caused me to believe, perhaps falsely, perhaps not, that comfort could be found in its upper reaches. I had done the same thing Susan was doing when she chose restaurants. I had built the perfect home. This was my miniature, my model, my "study" or "detail" to use a painter's terms. If it could be created here, in Plato's cave, it could exist upon a larger canvas, in a world of real persons, not shadows. Its reflection was strong enough to persuade me that other homes, even homes with a dead child, an angry wife, and dog-smelling furniture, could also be good homes. God, how little I knew Susan, I realized. What tragedies, and in what underground caves, had she been building her miniature happy homes upon? How empty my words of love must have sounded to her, indeed how empty they had been. She had taken them, not hated me for them, because they were the table and chairs that she was using to furnish the airy spaces she hoped, in rare comfort, somehow, someday, to move into and inhabit fully as a citizen of a larger world, in which we are not alone.

MY ROOM BEGAN, WITHOUT any effort on my part, to become a part of the larger house. More often Annie's children stopped by for a visit. They did their homework on the new computer. The dogs, I discovered, were sleeping on my bed when I was out. Annie stopped by on her way from the laundry room to visit. We caught up on family news, we avoided the old topics of conversation, the old battlegrounds. She spent a night with me in my narrow bed. We stayed apart for a while after this, and then she invited me up to watch a TV movie, and that night I spent in her bed. From my little room I opened the curtains sometimes and watched fallen leaves blow past along the ground above me, as the seasons changed. The old furnace at the head of my bed came on more frequently and made its raucous, fiery sounds. Annie and I fought, the old anger flared up, the rage, and I retreated to the depths and wondered how I had ever been lured out, and then we began moving in and out of the up and down of our house, our lives, together again.

22

The Land of Dreamy Dreams

MY STORY COULD END happily upstairs, with me safe in my wife's arms, but there is another thing that I have to tell.

Last year I concluded a lengthy and exhausting series of cross-country readings that ended with a couple of appearances in New Orleans, and I got the idea that I would call Annie in Pittsburgh and invite her to fly down and meet me in the land of dreamy dreams. We had worked hard at our marriage since the affair with Susan, forgiveness had been found. It was thrilling to feel the constant comfort of love that I felt for her while I was away. The trip had been successful, but I had been homesick the whole time. The idea of staying for a while in this beautiful city was almost like planning a second honeymoon.

I was staying in a fine old hotel on Royal Street, right in the heart of the French Quarter, and learned that I could keep the rooms for another week if I wanted. The weather had been beautiful, late springtime, in the eighties, and the air was full of the fragrance of flowers. Jackson Square had rocked all night with the backbeat rhythms of jazz and blues, street musicians occupied every bench along the promenade, and to wander among them holding hands with my wife seemed exactly the way I wanted to end my tour. These small romantic moments were the things Annie and I had begun to find together. I believed I had lived my entire life in search of what Annie and I now shared.

I had had little time to myself since I arrived in the city, no time for music and little leisure to enjoy even the good food. Both of us loved the city. We had friends in the Garden District we had stayed with many times, in the funny little guest cottage alongside their house. We had sipped sweet tea on the sunporch and watched the late sunshine break into prisms as it passed through the leaded glass of the windows on its way into the yolk-yellow rooms. We could stay with them again this week, if we wanted, we were always welcome, but my idea was that this would be a week to ourselves, just for us. We deserved it, didn't we, after all we had been through? We would hide ourselves away in the Quarter for a whole week and not come up for air. We would not even call our old friends in the District. We would browse the bookstores—Faulkner House in Pirate's Alley, Beaucoup Books down on Magazine. We would swallow Gulf oysters by the dozen at Acme Oyster Bar, eat crawfish étouffée at Les Pauls', drink gallons of chicory coffee and stuff ourselves with sugary beignets at Café Du Monde. Later we would diet, we would count calories and fat grams, but for now we would indulge ourselves in whatever pleasures we chose. Long gone were the days when the two of us could stay out late on Bourbon Street and drink Hurricanes at Pat O'Brien's—I remembered the boy I had been in graduate school and wished Annie had been in my life in those high old days—but there were many pleasures left to us nevertheless. The azaleas were long gone, of course, but as alcohol and danger were not the key to my happiness any longer, New Orleans is a flower garden all summer, and there were other dark blossoms of strange beauty and fragrance to replace what was already past.

There was so much I wanted us to do. Annie loved the out-of-way places, the voodoo shops and little art galleries across Esplanade. I wanted us to browse through these together. On her last visit she had bought an original Michalopolous oil, a painting of an eerie house in the District, with spatial distortions and garish colors, and had hung it in our living room in Pittsburgh. We were living in a different house by this time, not the old monstrosity where we had suffered so, but the painting reminded her, she said, of the architectural and emotional distortions of our life in those bad old days in that sad old house. Annie even liked the danger of New Orleans, a city teeming with murderers. These are not to be taken lightly, especially at night, off the beaten path, but for my romantic wife even these real threats were a part of New Orleans's charm. I called home from my hotel room and proposed the trip to her and immediately she was delighted. It was a wonderful idea, she agreed. She had missed me, and this would be a perfect way to reenter our daily schedule together. I felt successful and happy. Later she called the hotel again, when I was out, and left a message detailing her flight plans and time of arrival. An impulsive trip like this would be expensive, but we agreed it would be worth it. I had rented a car and would have no problem picking her up at the airport the following morning.

I had the remainder of the day to myself. For the first time on my long trip I felt a little lonely. I had missed Annie, but my days had been constantly filled with people. I had not had a free moment in weeks, and now here I sat in the caesura between the hassle of readings and appearances and the easy bliss I anticipated with my wife. I thought about taking a nap back at the hotel but chided myself for the thought. You are in New Orleans, I said, there is so much to see. I walked around the Quarter a bit, strolled among the street performers, past Tennessee Williams's home, past the rooms where Faulkner wrote *Mosquitoes,* through the French Market, where I bought a trinket for Annie. I stopped at an out-of-the-way diner down by the river and ate an oyster po'boy and drank a glass of sweet tea. I loved New Orleans, I decided for the one millionth time.

Then the most amazing coincidence occurred. As I was finishing my sandwich and tea, I thought I recognized a man standing at the register speaking to the bar maid about his bill. There was a friendly familiarity in the way that he went over the bill with the girl that I recognized before I even saw his face. I had not seen him in many years, not since the day in Alabama when he stiffed me for the bill for drinks.

I said, "Ramon?" and he heard his name and turned around, and sure enough.

His face was quizzical at first, and then brightened into a smile when he recognized me. There was no hint that any tension had ever existed between us. I couldn't believe my eyes, and my heart was filled with strange feeling. He was considerably changed, after all these years. His hair had thinned greatly and had turned a pale sort of gray and stuck straight up, unmanageable, from a pink scalp. His eyelashes were so white as to be almost invisible, and his eyes, obvious even in the riverside dive where I was eating, were a pale and wonderful color of morning blue. What was unchanged, unless now it was more exaggerated, was that wonderful perpetual look of near-adolescent surprise in his raised eyebrows, an innocent childlike joy in what age had revealed as boyish jug ears and big Adam's apple. He seemed much paler than he had ever been, and softer I should say, no longer the ex-quarterback but simply a middle-aged man in shirtsleeves. His shirt front was open three or four buttons down, as it had been when I last saw him—but now not from vanity, only carelessness of grooming. His pale, bare, almost hairless chest was a part of his boyishness. The shirt was soiled, his shoes were run down, his neck was dirty, his shirt collar was folded under on one side. And yet in a way he looked wonderful to me, a relaxed, noncompetitive version of himself.

Though the two of them, he and the barmaid, had been going over his bill for mistakes, it was clear this was a friendly conversation and that both were enjoying themselves. Even in jeans and loafers and a flowered shirt, I felt overdressed and inappropriate and "grown-up" in his presence. He was still a boy, uncorrupted and hungry for, well, for what I didn't know. Hungry to meet each new minute of the world and test it for danger and adventure, as he had always done back when I knew Ramon in school and in Florida.

Suddenly the comfort I felt in my love of Annie and the comfort of our home seemed anemic and pale by comparison to what I remembered as I looked at him. I recalled feelings of passion and joy that my present comfort suddenly could not match. I was afraid I had forgotten what it meant to be hungry for art or sex or whatever else we had been hungry for back in those good days. Alive is what I had felt then, mere satisfaction was what I was capable of now. Just how much I had loved life during those years came flooding back to me with such sudden force I felt tears well up in my eyes. The loss of that part of my past had never impressed me at all before, I had pushed it away from the front of my thoughts, in favor of more extravagant losses. Those years had seemed simply a way station on the road to

whatever destiny was to have been mine, this tour I'd just finished, a little shopping and good food with my wife. Now the
past overwhelmed me like a flood. I had been so young, my
God, newly married to my first wife at the time. Suddenly I
wanted to call her—my first wife, I mean, Elizabeth. I wanted to
say I was sorry and also to thank her for going with me on that
adventure. I could see her face as if it were yesterday. I saw the
little cubbyhole where we had lived so happily, where I sat at a
big typewriter in the bedroom and pecked out drafts of sen-
tences long lost to me. I loved life back then, that was the thing.
I hadn't realized I loved it so much. I even loved the unhappy
parts. It was all life, we didn't try to fix the bad, we just sucked it
in like the rest.

I was shocked to find myself comparing unfavorably the
love I felt for Annie to the urgency of feeling I had known back
then, not just for Elizabeth, for everything. Nothing today
seemed to mean as much. Even Annie, for whom my heart had
been so full only minutes before, began to pale as a recent memory. Ramon had somehow gotten a break in playwriting and acting since I had last seen him, and I learned from the overheard
conversation with the barmaid that he had directed *Hair* on
Broadway. *Hair,* my God, that was in another century, wasn't it?
Well, actually, it almost was another century. That's how long it
had been since I last saw or heard of him.

He said, "Buddy?" His head was cocked to the side, like a
question mark.

"Oh my God," I said, and stood up and we embraced right
there among the oyster shells.

The barmaid smiled warmly at us, until Ramon turned to
her with his beatifying smile and handed her a wad of money
and said, "Oh fuck the bill, just take what I owe and keep some

for yourself." He winked at me, "I ought to make this bum here pay it." The barmaid took his money and waved her handsome tip under both of our noses and handed him back what remained. She patted him twice on the butt as she turned back to her work.

I said, "I can't believe you recognized me." I meant this. Not only was I older, I hadn't yet grown my beard when I last saw Ramon.

He said, "I've seen your picture around. You're doing well."

We sat in the booth and talked for a very long time. I asked about Rabbit and Margaret Ann. I told him about the divorce from Elizabeth, my marriage to Annie. I eventually got around to telling him about Robin's death, and then told him how Erik was getting along, about his serving in the army during the Gulf war. I showed him a photo in my wallet. In it Erik's blond hair is almost to his waist. The photograph has caught him in the middle of a big laugh. "Everyone should enjoy life as much as Erik," I told Ramon. "He's a social worker in Maryland now, gave me my first grandchild this year."

Ramon and Margaret Ann were divorced, I learned. He had lost job after job in New York until they finally moved out of the city to try to get a grip on their lives. He had finally had one of those operations he'd always wanted, a heart valve I think. He was cheerful enough about his difficulties and I detected no self-pity, just the same wonderful, energetic, hypochondriacal Ramon.

"Do you live in New Orleans?" I asked.

"Oh Lord no," he said. "We've been in Iowa City for twenty years. I still teach at the same community college where they took me in after my last misadventure in New York. The class load is easy, and they let me do some directing. It's a good deal."

He was in New Orleans for only a couple of days, to settle the estate of an aged aunt who had died and left a small inheritance. "Margaret Ann lives in Cedar Rapids, so I see her every week. Nothing has really changed with us, you know, except that we're not married. She even cleans up my house about once a month, when she can't stand looking at it anymore. Harris— we stopped calling him Rabbit, oh, a long time ago—and his wife come down from Winnipeg a couple of times a year."

This is the way we went on for a while, about ourselves. I began to ask of the whereabouts of some of our old classmates. Ramon had kept up with our old friends better than I had. Tim and Ellie were divorced, he said, Ellie was now married to one of the Billips millionaires, one of the oil tycoons up in the Delta. Jonesy was dead, heart attack ten years ago, but Rebecca was doing great, living in Birmingham now, doing some kind of civil rights work. He went through the roll call of classmates and filled me in on those he knew about. Then he mentioned Elizabeth's friend, Twyla.

"You remember Twyla!" I exclaimed.

He said that he remembered my telling him about her, back in Alabama. He had made a point of calling her, getting to know her, after the "flap" between the two of us. His plan had been to poison her mind against me, maybe sleep with her a few times, he had been so angry and so embarrassed after he left the farmhouse.

I said, "This can't be true. You kept up with Twyla all these years?"

"Well, first," he said, "I never slept with her. She wouldn't have anything to do with me. Second, she and that guy she was married to finally had a kid, a boy. They got divorced, eventually, but she had this kid with him before that happened. I met the kid once, when he was about three."

I said, "Did you actually 'poison her mind' against me?"

He said, "Oh, sure, you bet. I had her hating your guts before I got through with her." He laughed a genuine laugh, as if we were sharing a joke, and finally I had to laugh too.

I harbored no ill will against Ramon. We went back so many years, had shared so much. It was typical of him to go to such lengths in a competition—what he saw as a competition—and in a weird way this was the type of nutty excess that I found myself loving about him over the years, even when I his target.

What I didn't expect was the fullness of feeling that welled up in me at the sound of the name of Twyla. I was brought up short. She might as well have appeared before me as an apparition, so vivid, indeed so enchanting was her memory. More than ever the extravagance of my feeling for her—and not just for her, for all those days of urgency and drama—flooded in on me.

And suddenly I realized I was still in love with this woman.

This might seem impossible after so long a time, but it was true. The overpowering, visceral memory of old feeling seemed in this moment a definition of love, and immediately I wondered whether all that I had felt over the years, and even those feelings of only an hour ago, were not a lie. I held this thought to myself and said nothing to Ramon right away, though he must have known.

He told me that she had remarried and was "sort of retired now," to recall his words. He knew that she had finished her major in English and had taught literature for a long time at the same private high school where her husband worked.

I said, "Are you sure we're talking about the same Twyla? The hippie girl? The nymphomaniac?"

He said oh yes, the same.

I said, "Retired? My God, that's right, that could be true." She could have taught thirty years since then. She would be in her fifties now. I hadn't considered that she would be a middle-aged woman, that she might look different. I had imagined only her slender legs and arms, the blond hair that fell over her shoulders to her hips, her sexual talk. Was she wizened now, was her voice crackly, had the veins of her hands turned purple, her skin become papery and loose as crepe? I hadn't weathered the years so well myself; who knew what had happened to Twyla.

Ramon waited just the right interval before he said quietly, "She is still the same. She is still heartbreakingly beautiful."

There was one other thing he still had to tell me. He seemed to have been waiting for this final revelation, as if all the rest of our conversation had been the setup for what was now to follow. I forced a suspicion out of my mind that my old friend Ramon was getting something more out of our meeting than I had taken into account. I slapped away the brief suspicion that this meeting in New Orleans was not as accidental as it at first had seemed. Alarms went off in my head, as the saying goes, I knew I should be careful. No matter. I was not cautious in the slightest degree. Insight was worthless to me. I had to know more, I had to talk about her, to recall every detail of the affair, to tell Ramon that I had secretly loved her for all these years, even to tell him about Susan, who had been a kind of pale substitute for Twyla, so that I might hear at least an echo of those long-dormant feelings once again. I was ready to beg him to tell me that she had left her second husband, that he was dead, that she spoke of me. I released all hold on good sense.

I had to get in touch with her, no matter where she was, no matter what miraculous bridges Annie and I had, over the last several years, built back across the chasm to our marriage, no matter what affection and trust and spiritual connection must be sacrificed to do so, no matter that the transformation and forgiveness we had pieced together in our painful alliance since the affair with Susan might be undone. I told Ramon everything. I poured out my heart. I told him how, with Susan, I had felt alive, exactly as I had with Twyla. With the two of them every feeling, even the disastrous ones, seemed part of an adventure that made life bearable, that made tragedy into exquisite melodrama and therefore tolerable, a pain worth experiencing as often as possible.

The word *comfort* to describe any part of love, which was the expression constantly on my tongue these days, never came to mind back then. Comfort had meant nothing in those days. Or maybe I was looking for comfort and only called it by another name.

Suddenly I realized I loved this woman elaborately, incautiously, indeed madly.

He said, "She lives just across Lake Pontchartrain, you know."

I looked at Ramon. His face did not reveal anything beneath its surface. He was an excellent actor. I managed to wonder fleetingly whether Ramon had some emotional stake in seeing my marriage unravel and fall apart, as I suddenly felt it might be doing. I wondered whether the collapse of my life's happiness were not a challenge of some sort to him, a particularly difficult scene he had suddenly become determined to master. I felt a loose string or two in my emotional fabric, and I picked and yanked at them without caution.

I said, "She does? She lives on the Coast?"

"In Bay St. Louis," he said.

I said, "She does?"

I ENDED MY CONVERSATION with Ramon quickly and scurried back to the hotel. My hands shook so violently I almost tore the pages of the phone book. I didn't care how he knew these things, I didn't consider again any motive he might have, any manipulations he might be involved in. Bay St. Louis, I found the town, I found the number, her husband's name, which Ramon had provided. I lifted the phone from the cradle and pressed at the numbers on the dial before me. She answered and her voice was the youthful music of my memory, and my feelings were exactly as if our last stolen grieving kisses had been yesterday. Twice, early in the conversation, I had to hold the phone away from my mouth and take deep breaths so that I was able to talk. I remembered with what ease her touch, her voice on a telephone had, all those years ago, been able to take my breath away. I spoke her name, I told her who I was. It occurred to me what a ruinous path I seemed all too willing to take.

Except that I was so breathless with emotion at our reunion the conversation began normally in every way. Her voice held all of the old music and something else as well, a quality of speech I had forgotten about, a distance I would say, as if she were mildly amused at everything we were saying, an ironic distance from the contents of our words. I asked whether she was free to talk, and she said, "Oh, yes, Albert is out on *the boat.*"

Something in the way she said the final phrase of her reply struck me as sarcastic, somehow, a tone I took to be a put-down of her husband and an invitation of sorts to me.

I said, "I'd love to see you."

She said, "Oh, well, *see me,* ah." She had placed a similar emphasis on words in that sentence as well, and I was baffled as to how to interpret her meaning. Eventually she said, "I don't look like I *used* to."

I said, "I don't care." I meant this, but there was that odd sarcasm again, if sarcasm indeed was the point.

It took me a while to understand that she had gone mad. Madness I realize is an old-fashioned term. Schizophrenia, depression, personality disorder, agoraphobia, even Alzheimer's I suppose—anything was possible. I don't know what name to give to her sad condition. She had lost her mind. That was all I knew, and that was irrefutable. Some things she said made sense and seemed true; others were quite insane. Her son was dead. The story was shocking. Twyla's son had been the postal worker in Pensacola who one day took a rifle and murdered his supervisor and a coworker and then turned the gun on himself. I remembered reading about the incident when it happened, but seven or eight years had passed, so the memory was vague. I got no other details than this, for she was weeping piteously by this time in the conversation. The broad outline of the tragedy was all that I could make out through the weeping, which itself sounded less like emotion than like a rote demonstration of emotion. I wondered if my own tears, those years ago, had seemed so false. She wept easily, but I could tell even over the phone that this crying was not cathartic or helpful or even interesting to her, but rather like something done in a habitual trance, like peeling potatoes or shelling peas or knitting. I continued with the conversation, which now began veering off into unexpected tangents because I think I still had not been willing to believe fully the extent of her deterioration. She spoke of alien abductions as if they were as commonplace as the weather. She seemed to believe that her late

son now lived on a spaceship. All this was said in that amazing
voice of hers, honest to God like silver bells at times, and tinged
with her strange irony, sometimes sarcasm, so I was unable to determine which parts of her story she actually believed and which
she considered to be an inside joke between the two of us. She
was a complete hermit, I finally figured out this much. She saw no
one, she never moved from her house. She did keep a telephone
handy for emergencies—her husband had insisted upon it—and
she seemed to think her late son might someday try to reach her
from his new home—the mothership, to use her phrase. She had
not one friend anywhere on earth who knew where she was (I
don't really know whether this was true, I don't see how it could
have been, if Ramon had managed to keep up with her, even in a
cursory way). Her husband, she believed, hated her, though it
was obvious from everything else she said that this could not be
true. He had moved out, it was true, but he had not fully aban-
doned her. He had made a sort of separate peace finally and now
lived alone on a houseboat or yacht or some such vessel, moored
in a harbor in Bay St. Louis, a few miles from the house. He came
in each day to check on her, bring her things, gifts, trinkets,
movies, groceries. Each day he stayed for a while, cleaned up the
house a little, prepared some food for her to eat, and then went
back to whatever life he had made for himself.

I ended the conversation in despair and confusion. I looked
at the furnishings of my hotel room and, though I had been on
the road for seven weeks, I did not believe I could tolerate another moment without my wife. Without her the world seemed
ready to fly into chaos. She was the completion of me. Without
her anything could happen, there would be no protection. I wept
for what I had lost, for my fathers, for my sons, for Elizabeth,
for Annie whom I threw away once and had seemed ready to

throw away again, my God. Could I have almost allowed this to happen again, even after all we had suffered and come through together? I had felt changed, transformed forever by the truth, and yet I seemed still only to be the impulsive child ready to dive onto his head into unconsciousness for no better motive than a new TV. I was still the monster who had tried to shoot his father through the window, who set an infant on a strange horse, and fucked a woman with an Amazing Technicolor Fucking Machine. I wept for the demon whose face was my own. I wept for the burden of my inner midget, whom I recognized now as an eternal assurance that I was all alone in the world, and would be so forever, without my wife this was true, anyway. I wept for Ramon's health and for Margaret Ann and for poor dead Jonesy and Rebecca and Susan and my mad old lover Twyla and really, as corny and untrue as it may sound, for all the world of woman and man. During this phone conversation with Twyla, I never brought up the name of my son or the awful circumstances of his death. I thought of doing so, but I just didn't. What was the point? Especially what was the point if I had learned nothing from it of the value of faithful love? I didn't bring up the name of Ramon, either, though I would have been glad to have someone with whom to discuss his motives, even someone as crazy as Twyla. Could his motives have been so complex, his manipulations so profound, his heart so unkind? Were my motives and manipulations any less unkind, I who had once survived such demons and managed to keep a wife's love? I wept for everyone, for all the madness in the world, for murderers, for suicides, for divorce, for fathers and sons, and for that reckless stunted creature, that sickness inside myself, that put into jeopardy the fragile souls of those most dear to me, and allowed me to call my actions by the holy name of love.

EPILOGUE

Not too long ago Annie got a letter saying she had inherited some money from a dead relative. It was one of those storybook deals, a great-uncle she never met. We're a middle-aged couple, in our fifties, barely making ends meet, you know, so we were thrilled. It wasn't a lot of money by some standards, but it was a year's salary for the two of us. The taxes were all paid. It was a good deal.

We didn't believe it at first. We read the letter over and over. We called the phone number on the stationery and talked to somebody at the bank. It was true all right. Then we made jokes. We said we could pay off our Visa card and go out to dinner and have enough left over for the parking meter. Then we imagined a new house for ourselves. Each of us would have our own private study. There would be many bathrooms, all with skylights. Then we imagined South Sea vacations. We would get good tans and drink rum drinks out of a pineapple. (Not really *rum*, you know. This was part of the fantasy.) We would take our grown children with us, their families. Then we became philanthropic. We would set up a scholarship fund for the education of needy children. We would give it all to the Rainbow Kitchen. We imagined many grateful homeless people. Then we got practical. We would pay off the car, get the house painted, get a stove with a self-cleaning oven, put some away for retirement, buy CDs, IRAs.

We sat together in the living room that afternoon and dreamed of all the things we'd ever wanted.

Then I said, "I've always wanted a gun."

My wife looked at me. "A gun?"

I said, "It's not a good idea. It could be dangerous. I realize that."

She said, "A gun."

I said, "One of those AK-47s you hear so much about."

I thought she would say, "No, really, how should we spend it?" She said, "With a banana clip."

I looked at her.

She said, "I always wanted a Derringer. Chrome-plated, with a pearl-handled grip."

I said, "You could keep it in your purse."

She shook her hair. She said, "Or my garter belt."

She's a beautiful woman.

I said, "Right. Your garter belt."

She said, "Do you remember in *Pulp Fiction,* when John Travolta left his AK-47 on the kitchen sink?"

I said, "I loved that part."

She said, "That was the sexiest part, to me. The weapon, the dishwashing detergent, side by side, oh man."

I said, "I'll need bullets. A lot of bullets. And probably some new clothes."

She said, "From Banana Republic."

"Right."

She said, "Teflon bullets, if we can get them. They penetrate bulletproof vests."

I said, "Like on *Homicide*. But not all Teflon. We'll want conventional stuff too."

She said, "Exploding bullets. They'll be legal soon."

I said, "Right! Jeez, I almost forgot about exploding bullets."

It was mid-afternoon. We were rich. We sat together on the sofa and watched O. J. for a while. We held hands. We made love on the couch. Later on we did the same thing during the impeachment trial. We like sex and violence, maybe, or maybe we like sex during trials of the century.

My wife straightened her clothes.

I said, "You should have an assault weapon of your own. In addition to the Derringer."

She became thoughtful. She said, "You know what's wrong with this murder trial?"

I looked at the screen. Johnny Cochran leaned close, to talk to O. J. They both laughed.

My wife said, "No guns."

I said I hadn't thought of it before, but she was right. A stabbing was all right, but something was missing, it was true. It's just not the same without firearms.

She said, "Now the Betty Bradley trial—that was a murder. Guns blazing, empty shell casings, the smell of cordite in the air."

I said, "Or the woman who killed the diet doctor, remember? The schoolteacher."

She said, "Exactly."

We watched O. J. a little longer. It was pretty disappointing, so after a while we turned it off and sat together on the couch.

Finally my wife said, "Anyway. I'm an heiress."

I said, "We're rich."

She said, "A Derringer is just a start. An AK-47 is training wheels. We'll fill this house with guns."

I said, "I love you. I've never loved anyone else."